AN ORDINARY MAN'S GUIDE TO GROWING UP MUSLIM IN INDIA

Neyaz Farooquee is a journalist based in Delhi. He was a fellow at the New India Foundation and a non-fiction fellow at Sarai-CSDS. He currently works with the BBC, and was previously a staff writer at *Hindustan Times*. He has also contributed to the *New York Times*, *Al Jazeera*, *Caravan* magazine and *Tehelka*.

Praise for the book

'Farooquee has achieved in this book what writers such as Ta-Nehisi Coates have done for Blacks in America, making voices of the marginalised minority heard. Both the author and the publisher (the book was written using a grant from the New India Foundation) deserve praise for addressing this subject at a time when communal polarisation has deepened across the country.'

—*The Hindu*

'The book certainly brings some sense of closure on a personal level, but a lot remains to be written – and justice for most disadvantaged sections of our society remains elusive.'

—*The Times of India*

'Neyaz Farooquee's *An Ordinary Man's Guide to Radicalism: Growing Up Muslim in India* is a poignant reflection on these and such other existential dilemmas facing India's largest minority. Farooquee is a welcome addition to the tribe of young writers whose work is immersed in the lived realities of ordinary people.'

—*Open*

'Farooquee's memoir is novel in the sense that it inaugurates a subgenre as there are hardly any platforms where the Indian Muslim experience has been articulated as clearly and candidly as it has been in this book.'

—*Frontline*

'Farooquee's book is not just an examination of the assumptions others make about Muslims. It is also, at its best, an interrogation of the assumptions that many Muslims make.'

—*India Today*

'Farooquee successfully emphasizes the increasing social segregation on communal lines in urban India. The book is a welcome addition to the corpus of literature that helps us understand the fears and insecurities of Indian Muslims and their sense of victimization at the hands of both the State and the media.'

—*The Telegraph*

'Revolving around the theme of Muslim vulnerabilities in India, Farooquee's book opens up a Pandora's Box, raising questions on crucial issues of power and class, identity and suspicion, nationality and citizenship and, importantly, the rhetoric of political "appeasement" and actual deliverance.'

—*Dawn*

'The memoir, tries to clear the many myths and stereotypes about Muslims in India and highlights the diversity within the community and their lived reality.'

—*Al Jazeera*

'[T]his book is perhaps the best to understand how the barb of majoritarianism is unleashed on the face of a minority community having created a pretext. This will also help the reader know many untold stories related to the Batla House encounter or several chilling questions – still unanswered – the mainstream media has hardly touched upon.'

—*The Book Review*

'This autobiographical book brilliantly tells us the process through which the Muslim community is put on the path of alienation through a systematic othering by the Indian state. What is noteworthy about the book is the complete refusal by the author to put the blame for this state of affairs on any one political party ... A dispassionate analysis will tell us that the story is perhaps more complex.'

—*Sabrang India*

'The fears that Farooquee wrote about have only grown. But the courage he showed – by writing this book and by staying firm – continues to inspire. For every young Muslim who is unsure if he or she belongs, this book is a guide. It is not a guide to radicalism, but a guide to living a good life.'

—*New Age Islam*

AN ORDINARY MAN'S GUIDE TO GROWING UP MUSLIM IN INDIA

NEYAZ FAROOQUEE

First published as *An Ordinary Man's Guide to Radicalism* by Context, an imprint of Westland Publications Private Limited, in 2018

Published by Context, an imprint of Westland Books, a division of Nasadiya Technologies Private Limited, in 2026

No. 269/2B, First Floor, 'Irai Arul', Vimalraj Street, Nethaji Nagar, Alapakkam Main Road, Maduravoyal, Chennai 600095

Westland, the Westland logo, Context and the Context logo are the trademarks of Nasadiya Technologies Private Limited, or its affiliates.

ISBN: 9789379853608

10 9 8 7 6 5 4 3 2 1

Typeset by Mukul

Printed at Manipal Technologies Limited, Manipal

For Abbu and Ammi.
And those who are seeking justice.

Taught Man What He Knew Not.
And Then He Blew It Out.

Contents

Prologue: A Person Like You

HOW DO YOU REACT when something like a police encounter happens in your locality, and a few doors down, two men are killed – two of your neighbours, who have been labelled terrorists. Imagine, for a moment, that this happened not in Imphal or Srinagar, where such occurrences are not unheard of, but in your safe, cosy neighbourhood.

Let's get to the facts.

It was September 2008 in south Delhi's Jamia Nagar, in the vicinity of a central university called Jamia. Few here believed that the encounter was genuine, but an inspector of the Delhi Police was killed. This gave an unfortunate twist to the story and added credibility to the police version. Students were found to be anti-nationals. But the locals, including myself, found the story hard to believe.

I was twenty-two when it happened, living alone, about 200 metres from where the two young men died. When I read the reports in newspapers, I remember thinking that they sounded rather like me. It was so close that it scared me. It was as if they were me – only the names were different. They were living alone, away from their families, just as I had been since childhood. One of them wanted to be an IAS officer, another a pilot. One of those killed was studying at

Jamia Millia Islamia, like I was; the younger, about seventeen, and just a few months old in Delhi, was preparing for the Jamia entrance exam. Alongside that, he was attending English coaching classes, like I had once wanted to.

Going by media reports of the time, the rooms of the Terrorists were messy, as mine was. The lights in my house were usually on till late at night, or perhaps I should say, early in the morning. Neighbours would say, Neyaz is a very hardworking boy, he studies all night. My friends and I knew just how hardworking I was. They didn't open the door when the police knocked. I wouldn't have either – even God would have been hard put to wake me up if I didn't have an important class. Anyway, according to the newspapers, the lights were on late into the night in their home too.

Based on the stories of their activities, narrated mostly by anonymous sources, the papers confidently announced that these boys were indeed Terrorists. They may as well have been: it was too early to call, but the news reports betrayed no doubts about their culpability.

The encounter followed within a week of the serial blasts in Delhi that had killed thirty people. For a week after the blasts, the police had been raiding suspected Terrorists and their Hideouts, including in Jamia Nagar, and it was in the news all over. The men killed in the encounter had, as it turned out, submitted their original IDs and addresses to the caretaker of the building (who claimed that he had in turn submitted these to the local police station). Following the encounter, locals asked: why didn't the Terrorists run away from Jamia Nagar? The police, for their part, claimed that the Terrorists had been over-confident because they were disguised as Normal Human Beings. In a single statement, they rendered everyone a suspected Terrorist.

The police decoded all these Facts in a flash, like experts in Bollywood movies. And the media conveyed these to you and me, since, you know, that's their job. A nation's conscience was satisfied.

But mine was not. Not at all. Maybe I was not part of the nation, I thought for a moment. Or perhaps I didn't matter. I was scared. I had my doubts. So did every young man in our locality. The speed with which the authorities, and the news reports, reached their conclusions made us suspect there was something fishy; that there was more to it than what you and I knew or were told.

I had come to Delhi to study when I was barely old enough to wash my bottom. Having lived alone for eleven years, away from my parents, my thoughts were defined by friends and acquaintances in Jamia Nagar, and by the remnants of my past. The rest I learnt mostly from *The Hindu*, the newspaper I subscribed to. I didn't have TV; *it spoils kids.*

I grew up in a religious family, where half the worries of my parents and grandparents revolved around achieving piousness and seeking God's approval of their deeds. Not that I was raised as a religious bigot or anything like that. Far from it. My grandfather, Dada, taught me *Sare Jahan Se Achha* by the poet Allama Muhammad Iqbal, who also wrote, in case you don't know, a poem called *Ram*, in which he called Ram 'Imam-e-Hind', Leader of India. Iqbal is also famous for his *Shikwah*, a complaint to God, for having let down Muslims. It earned him the wrath of the clerics, who issued a fatwa declaring him an infidel. Kufr ka fatwa. But the man responded with *Jawab-e-Shikwah*, Answer to the Complaint, and shut everyone up.

Ki Muhammad se wafa to hum tere hain
Ye jahan cheez hai kya, luh'o qalam tere hain.

If you love Muhammad, I am all yours,
This world is nothing, the pen of destiny is all yours.

Dada also taught me *Is khak se uthe hain, Is khak me milenge*. I have risen from this soil, and will mingle with this soil. He taught me to use adab rather than salam while greeting an unknown person, as one might not know their faith and sensitivities.

I had been taught all this before I came to Delhi in 1997 to study, to learn new things and to uphold my family's honour. Dada was a respected figure and my parents, with their good deeds, had not let down his legacy.

I was considered bright and was despatched to a school in Delhi. (English was my forte; I knew the meaning of the word 'traitor', for example, and I knew the right word for the female chest.) I cleared the entrance test for class 6 in Jamia School, in which only six students were selected from more than a thousand, to join the batch of twenty-odd class 5 passouts.

At this new school, everything was different. For example, where I came from, the medium of instruction was Hindi, but at Jamia School, it was Urdu. Studying in a Muslim school, with only one Hindu classmate, and living in the Muslim ghetto of Jamia Nagar, I learnt many new things – from friends, from seniors, from the locality.

I learnt about Them.

That they discriminate against Muslims in IAS entrance exams and that's why there are hardly any Muslim IAS officers (Dada wanted me to become one). That they justify the demolition of Babri Masjid in Ayodhya. Of course, every educated Muslim knows what they are doing in Kashmir. And in Palestine.

I am not sure how much of all this I truly comprehended, but I did imbibe something of it.

My family didn't want me to attend Aligarh Muslim University, where, reportedly, students were involved in regular fights on campus – although this is hardly novel in Indian universities. So they chose Jamia instead.

As the days passed, I slowly realised that making it to the IAS was a far-fetched dream. Then, somehow, of all things, Medicine came to mind. I tried my best but did not clear the entrance test, and ended up studying Biosciences. This was the best I could do, given the amount of time I spent on my course books.

But those three years of undergrad were the best time of my life. I made many friends in college. It was a secular environment, or so I thought. After all, there was a Hindu as well in our group. And what's more, his religion was never on our minds. Sure, the rest of us used to go to the university mosque to offer Friday prayers; that was natural. By some chance, everyone in our group was a medical discard: none of us had qualified for entrance to medical college, and we had all landed up in BSc Bioscience, the poorest cousin of MBBS, behind even Biotechnology.

We were always having discussions (we called it bakchodi in our Delhi lingo) on a range of issues – from Islam and Muslims to India's nuclear deal with the US, to porn, or the Size of the girl who had just passed by. It was always lively, definitely livelier than coursework.

By the final year of undergrad, I began to worry about my future. MSc Bioscience or MBA? Only these two options seemed viable. I decided to pursue an MBA because I didn't want to spend my life in labs examining rats and cockroaches and fungi. But the events of that September morning in 2008 changed the course of my life, literally as well as figuratively.

In the encounter between the officers of Delhi Police and those they called terrorists, two men from the Terrorist side were killed and a police inspector was shot (and eventually died that evening).

With every passing day, between police flip-flops and the media's hysterical reportage, it seemed to the residents as if the aim of the EncounterTale was to defame Jamia Nagar's Muslims, our colony, our university. No one appeared to have a doubt about it. But the encounter was not the end of the matter. The police continued picking up students for their alleged links to the Terrorists. Like they did from the Lajawab tea stall in Batla House colony. Apparently, a student was telling his friend that one of the Terrorists happened to be a classmate of his friend's, and before he could finish, he was in a For You, With You, Always van. Nobody knew where this news came from, but it stuck. And it scared us.

All my friends were scared. We stopped going outside after sunset. No Lajawab, no Bismillah tea stall, and rarely beyond Azmat's kebab shop, which was just at the mouth of my lane. Who knew who was listening to your conversation and how he would interpret it. Each of us thought he could be next. I have nothing to hide, but ... but what if they arrest me?

Like me, none of my friends had parents in Delhi. Nobody would be there to defend us if we were arrested. We weighed our options; the future seemed dark. I thought a lot about going back home. Then I would remember the news that a few of the Terrorists had escaped from that building – one that had only a single entrance – about 200 metres from mine. God only knew how they managed that feat; nevertheless, it was all over the news that they did. I thought, if I left, they would say one more has run away. I scrapped the thought of going home. If that sounds paranoid to you, you can thank your stars you were not born into a Muslim family. Or you too might know what we went through all those days in that ghetto of – what many call – Pakistanis.

I had sleepless nights. The only source of succour was a man I had loathed since I joined Jamia Millia Islamia.

Bastard had defended Salman Rushdie.

But this time he was defending us, the Suspected Terrorists. To each of us in the crowd of hundreds of young Muslim students crammed into the university auditorium, Professor Mushirul Hasan said: 'You are as patriotic as anyone else. You don't need to prove your patriotism to ANYONE else.' There was a deafening applause.

The next day, he organised a peace rally. All of us terrorists, suspected terrorists, radicals, extremists and fundamentalists participated. Our 'trainers' too, from the jihadi laboratory called Jamia.

Eid came. It was mid-session and, normally, there would have been no question of going home. But I went home to clear my head. After a week I was feeling better, and returned. On the way, when the train stopped at the Gorakhpur railway station, I went to buy a magazine and saw the cover of *India Today*. It took me back in a flash to the darkness of the previous days.

The article quoted one of the arrested men: he would bomb a market even if his mother was there. This was scary, but it was also difficult to believe. It appeared like a cooked-up story, part of the frenzied and indiscriminate reporting in the aftermath of the encounter. Surely such hardened criminals wouldn't open their mouths so easily? Perhaps they were tortured into saying all this? In the coming days, in a jan sunwai, public hearing, organised by a group of Jamia teachers, the parents of the arrested men stated that they had not been allowed to meet their sons for days after their arrest.[1] In fact, they didn't even know where their Terrorist sons were being lodged, and only saw them when they were presented in court. The parents said that their sons had been presented in scarves even in the courtroom. It was only when their lawyer protested that the men were told to remove the scarves. Their faces were badly bruised. I was present at the meeting where the parents recounted this, and remember their faces and voices vividly to this day. And yet – and yet, the great journalist had scooped a 'frank interview' with them. Not one but two meetings, and within a few days of the arrest, he says in the story.[2] I was impressed. I became determined to be a journalist; not that I would change the world, but I would be at least one less person, I thought, who would propagate half-truths – or lies – in the garb of journalism. So, when I completed my graduation, passing by an insultingly small margin, I sought admission to Jamia's AJK Mass Communication Research Centre for a Master's in Convergent Journalism. On graduating from there, I got a job at a leading English daily in New Delhi.

It's been over a decade since the encounter, but the questions remain. Were they really terrorists? If not, then gross injustice was done to them, their families, their friends. If yes, then there was gross injustice done to Inspector Sharma, his family, his friends, and those killed in the bomb blasts. In what circumstances was the inspector shot? Was he shot by the men inside the flat? Was he shot in friendly fire? The track record of the police team involved in the encounter, the Special Cell of the Delhi Police, was hardly spotless, if one were to go by media reports. There had been several allegations of the cell's involvement in questionable encounters.[3]

What's the complete truth? No one knows. Truths are as diverse as the narrators are.

Even now, every so often, plainclothes policemen appear in Jamia Nagar, driving cars with no number plates. Often at midnight. When residents oppose their presence there, even manhandling the policemen sometimes, the police say they have come to pick up a chain snatcher, or an auto thief or a Bangladeshi. Even now, almost a decade later, such highhandedness only adds to people's doubts about the genuineness of the encounter in 2008.[4]

Over the years, I went through a transformation without realising it. This village kid from a religious family grew up into a city-dwelling young man with a sense of gnawing victimhood – real and perceived. I made friends of all hues, watched birds, enjoyed the beauty of the mountains, jungles and lakes, made sense of religion, and learnt that you can't clap with one hand. And also unlearnt many things.

The encounter had driven me nearly berserk, like it did many youths in Jamia Nagar. I was on the brink of breaking down. In frustration, I thought about ways to deal with what I – we – were facing. It set me wondering about why the youth in disturbed areas took up arms. Why, and also how? What made them so desperate that they felt the need to do that?

In the bomb blasts and other terrorist attacks in Delhi and across the country, and the counter-terror operations that followed these, innocent people have suffered beyond measure, and my small struggles are by no means comparable to theirs. But the many stories of small sufferings, small achievements, small men in Jamia Nagar that are lost in the noise still need to be heard. You have heard the news, but there is so much that never makes it to newspapers and television studios.

My own story is one of a kid who came to Delhi with many hopes; of a young man who lost his way; and then, if I might say so, of someone like you.

Will you read my story?

Part One

1

A Solitary Exodus

AMMI SEEMED TENSE THAT morning.

There was nothing new in her daily routine: offering morning prayers, cleaning the house, preparing breakfast, waking us before Dada came back from his Panchayat meeting (and shouted at us for sleeping when 'the sun has risen high and noon is approaching').

But she looked sad that day. We did not hear the murmurs of her duas for our family's well-being, the children's education, the girls' marriages, the health of some ailing lady in the village, or a good harvest – duas that usually continued long after her morning prayers were done. That morning, after Fajr namaz, as the darkness of the night gave way to dawn, she did not stroll down to the fields at the back of our house, with her tasbeeh in hand and specific duas on her lips: duas which had brought us happiness and progress all these years. She did not survey the anar, jamun, shahtut, nimbu, aam, tamatar and sabzi that grew on our small backyard farm.

We had learnt the names for these fruits in English, and repeated them some evenings as part of our homework: anar is pomegranate, jamun is berry (not blackberry, just berry, you idiot), shahtut is mulberry, nimbu is lemon, tamatar is tomato, sabzi is vegetable. And even a nursery kid knows aam is mango.

There will be one less voice repeating those lessons now, she thought. Her ten-year-old son was going away to a far-off land. She was worried he would not get home-cooked food in that alien place. *Who will wash his clothes? No doubt he will study, learn new things, preserve the honour of the family. Oh, but who will take care of him if he falls ill? And then, the consolation, the only consolation, is that he will be an educated man, a bada admi, when he returns. Everybody knows he is very talented. Have you seen his writing style? The way he writes in Urdu? Pick any language, Hindi, Urdu or even English. Give him a book and he will finish it in just one day. Like his Baaji.*

Her favourite story was of how on Republic Day, in front of the entire village, I had given a rousing speech on Sir Syed and Rajendra Prasad in flowing Urdu, like a grown man. After the speech, the principal Masoom Sir had announced, 'This boy has continued the legacy established by his older sister in this school. I congratulate Janab Nabib Sahab, who is sitting with us on the dais, on behalf of the teaching fraternity. Sir Syed School is very proud of this child.' Dada, who had written the speech, looked very proud too.

And why not? They were talking about his granddaughter. And grandson. His. Whom he had nurtured like one nurtures a mango tree, willing to wait years for it to fruit. He saw the coming of fruit that season.

Or Ammi would say, 'What about the prediction that mute woman made a few months ago? The one who came to the house, begging. She was trying hard to speak but all that came out were sounds. And you know mute people don't lie.

She had the serenity of a saint and looked sincere even from a distance, everyone could tell with one glance. God only knows who she was; even angels come in various shapes.'

Through gestures, she had made many predictions for the family. That Baaji would soon get married and get a husband who would treat her like a queen. That she would be the one to whom the keys of the house would be entrusted. Ayaz, my younger brother, would earn money, big fat money. Here, she mimicked the action of an official asking for a bribe. He wouldn't study much, but he would fly to a distant land to earn, like my father had.

And I? I would study like no one had in the whole family. The womenfolk of the family and the neighbourhood were witness to this. One of them said, and they all agreed, 'Exactly. He can't do anything else, only lick his books.'

Preposterous. As if I didn't go out to play. Or take the wheat to the flour machine. Or help on the farm during harvest.

Rubbish, plain rubbish.

But now, the prediction was coming true.

Proud and happy though she was, Ammi was worried. *And how old is he? You can see for yourselves, he is just a little kid. How will the poor soul manage? His father is already out in the Gulf to earn bread and butter for the family. Now the elder son is going away too.* It would take a day to reach Dilli, where he was going; even home-cooked food sent to him would perish before it reached Babu. Farooquee Babu.

Babu – a term of endearment but also the word for bureaucrats. Dada had wanted his Farooquee Babu to be an IAS officer. For the prestige that an officer brings to a family. Everything else pales in comparison.

The entire house was awake early that day and everyone looked perfectly happy, as if they were thankful I was leaving. When my sleepiness fell away, I realised it was only I who was happy. Then, as the minutes passed, I gradually went quiet. I didn't want my voice to give away the fact that I wanted to cry.

I loved playing cricket, like most children in the village. Dada had played football, as did Abbu in his day. In fact, Abbu was quite a star in our village and its surrounds. But by the time I grew up, football was slowly giving way to cricket. I played a bit of football, kabaddi, thuthur-muthur and badminton, but cricket was by far our favourite.

The wall of our primary school was wicket and wicketkeeper. Older boys played in the village field – part of the graveyard that had been flattened over the years. This was further than I was allowed to roam. So the roads and the small open space in front of our house became our Eden Garden and Lords.

We would request someone going to Thawe, the local market, to bring back a cricket ball for us. Coscos were costly; leather balls were even costlier and also dangerous. We played with rubber balls that were about one-tenth the price of Cosco balls. Only, these balls were small and feeble and disintegrated after a few hard shots. More often, we would lose them in a nearby field or in the many construction sites around. Or it would fly to a neighbour's compound, and he would return the ball only if his kid was playing too.

When we had exhausted our pocket money, there was a fallback.

Collect polythene, steal some bricks from outside Badey Dada's house, where a pile was always stacked against the wall. (Careful, the pile might collapse and alarm him.) Light a fire. Put all the polythene on the bricks and melt them.

Take a chappal and gently beat the melting polythene with it to give it a round shape. Don't use hands – it's sticky. Don't let it touch the soil, or it will lose its stickiness. Mould it well before the polythene cools, otherwise it will become a smelly, irregular lump. Voila! In a few minutes, your cricket ball is ready.

And for the bat? Just cut a branch from one of the shisham trees nearby and shave it into a bat. Jamun wood doesn't make for a good bat; it's too weak. Goolar is good, but we were not allowed to cut it – it was next to the pond and we might fall in and drown.

Our cricket pitch was also the place where the village school held its prayers.

Iqbal's *Lab Pe Ati Hai Dua* to start the day. And Rabindranath Tagore's *Jana Gana Mana* to end it.

It was where we had our ghur – what urbanites know as a bonfire – in the winters. The menfolk of the neighbourhood sat around it and talked village affairs, harvest, politics and religion.

The pitch-field overlooked our school wall, painted with a map of India depicting all its states. The map was coloured in bands of saffron, white and green, like our flag. My state was part saffron and part white. The wall also had quotes from the leaders of our freedom struggle. And the sort of slogans that every school sports:

Unity in diversity.
Work is worship.
God helps those who help themselves.
Honesty is the best policy.
Miles to go before I sleep.

Next to the run-down school building was the haloed circle made of slanted bricks, at the centre of which a flagpole was installed on Republic and Independence days. When the festivities ended and the flag post was removed, we played thuthur-muthur there: one team stood at alert inside the circle and the other team waited outside. Their job was to drag those inside the circle out – pull them out or head-butt them, whatever worked. When the outside team entered the circle to ambush the inside team, the defenders could beat them ferociously within that millisecond.

Brave were the ones who played bare-chested.

When we sat by the ghur in the lazy winters, perhaps the school itself, obscured by dense fog, reminded Dada of his (meagre) student days. He would often recite a Sanskrit shloka that he had learnt in school, which defined the qualities of an ideal student:

Kak cheshta, bako dhyanam
Shwan nidra, tathaiva cha
Alpahari, griha tyagi
Vidyarthi pancha lakshanam.

Crow's perseverance
Crane's concentration
Dog's sleep
Eats less

Leaves home to study.
These are the five signs of an ideal student.

I was supposed to emulate this. But it constantly disappointed him that this young generation had no idealism left. Sleeping on after the sun rose – which was late for a student or a farmer – would invite Kabir upon me:

Ati ka bhala na bolna, ati ki bhali na choop,
Ati ka bhala na barasna, ati ki bhali na dhoop.

Too much speaking is not good, nor too much silence;
Too much rain is not good, nor too much sunshine.

The day I was leaving, my sisters didn't want to go to school. Bhayya was going to Dilli, and they wanted to say Salamalekum before he left.

Salamalekum is not the right word. It's Assalam-o-Alaikum – Peace Be Upon You. In response, you say, Walaikum Assalam – Peace Be Upon You Too.

But Dada had made it clear: nobody misses school. 'I have told your principal, he will let you off for a few minutes when Babu is leaving.'

Baaji would be at home as she had finished her schooling. My younger sisters went to the neighbourhood school, which was right next to our house. I had studied there too before moving to a hostel in Gopalganj for a few weeks and then to the school in the neighbouring village where Baaji had completed her schooling.

There, she had given her speeches for Independence Day and Republic Day celebrations – and I had repeated the ones I could. On Mahatma Gandhi, Maulana Azad and Chacha

Nehru. On Babu Kunwar Singh, Maulana Mazharul Haque, Shibli Nomani, Muhammad Iqbal, Khan Abdul Ghaffar Khan, the Ali brothers. And on the Revolt of 1857, Chauri Chaura in 1922, the Jallianwala Bagh massacre in 1919 and about India's independence.

There, I had also told jokes from the dais every Thursday – our activity day and half holiday.

There was a rich shopkeeper. He was thankful to God for what He had given him. To thank Him, the man had hung a frame in his shop with a dua written on it: *Ha'za min fazali rabbi*. This is by the grace of my Lord. A thief raided his shop and stole all the material, and wrote just below that dua: *Innallah ma'assabireen*. God gives to those who are patient.

One more?

An old lady died in her childhood.

Clap clap clap. Giggle clap giggle.

These were jokes that my younger sisters would retell when their time came.

Ayaz had missed school but still missed my departure. He was unwakeable. Dadi called him Kumbhakaran. Later, he complained bitterly that nobody had woken him up to see me off. I thought he refused to wake up because he was angry with me. I had given him a tap with a cricket bat the day before because he had batted the whole time and, when it was my turn, the scoundrel ran away. After a long chase, when I couldn't catch him, I threw my bat at him in frustration.

Though this misbehaviour would not have been tolerated ordinarily, I was let off with just a glare. For one, I was generally considered a sincere child; and, two, I was going away the next day.

The train that afternoon was at 2.35 p.m. from Siwan, the nearest major railway station, about 30 km from the village. It was the train that important people like netas and bureaucrats preferred when they had to travel to the North. It connected us to the outside world – except to our capital Patna, because there was no train-bridge nearby for us to cross the Ganga.

It took forty-five minutes of hanging from – or standing on one foot in – the local train to reach Siwan. Or a one-hour bumpy drive by jeep. Or two struggling hours in a bus. But before that, we needed to buy our tickets from Thawe, our local railway station, as Siwan station would be very crowded. You hardly ever got tickets for reserved seats during summer vacations, so the idea was to get a general ticket, enter the reserved bogey somehow and pay a fine to stay there. No one who travelled by train had to be told this; it was the norm.

Further, Neshat Chacha, our neighbour, said that it was a total waste of time scrambling to get reserved tickets. He worked as a guard in the local metre gauge trains. In the beginning, he was posted in Jammu and Kashmir but managed to get a transfer to the Thawe route, which was close to home. Later, when he would be promoted to broad gauge trains, he would choose to remain on the local route that kept him close to home. He was one of the rare people in our village who had a government job. He was a favourite of the youth in the village during the sugarcane season. The trains running between the fields and one of the mills passed through my village. The young men of the village would issue a gentle reminder: Guard *sahab, sab khairiyat hai na*? All well, na?

The train, (over)loaded with sugarcane, ran so slow that, the joke went, you could cook your lunch on the train and be done before it had left the village. Well, they often did 'cook' the sweet dish, and whenever they did, some of the delicacies got delivered to guard sahab's home too.

But guard sahab had not seen anything.

That morning he explained that we didn't need to queue up at the ticket counter in Thawe. 'Go round the back and tell anyone sitting at the counter my name. He will promptly issue you a ticket.'

He elaborated: 'Pay a fine when the TTE comes for the ticket. After that nobody will say anything to you. And if you can somehow save yourself from encountering the TTE till Gorakhpur, you can even avoid the fine. After Gorakhpur, you don't find many TTEs.' TTE: Travelling Ticket Examiner.

His experience as a railwayman was impressive. 'Try to enter coach S-5 or S-6. You will find many people in the coach from Siwan and Gopalganj. Talk to them politely and adjust with them.' With a smile, he added, 'slowly slowly'. It was the same smile that he had smiled when his attempt to squat on our land failed and he had to apologise to Dada – his father's younger brother.

Dada always insisted on setting out early. You never know when a vehicle might break down. Or what the future holds. Better to go a little early. So, food was being cooked early and packed for the long train journey. For me, and for my cousins Aamir Bhayya and Bhuttu Bhayya, who would accompany me to Delhi. Bhuttu Bhayya was to join us at Thawe bus stand. I would live with him in Delhi. Aamir Bhayya would return once I was settled there – once a proper school uniform had been bought, good hotels identified for me to eat at and I was familiarised with the safest route to school.

Aamir Bhayya, the son of my khala, Ammi's elder sister, lived with us because there were better facilities for education around my village, and also because of the environment that Nabib Sahab's home offered.

Janab Nabib Sahab is an enlightened man, the whole world knows. Though hardly educated – except for a few classes taken in his spare time away from the task of grazing the buffalo – he gave his kids a sound education. His eldest son went to college, which the family could barely afford. It is another matter altogether that the young man had to discontinue his studies to find work, feed his family and marry off his sisters. But no doubt he was groomed to be samajhdar like his father, thoughtful and wise. And Nabib Sahab's younger son was sent to Siwan and Patna to prepare for MBBS, at a time when few in the village had the luxury to step out to study.

Dada had told Ammi to cook vegetarian food as we were travelling by train and a lot of our co-passengers would be of the Hindu biradari. He was fond of saying, '*Ek qadam hum chalein, ek qadam aap chalein*' (I will take one step, you take one).

He not only preached, he set an example. Sometime in the 1970s, when Hindus from a neighbouring village had opposed the slaughtering of a nilgai – 'blue cow', though it is in reality an antelope – that had strayed into the village. Farmers didn't usually oppose the killing of nilgai that entered the farms because they destroyed crops, but they did this time. Nabib Sahab summoned a meeting of the villagers and told them that everyone's sentiments should be considered. Because he was a respected figure, the entire village took a vow that no one would slaughter a cow there anymore. Those who wished to eat beef would procure it from a licensed slaughterhouse.

My family still respects that unwritten treaty. For that, we are respected among both Hindus and Muslims.

So, our meal in the train had to be vegetarian, and it had to be something that wouldn't spoil in the July heat and humidity. My choice was sattu paratha and aloo ki bhujia. That morning, Dada returned early from the Panchayat meeting that followed his prayers and tended to go on forever. He enquired if my luggage was packed. Ammi had packed it before I woke up. As I was going to Dilli, she had ironed my clothes as well. 'How many bags?' Dada asked.

'Two,' lied Ammi. There was one for clothes, one for my books and another for eatables like bhuja, halwa, achar. Dada wasn't impressed. 'Two? And another one for food?' Two bags were already more than his prescribed limit of luggage per person: 'Light enough to carry, or maybe to run with, in case of an emergency.'

He asked mockingly, 'We will see him off at Siwan but what about Dehli? Who will carry his luggage over there? Farishtey?'

Ammi muttered something inaudible but she knew what to do. She would reduce the bhuja – snacks typically made with chana, chawal or makka. She took out the bright red shirt and bluish trousers which were my least favourite. She had insisted on packing those: 'You should wear more bright colours. Your dress like older people. Like your Dada. Always grey clothes.'

I had my breakfast sitting close to Ammi, while she was busy with her chores near the chulha on the first floor of the house. The ground floor was overcrowded, so whatever

Dada managed to save from the money Abbu sent, he used to build the first floor in stages – pillars first, walls next, roof thereafter and then he shifted the chulha to the first floor. It had a bigger courtyard and more open space.

The chulha should be in an open space because smoke kills.

As I ate my breakfast, instructions kept coming at me from all sides. 'You are very lazy when it comes to food. Don't worry about money. You must eat fruits, whatever sort you like. Hotel food is not good for your health,' said Ammi. 'You like grapes, na? Nowadays, all kinds of fruits are available in the market in all seasons,' she went on, while her hands shaped perfectly circular, thin parathas that would be packed for the journey. 'Sayyada, tell him where to get fruits.' Sayyada, my Chhoti Ammi, my father's younger brother's wife. She had gone to Delhi for treatment and knew every corner of the city. *Shaher ka chappa chappa.*

'Anywhere,' she said as she cooked the aloo bhujiya. 'You go anywhere, you will find fruits. You just have to be a little careful with the rate. Bargain. Just halve the price they ask for.' I nodded in agreement.

Dadi was churning the buffalo milk with a stick we call rahi – I don't know what people call it in cities. She was rotating it as fast as she could, so that her Babu could take some butter with him to Dilli. Or at least have some before leaving.

In her shaky voice, she said, 'Babu?' Mmm.

'Don't forget to drink milk daily. How thin you look. Like a bimarua laika.' Diseased kid. She looked around. 'You all are sending my kid to I don't know what godforsaken place. Who knows him in pardes? *Abhi to iske doodh ke dant bhi nahin toote hain sahi se.*'

This was not true. And I knew it was just a muhawara. Like Dada once said when I complained about my teachers: *Nach na aawe aangan tedha.* You can't dance, so you complain the ground is uneven. Or when he mocked Dadi for speaking out of turn: *Adhjal gagri chhalkat jaye, bhari gagariya chuppe jaye.* A barrel half-full of water makes a noise; full ones are quiet.

Dada too was rushing through breakfast. He wanted to instruct the tractor driver Naresh Bhai and the daily-wagers who worked in our field, because he wouldn't be back until the evening.

Dadi, meanwhile, continued, 'Achha, Babu, will you take some arwa rice? The harvest has been very healthy this season.' I was quiet. She said. 'See, it's shinier than last year's. Thanks be to the uparwala that it rained in time. Where will you find this rice grown in your own fields in pardes?'

Chhoti Ammi and Baaji were assisting Ammi with packing the food. They both looked at me, suppressing their laughter and avoiding Dada's gaze.

I had to smile back.

Dada shouted, 'He is going to Dehli, not Siswan.' Siswan, in the neighbouring district Siwan, is Dadi's ancestral village and, coincidentally, Ammi's too.

It was time to leave. Ten thirty. Dada would brook no delay.

Ten thirty meant ten thirty.

He was waiting outside with Aamir Bhayya's bicycle. Four people wouldn't fit on our scooter, so Naresh Bhai was to accompany us as far as Thawe on his cycle.

Thawe is some 4 km from my village if you take the brick-soling road that passes through Pakhopali bazar, and hardly 3 km if you pedal along the railway track. It's a local pilgrimage site because of a popular Durga mandir, and there's also a crumbling haveli nearby. Every year, a large number of devotees from near and far visit the temple. It is believed that Goddess Durga rested at that spot on her way to visit Nepal. Thawe was also a small centre for Bhojpuri song recordings. The town used to produce a large number of religious songs at one time but, of late, it had become notorious for producing vulgar songs that were immensely popular. The year I was coming to Delhi, '*Ja jhar ke*' was a big hit. Younger men loved it, older men frowned upon it. You could read it as you liked: work on your looks before you step out, shake yourself up, revv up your vehicle. But for those who could read between the lines, the song could seem like a reference to masturbation.

From Thawe, there is a bus to Siwan.

Dada would ride pillion with Aamir Bhayya on the cycle and pedal it home on the return journey. I would sit on the carrier of Naresh Bhai's cycle, and he would go back home after dropping us at the bus stand.

My bicycle. Hero, size 20, red. I had raced it over every bump and every turn in the village, every field of ours, from the railway tracks to the qabristan to my school in the neighbouring village. I was leaving it behind for Ayaz. Aamir Bhayya would park the bicycle at Moinuddin Chacha's barber shop in Thawe. Moinuddin Chacha and his family were the sole hairdressers in the village. At weddings, he was the one who invited the villagers on the host's behalf and distributed the wedding cards. He was a many-roles-in-one man, who also acted as chef during celebrations until the fancy catering services arrived and he was relegated to assisting them. He also carried wedding gifts to the homes they were meant for. And he was single-handedly responsible for making the village's katua kids katua. Circumcised.

That was a festive occasion in our house, which was specially repaired, painted and decorated. All the relatives gathered and a milad, an assembly of maulanas who talked about religion, was organised. It was like a wedding party. When the moment arrived, I was made to sit half-naked on a mortar – the wooden kind, which was used to pound cereals and spices. Moinuddin Cha sat in front of me, holding his knives and scissors. People held me, and an older cousin went out on to the terrace to distract me. 'Look! Aeroplane.' But another cousin had been circumcised earlier that day and been fooled by the aeroplane, so I knew what was coming and was determined not to be distracted by any aeroplane. Relatives, all gathered for the sacred occasion, formed a ring around me to watch the proceedings and suggested other ways to distract me. And then my cousin asked, 'You want my watch? Here.' I used to like it very much and looked up instantly. Before I realised what was happening, it was gone.

It.

I was skinless, and permanently and identifiably a Musalman – it's the one thing that helps everyone, both Hindus and Muslims, identify the Other in case of a riot. After the ceremony, my cousin and I lay on separate cots, naked, while our, um, things turned into a massive tourist attraction. We got a lot of money from visitors and all kinds of food and fruits to eat. For the next few days, our things enjoyed (almost) unlimited freedom. When we left the cot, we wore a white kurta without a pajama, and ran around half-naked. (Netas wearing white kurtas have hogged all the limelight, but it is equally a sign of recent circumcision. If you spot a man – well, boy – in a white kurta, there is a good chance that he has been circumcised recently. You can ask him about that; and he will not take offence if he is a man.)

For many days after the ceremony, whenever Moinuddin Cha visited my neighbourhood to trim someone's hair or beard, the sight of his scissors invariably unsettled me – even if I was in a pajama. He doesn't practice his ancestral profession anymore. His sons are now in Saudi Arabia, earning the money and pride that had eluded his family for generations. He owns a pucca house too.

It was the month of July when I left, the season to sow paddy. The monsoon rains were nowhere in sight (except for a few guerrilla showers). But you could not leave your fields banjar either, so the pump-set tried (not very successfully) to stand in for nature.

'Naresh, you will come back from Thawe and take the tractor to the qabristan wala khet. I have told Mukhiyaji to give you diesel. Take 20 litres so we have enough for tomorrow as well.' Mukhiyaji was not really the elected village head. Villagers had given him the name, mocking him for his never-ending netagiri – having an opinion on everything, meddling in everyone's affairs and spreading news, all sorts of news, around the village.

Naresh Bhai asked, 'Which field? The smaller or the bigger one?'

This annoyed Dada. 'Why are you so distracted? When you know the smaller field has already been planted, why would you run a tractor on it?'

Naresh Bhai realised his mistake and did what everyone did when Dada was angry: shut his mouth. But Dada continued, 'Tell me, did you go with a sieve when God was giving out brains?'

Taibun Dadi was sitting hunched at a little distance. She was as old as my Dadi, and took care of our fields and directed the labourers when Dada was busy or not around. She was a fixture at home during the harvest season. She knew more about our fields than anyone else in the family, except Dada and Dadi. She knew the exact size of the farms, the date when the seeds were to be planted, or needed to be irrigated, or when the weeds had to be rooted out. She also had a brilliant network of informers who provided her with the names of the men and women whose cattle wandered into our fields.

That day, she was asked to supervise the labourers who were planting paddy.

Nabijan was to stay at home and take care of the buffalo. Nabijan. He had been living with us since he was a child, and grew up with Baaji and our cousins. After their father died, his elder brother had more or less thrown him out. He was the only non-family adult male allowed into the house.

When he grew older, Nabijan often threatened to run away because he thought he wasn't being treated well, or sensed better job prospects near his home, about 30 km from ours. He did run away twice or thrice but returned on his own.

He was a bit slow to react, and for us – my siblings, cousins and I – his slowness and simplicity were often a source of cheap amusement. We would, for instance, test his knowledge. We posed to him the same questions that elders asked us.

'Nabijan, tell us, is wheat flour ground or rice flour?' Haha, neither. You grind wheat or rice, not flour. Flour is already ground, buddhu.

'Achha, tell us, if an electric train runs from east to west and the westerly wind is blowing, to which side will the engine's smoke go? East or west?' Haha, hehe. You are so big, and you don't even know that electric trains don't expel smoke? Giggle.

He was the standard against which all of us siblings and cousins were measured:

You eat like Nabijan, with your mouth wide open.

You will get a husband like Nabijan.

You will get a job like Nabijan's.

Once, he ran away to look for work elsewhere, and returned after wandering for a few weeks. That evening, he was asked how many rotis he would like to have for dinner. He said he wasn't hungry, but ended up having eight rotis. He would only eat cold and hard rotis, because he believed that if he ate hot rotis directly from the chulha, his marriage would be delayed or, worse, he wouldn't get married. Alas, his fears came true; he is still to get married. Nabijan would sit hunched while eating, his lota with drinking water close by. When he was fully engrossed in his food, my cousins would surreptitiously take his lota and hide it somewhere. He would realise it was gone only when he had finished his food. He never drank water directly from the tubewell, so he would wander around for hours in search of the lota. We would hide it where he would not think to look for it: in his room.

In the mornings, when the milk was abundant, he would take some in a bowl and break his cold, hard roti into it. While he was doing this, one of my cousins would involve him in some trash talk to distract him, and another would quietly extract the bowl from under his hand. Unaware that the bowl had been whisked away, he would end up with a pile of roti on the floor.

We would have a good laugh.

When he realised that he had been made a fool of, Nabijan would get angry and threaten to run away again.

But he didn't. Almost never.

That morning Dada told him that if he needed khali to feed the buffalo, he could take it from Tahir Cha's shop. Khali, the stuff left over after mustard oil is pressed, is offered to cattle with hay. Cattle tend to like the recipe. 'Tell him I have told you to get it.'

Nabijan swung his head in affirmation, at least a metre to each side, as he usually did.

It was time to leave.

Aamir Bhayya carried my bags outside. I walked down to the ground floor with Ammi, one (slow) step at a time, holding the concrete railing. How many thousands of times I had slid down that railing, and how infuriated Dada always was when he caught me.

14, 13, 12, 11, 10, 9, 8, 7.

Then the sixth step, my favourite, because it was the highest step from which I could jump all the way down without hurting myself.

5, 4, 3, 2.

Finally, the first step that brought me to the courtyard, where we often sat on holidays. Where we blocked Ammi's way and demanded pocket money for balloons or ice cream or groundnuts. Or listened to Dadi's stories of djinns and churails. That a churail has her feet backwards, the only way to identify the evil spirit. And that djinns wear white clothes. They are tall, as tall as the palm tree. They are creatures of god, just like humans. And there are good djinns and bad djinns, just like humans.

Once Ustaaniji, the woman teacher in Dadi's village, was out for a stroll after midnight in the month of Ramazan. A pious woman, she prayed and recited verses from the Quran the whole night. She happened to pass near the village graveyard. That's where she saw them, the djinns as tall as palm trees, as white as the sky, praying in congregation. Luckily, they were good djinns. They didn't disturb her, and she was careful not to disturb them. They saw her and said salam to her; she responded and kept walking, reciting the Quran, rosary in hand.

Another day, a boy from my village had gone to defecate in the graveyard just outside our village. Some djinns spotted him and slapped him so hard that he was ill for a week with high fever. He hadn't seen anyone around, but he knew it was a djinn who had punished him for defecating in the qabristan, where our forefathers are buried, and where djinns often visit.

Djinns, by the way, can see us but we can't see them unless they wish us to. They pray in masjids at midnight when no one is around. Young women should not go up on the roof or step outside in the darkness of the night as there are bad djinns too. It is also better not to sleep in the passage of a house, as djinns use it to pass through and, if they happen to be bad, they might choke you. If anything like that happens, God forbid, you must recite the darood and kalma. Then they leave you alone.

The stories made the darkness of night around us scary. For several days afterwards, the movement of the shisham tree behind the house, or the jamun tree to the south of the house, or the banana tree in our backyard would give us the shivers at night. Going for a pee to the toilet at the western corner of the house, though well inside the building, became a group outing.

When we reached the courtyard, Ammi gave me some money. 'Buy dry fruits with this.' She issued last-minute instructions, difficult to decipher, bundled in emotions and a breaking voice. 'Your Abbu will send money every month directly to you. I have given Aamir Babu some money to buy what you need. He will give you the rest before he returns.'

Chhoti Ammi came up with her gift – a small sum of money. I said no.

It's never good manners to take or ask for money from others. If you need anything, you should ask your parents.

She tucked it into the pocket of my (new) shirt.

'Don't forget to offer namaz,' Ammi reminded me.

Panchon waqt ka. All five times.

I had forgotten the namaz you offer before embarking on a journey, but it was too late now.

The whole family had assembled at the door of the house. My sisters and cousins had sneaked in through the back door before anyone could send for them.

I didn't see Dadi anywhere.

In all the excitement of going to Dilli, I had not considered the fact that it would mean separation from everyone who stood there to see me off. I wouldn't be able to see them when I felt like it. And I would only be able to return for Eid if it fell during the holidays. I wouldn't be there when Abbu came back for his vacations, while all my siblings would be.

When my relatives visited to meet him, I would miss all the spontaneous festivities that followed. I hoped for a miracle, the kind of miracle that you know can't come true. I waited for someone to say one *last* time: don't send the kid.

No one did.

Outside, it was gloomy. The dog that I always kicked sat at the entrance. He seemed sad; who would kick him now? The sparrows in the veranda did not move; they waited in their nest, perhaps for me to try and catch them one last time.

Those last few minutes in the veranda, it seemed like time had stopped. Death must feel like this. The sher in Urdu that were painted just below the ventilators stared at me. I had spent hours decoding them, sitting in the veranda, watching the torrents of monsoon rain or bemoaning the uselessness of summer noons when it was too hot to play outside.

Sparrows had whitened the shers with their shit. A couplet encouraged me, saying:

Ghubar-e-raah ho kar chashm-e-mardum me mahal paya hai,
Nihal-e-khaksari ko laga kar hum ne phal paya hai.

I was the road's dust once to find an abode in men's eyes.
It was soil that I embraced to bear such fruit.

To walk on that road and find an abode in men's eyes, I needed first to pass the words Bismillah-ir-rahman-ir-rahim, written just above it. In the name of God I begin. The writing had its own sense of style – of the calligraphic genre of Arabic, but with a healthy touch of Urdu.

Another couplet in the veranda advised me:

Na kar apno se tu imdad ki ummeed mushkil mein,
Nikala hai kahan nakhoon khare kafe pa ko.

Dada said that it meant not to trust your own people blindly. Do the toes of your foot take out a thorn from your foot? No. For that, your foot must rely on the fingers of your distant hand. So, always be careful, he would say, especially of those who claim to be your own.

We interpreted this as a taunt to Badey Dada, Dada's elder brother. Whenever he got a chance, Badey Dada tried to squat on our land. Once, his family had mocked us when we had to go on a tractor to Thawe because we didn't have a car like they did. Angry about that humiliation, Abbu bought a second-hand pumpset-jeep – that's a jeep with an actual pumpset for an engine, once a common sight in our parts – on credit the very next day.

Badey Dada was building a huge house, unfit for a small village set-up. He spent a mind-boggling sum of money on it because his son, who was in Saudi Arabia, was earning a handsome income, more than any one of us could ever imagine earning. About their palatial house, Dada would quote the poet Ghalib's couplet:

Aur bazar se le aaye agar toot gaya,
Saghar-e-jam se mera jaam-e-sifal achha hai.

My clay-cup is better than Emperor Jamshed's,
If it breaks, I can at least buy another in the market.

Emperor Jamshed was the great king of Persian legend who possessed a cup filled with the elixir of life, the possession of which was considered by many to be the reason for the success of the Persian Empire.

On the other side of the veranda was a couplet that said:

Tishnagi bhi ek sharf hai warna ae lab,
Waris-e-zamzam nahi ki malik-e-kausar nahi.

Thirst is also a virtue; if not for it,
Your lips wouldn't know Zamzam (the sacred water of Mecca) or Kausar (the fountain in heaven).

Between the two, in the centre of the veranda, meant to be read before a journey, was this dua:

Bismillah-e-tawakkaltu alallah-e-lahaul wala quwwat illa billah.

In the name of God, I place my trust in God, and there is no power (to do good) and no might (to abstain from evil) except with the assistance of Allah.

Outside, the house had a chhajja – a concrete shade that protected the windows and the entrance from rain and harsh sun. This too had a dua written on it:

Qullu nafsun zayaqatul maut.

Every creature will have to taste death.

It was a reminder that one should be pious and pray for one's salvation. Because this world is merely a transition, and everyone will eventually die before being resurrected by God on the Day of Judgement – when your piety will decide if you go to heaven or to hell.

The pigeons at Badey Dada's house – in front of ours – sat guturgu-ing. One stone and they would have flown off to take another aerial survey of the village. And witness the first meeting of eyes on rooftops of young girls (there on the pretext of spreading washed clothes to dry, for example) and boys (wandering around pretending to stock firewood or some such serious work). Crisscrossing the jamun, goolar, sheesham, rising above warehouse, past the pond, into the fields beyond that – the places where I played and grew up.

Dadi appeared with a glass of water. She always offered water to Abbu and Chhote Abbu when they went away to the Gulf countries. Now it was my turn. I wasn't thirsty but obliged her because you are supposed to respect your elders. I managed to drink half a glass without making eye contact with anyone.

She put a wrinkled hand on my head, and said, 'Babu, when you come back, we will marry you off.'

I tried to hide my embarrassment.

'It's no mean task to find an achhe rahen-sahen and chaal-chalan wali girl nowadays.' Good-natured and well-behaved. 'You understand?' she said, as if seeking my approval of her wisdom. With a glitter in her eyes, she scanned those who stood around and said, 'But, Babu, you don't have to worry. I will not die before I find a good girl for you.'

She gave me a fruit, which Ammi had bought for her in Gopalganj market when she went there to buy some clothes for me to wear in Dilli. 'And don't eat anything anyone gives you on the train.' She reached into her kurta pocket and coins jingled, like the ones she gave me to get her paan. She took me aside, away from the eyes of the other kids, and whispered, 'Take it, Babu, buy mithai when you reach Dilli.'

Dada was getting impatient. 'Oh, finish your rituals now. It's getting late.'

I said my final adieus. Assalam-o-Alaikum, Dadi; Assalam-o-Alaikum, Ammi; Assalam-o-Alaikum, Chhoti Ammi; Assalam-o-Alaikum, Baaji.

Walaikum Assalam. Peace be upon you too.

Assalam-o-Alaikum and Salamalekum from my sisters and female cousins, in tandem, sounding like a thousand-people chorus. Some from behind the curtain at the entrance and some not. I said Walaikum Assalam so many times.

Assalam-o-Alaikum, Nabijan bhai.

Ammi must have been happy to hear this. Whenever I had shouted at Nabijan, she reminded me of hadees, lines from Prophet Muhammad's sayings: one, Those who do not treat their servants well are not of us; and the other, Treat your servants as you would treat your brother.

And if such misbehaviour reached Dada's ears, it invariably invited the poet Iqbal's couplet:

Iqbal bada updeshak hai, Mann baton me moh leta hai
Guftar ka ye ghazi to bana, Kirdar ka ghazi ban na saka.

You are a good preacher, you charm with your words,
You are a champion at talking, but not in your deeds.

Or another couplet that made us laugh, for reasons undecipherable to elders – it featured the name of my younger brother Ayaz and that of Mahmood (his original name was Mehboob), a servant at our Badey Dada's home. The servant was rather less lucky than others of his kind; he seriously lacked servant-sensitivity, and would advise our octogenarian Badey Dada, in all innocence, to marry again when Badi Dadi died.

Ek hi saf me khadey ho gaye Mahmood-o-Ayaz,
Na koi banda raha, Na koi banda nawaz.

The king and his servant stood in the same file facing God,
And thus melted the difference between commoner and king.

Such hadees and poetry were commonly quoted at home, as were Kabir's couplets, Khusrau's riddles, Guru Nanak's teachings and those of Chanakya. And then there were local idioms and wisdoms and whatnots. The men and messages varied. Of late, Muhammad Iqbal had come to be quoted quite often, for example that last couplet.

Dada's warning swiftly mobilised our caravan. Baaji ran indoors. Ammi was in tears, I saw from the corner of my eyes. I was still avoiding eye contact.

I wouldn't cry. Otherwise Baaji would make fun of me later.

You cried.

Like a child.

In front of everyone.

Aaw!

I was leaving behind a world to which I would soon become indifferent, nonchalantly forfeiting all its ideals. In time yet to come. But soon, very soon.

For now, I could not stop hiccupping. They, Dada, Aamir Bhayya and Naresh Bhai, walked at a brisk pace. I trailed behind.

Resisting the temptation to look back. One last time.

Before I was transported to a distant land. Where I wouldn't know anyone.

Where I wouldn't find Ammi. Or Dada.

Where I would have no friends.

And from where I couldn't even come to visit home alone. I could, but I wouldn't be allowed to.

I don't remember who noticed me crying like an idiot. Dada didn't look at me. Aamir Bhayya did not say anything. Naresh Bhai tried to console me, but Aamir Bhayya said, 'Let him be.'

Our route crisscrossed through the village. Walking. Dada first. Naresh Bhai following with his cycle (and luggage). Aamir Bhayya following with his cycle (and luggage). I was trailing behind (no luggage).

Past Maroof Da's house, where I had watched many a madari perform with his monkeys.

Then Qabool Da's house, behind which were the mango trees on which we played dola pati – jumping from one branch to another – in summer.

Idrees Da's house.

Our mason-on-demand Jameel Cha's house.

Naresh Bhai's mohalla, where all the Bahujans lived.

The house of my school teacher in Gopalganj, Hasnain sir, and his Ansari mohalla.

Noorul Haq Cha, our cycle-repair mechanic's house-cum-shop.

The house of Mushtaq Phoopha, who sang at the mushairas Abbu organised when he came home from Saudi Arabia on vacation.

Mandir-o-masjid giraane ka naya chhodo chalan,
Desh ki azmat bachao ae mere ahl-e-watan.

Stop this rush to demolish mosques and temples,
Save, O my countrymen, the greatness of this county, instead.

The sudden greenery of monsoon lent the railway tracks a certain beauty. You could almost forget the smell of the shit that lined the tracks.

The village was more or less behind us when we heard someone wailing. 'Chacha? Nabib Cha?'

Muzaffar Cha was running towards us, holding out an arm. 'It bit me, it bit me. A scorpion bit me.'

People in the village would often come to Dada for help with scorpion stings. Dada was in a hurry to catch the bus to Siwan, but he could hardly say no to such an emergency.

'Where? Where did it bite you?'

It was on one of his fingers and he had tied a piece of cloth close to his elbow to stop the poison from spreading.

'How did it bite you?'

'I was removing the bricks that lay in my osara to make space for some cattle.'

Dada picked up a few pebbles and asked him to sit down. He held Muzaffar Chacha's arm near the elbow and slid his hand down slowly, muttering a verse. At the end of each cycle, he put one pebble aside to ensure that the cycle was repeated the exact number of times.

In a few minutes, Dada gave Muzaffar Chacha a few instructions and excused himself, explaining that we needed to leave soon or miss our bus. The villagers who had gathered around us told us that there was one Atul Bihar's bus. 'It's a good service,' they said. 'It doesn't stop anywhere in the middle like the local buses do, Chacha.' Muzaffar Cha offered to send his son to help us carry our bags. He was still holding his arm but he looked relieved. How, you might wonder, does repeating a verse treat the poison of a scorpion? But it had done just that for many years in a village where there was no qualified doctor. The nearest hospital was kilometres away, and not easily approachable. Also, scorpion bites were common enough when people went out to defecate or graze livestock or collect firewood.

Placebo effect, many call it.

I never gathered the courage to ask Dada how it worked. The only person he had taught the verse to was Baaji. When I had asked her, she said she couldn't tell me. If she did, its effectiveness would lessen. By the time I grew old enough to understand it all, Dada was no more and Baaji had forgotten the verse. The healing verse that had cured, or fooled, many a scorpion-bit villager was lost forever. We hurriedly relaunched our journey. I sat on the bicycle carrier and watched the fields go by. There were fields on both sides of the tracks. The side I faced had patches of grey interrupted by green, paddy drowning in muddy water. In the distance was an abandoned brick kiln that Dada had started in partnership with someone from the neighbouring village. The venture had failed, and was now a green hillock of weedy misfortune surrounded by this grey lake of misfortune. Behind me, the grey extended further; last year's flood waters still made their presence felt, though this year's monsoon was yet to show its true colours. The tracks stopped the floods from entering our village, which was good, but they also didn't allow the water that had sneaked in to retreat. The stagnant water ruined that year's harvest.

By the time it began to dry, another monsoon would arrive. It was a yearly ritual. It would rain, and we would hear that an embankment had broken somewhere in a distant land, and then it would become unstoppable, the flood. Slowly, all the villages around us would get inundated. One by one. On a first come, first served basis. A scenic devastation, in other words. It was a little worse every year.

My village was relatively less affected. Often, the floods in Bihar were so intense that they washed away villages, highways (where they existed) and railway tracks (where they existed). Its intensity drowned out the languages of privilege and protocol. Journalists and netas had to defy the rule of gravity to certify that the misery was genuine. And get a good photo-op.

But also for funds to be released. Or remedial action to be intensified.

Or for the news to be featured in a prime-time news bulletin or on the front pages of a newspaper – to attract the attention of wealth and power. To a world so far removed (geographically and mentally) that people didn't even visit for poverty tourism.

On the far side of the fields was the graveyard where we sometimes played. It had a single banyan tree that looked haunted. No one was playing there as we passed. A few (living) souls crossed it on the way to their fields. I was not allowed to go to our fields during schooltime. But when I came back during my vacations, I would be able to go there without any restrictions during sowing and harvesting. Bathing in the waters pumped out for irrigation was such great fun. I would sow the paddy as Taibun Dadi did, as Chandrika Dada did, as Indrasan Chacha did. I would spread the fertiliser in the field as Dada did. I could be out in the fields the whole day. It would be fun. I had heard they had very long vacations in Dilli, like a month or two months.

We passed the abandoned railway cabin (where thieves hid to snatch villagers' cycles, watches and money), the village school at Semra (where Dada had studied), Bihar Cinema (where I wasn't allowed to go), the railway station (where we bought our train tickets for Dilli), Thawe market (where they sold fish as well) and, finally, reached Thawe bus stand. We parked our cycles at Moinuddin Cha's shop, and waited at the main road near the bus stand. Jeeps and small buses passed by, but we didn't take them. They stop anywhere they feel like, dropping you off in the middle of nowhere.

As we waited, Aamir Bhayya asked if I would like to eat some pudukiya. Across the road was Gauri Shankar halwai's shop. His pudukiya sweets were famous, and there was a good reason for this.

One evening Gauri Shankarji was returning home, dejected that he couldn't sell his pudukiya. The sweets would now go waste and his family would go hungry. On the way back, he met a djinn. Gauri Shankarji was scared to see him, but good djinn that he was, he pacified the man and asked him why he was sad. When Gauri Shankarji explained, the djinn, moved by his story, bought all the pudukiya in his basket. And before vanishing told him to always use original, pure ghee to make his sweets. It's believed that Gauri Shankar's shop still follows the djinn's advice, and that's the (open) secret of his tasty pudukiyas. Shops claiming to be Gauri Shankar Sons have appeared at many places in Thawe and Gopalganj, and all do brisk business. Like the one opposite this bus stand.

Eventually, a bigger bus arrived. The conductor put my luggage on top. There was no vacant seat, so we stood in the aisle. This didn't please those who sat on the seats.

We were disturbing their view of *Mohra*, playing on the TV screen installed inside. *Tip Tip Barsa Paani* – I stole a glimpse from the corner of my eye so as to not let Dada know I was looking at that fahshipana.

We spent about two hours in that crowded bus which stopped more than it ran. It was the first time I was in a place as big as Siwan. It had two-way roads and even street lights. There was a traffic policeman, like the one in my books, wearing a white shirt and a hat. The traffic policeman STOPed and GOed people with his hands. Few paid heed. There were big, shiny shops. There were endless lines of hawkers.

Everything seemed so big and so far from Gopalganj. The train was running late as usual. We walked up the platform to where we thought bogey S-5 or S-6 was likely to stop. It was close to the sound system and we could hear the announcements clearly. The speakers were apologising, in a strangled voice, for the inconvenience they had caused: 'May I have your attention please? Train number Two Five Five Three, Barauni–New Delhi Vaishali Express via Gorakhpur, Lucknow and Kanpur, has reached something something junction. The train is late by one hour and fifteen minutes. The inconvenience caused is deeply regretted.'

The inconvenience caused to us had increased to more than two and a half hours by the time the train arrived.

This was the first time I was taking a train. I had only seen trains from the outside when they passed through my village. I had never taken a ride because I never needed one.

My only train-related experience until then was running on the narrow metal tracks.

Who can run fastest? Who can go farthest? Without falling over?

I didn't always lose.

Many a time I had thrown stones at a running train and run away as fast as I could, holding my pants. My friends and I would also gauge just how far an approaching train was from us. All you needed to do was to put your ear against the track to hear the humming sound and feel the vibration. 'Oh, it has whistled; it's approaching the dhala.' The crossing before our village. 'Put your ear here, you can hear it.' In summer, the tracks often left your ear blushing red, but that was a different matter.

Here, in the new and beautiful world of Siwan, my smile returned (slowly, slowly). My cousins reminded me that I was finally gaining freedom from Dada and his diktats. I could do anything in Delhi. Nobody would be there to nag me or stop me. I thought that no one would stop me from playing cricket till late or staying outdoors after sunset. No one would tell me to study the whole time. Only later, when I reached Delhi, did I realise that he had told a lie to help me forget my homesickness. Bhuttu Puttu would keep a hawk's eye on me. I was free when he wasn't there, but anonymous reports of my daily doings somehow always reached him by the evening.

Those who lie go to hell, the Prophet Muhammad said. You are allowed to lie only when it is to save someone else's life.

As the time of the train's arrival approached, the hopeful crowd on the platform swelled. There seemed to be way more people on the platform than there were at the Eid mela in our village. And this big crowd was going to rush into the train.

Beggars begged (in Allah's name, in Bhagwan's name), chips sellers chipssold, groundnut sellers basketbutted the crowd to make their way through the rush. Giftssellers carried around keychains, luggage chains, torches, battery-operated (toy) cars, lighters and whatnots.

Aamir Bhayya spotted a vacant place on a concrete bench. Dada sat there, I stood next to him, and my cousins wandered around.

I won't tell Dada, but I know what they are up to. Hmm. There was nothing to do but wait for the train. But if you were with Dada, he would not allow a moment to pass without imparting some knowledge or testing you on past lessons.

'Mohammad Sahab said, study even if you have to go to Cheen. You know what that means, don't you?' (Dada always enunciated the Prophet's name with a thick O: Mohammad.)

Reluctantly, I said no. He had explained it to me earlier.

'It means that you should do everything you can to get an education, to learn things. However far it is, from whoever it is, older or younger. You must be ready to face any difficulties in order to acquire knowledge.'

'But, Dada, why Cheen?'

'As you know, Mohammad Sahab was born in Saudi, and you have to cross many countries to reach Cheen from there. You know, na, Cheen is our neighbour?'

'Yes, yes, I know. Across the Himalaya.' *Parbat woh sabse ooncha, hamsaya aasman ka, Woh santari hamara, woh pasban hamara.*

Dada said, 'So if you want to reach Cheen from Saudi, you have to cross Iran and Pakistan and many other countries and mountains.'

'Achha.'

'Imagine how difficult it would have been to travel that far when there was no bus or train?'

I thought. And asked, 'Achha, Dada, how far is Dilli?'

The change of topic annoyed him, but he said, 'Check your ticket. It is printed there.'

'903 km, Dada.'

Aamir Bhayya came across to hand him tea in an earthen cup. 'It's not good. But what will you get at the station anyway?'

'Dada, be careful. There are pigeons sitting above,' I said. Dada smiled. He knew what I was talking about.

Once, Abbu and Ammi had gone to Patna zoo with some relatives. Abbu bought tea for everyone and told them to be careful as there were crows in the trees above. Before he could finish, a crow had done its job in Abbu's own tea. When we heard the story, we laughed our hearts out. And my youngest sister had asked, 'Abbu, how did it taste?' Abbu ran to catch her, finally getting hold of her on the terrace, as she zigzagged between the chulha, the firewood and the grain that was spread on the roof to dry. Cuddling her, he joked, 'Come, have it and tell me how it tastes' – pretending to pick up the crow shit that was spattered on the terrace railings – 'It's right here, for you.'

Dada finished his tea. Now it was time for another exercise.

'So, you know where all your train passes through?'

'No.'

'Look at your ticket. It's written there, next to Via. They just announced it too.'

'Gorakhpur, Lucknow, Kanpur.'

'So what are all these cities famous for?'

'Lucknow is the capital of Uttar Pradesh.'

'And?'

'Nawab Wajid Ali Shah was nawab there.'

I remembered this because I was often mocked and called Nawab Wajid Ali Shah for being lazy and passing on the work I had been asked to do to my younger siblings or cousins or Nabijan. The Nawab of Awadh was famous for his indolence. When the Angrez attacked and captured his city, he didn't escape even though there was time enough to do so. The British asked him why he had not left, and he said it was because all his servants had run away and there was no one to put sandals on his feet.

'And what about Kanpur?' Dada asked.

'Alam Phoopha lives there?'

'Nana Sahab Peshwa fought the Angrez there.'

'Okay.'

'And Gorakhpur?'

'Hmm ... don't remember.'

'How is it that you don't remember? You don't know Chauri Chaura? You spoke about it at the Republic Day function. It's there, right next to Gorakhpur.'

It's not that I had forgotten. I was probably not paying attention to Dada's questions. When Dada was teaching me his interpretation of the world, I often had something else on my mind. While everyone else in my neighbourhood got to play the whole day, sleep till late, go to the nearby canal and bathe, I remained chained, metaphorically, to values, hopes, Dada's diktats, Ammi's watching eyes, Dadi's sensing nose and ears.

Dada's teachings kept coming all the time, all days of the week, all through the year. Anything you picked up in your little world, he would have told you something or the other about it already. Some history, some geography, some moral lesson, there was always something. The abundance of it made a lot stick. Some vividly, others less so. Often in flashes, here and there. Like the pieces of a jigsaw puzzle – one leading to another, taking time to join and form something coherent.

'Yes, yes, Chauri Chaura,' I said.

They had burnt a thana over there. Policemen and many other people died, so Gandhiji ended the adam ta'awun ki tehreek. Non-cooperation movement. Gandhiji had called for civil disobedience against the British after the Jallianwala Bagh massacre. Jernal Dyer had killed many people in the firing there.

'It will be on your right. Just before you reach Gorakhpur. You can see a small memorial erected there.'

'Achha, Dada, where is Aligarh? Nahid also went by Vaishali Express.' Nahid, my cousin, had recently joined AMU.

AMU was started by Sir Syed Ahmed Khan. It used to be called Mohamedan Anglo-Oriental College. Mohamedan is not the right word. It was invented by the Angrez. Mohamedan means we pray to Mohammad Sahab, and that's not true.

'Aligarh is near Dehli,' Dada said.

The speaker announced that the train would arrive in a few minutes at platform number two. A sea of heads rose unevenly, looking towards the side the train would come from. I tried too, all I could see were legs and waists. As the train approached the platform, I was given a wartime briefing.

'You don't worry about anything. Run and enter the coach with either Aamir Bhayya or Bhuttu Bhayya.'

'Who will carry my bags?'

'I said, na, you just have to worry about yourself.'

The train arrived and legs ran. People scurried about like insects. The coaches S-5 and S-6 went past us. As did the general coaches, AC coaches, pantry car and sleeper coaches.

Aamir Bhayya ran.

I ran.

Bhuttu Bhayya ran.

Dada tried to run.

I kept my eyes on Aamir Bhayya. He reached first and when I caught up, he tried to push me inside coach S-5 which was already full. I got inside before my cousins could.

Then a mob (of travellers and see-off-ers) threw their love at us with full force and there we all were, inside the coach and almost out the other side. The crowd jostled with each other to reach their seats. Goingcominggoingcoming. Dada waited outside. There was no way I could say salam or shake hands with him.

At home, I tried to avoid Dada as much as I could. His poetry-jibes, his admonishments, his never-ending sermons that embarrassed me in front of my friends.

How important it is to be a just and upright man.

That one should never miss a chance to learn anything and everything.

How important it is to be united.

That one must be a good shehri. Citizen. And all that.

I hated him when he shouted at me, this is wrong, that is foolish. Once in a while, when I was sure his behaviour was unacceptably harsh – for example, when he didn't allow me to play with my friends in the village – I even invoked a hadees that I had learnt from my cousin: 'Those who do not treat children well go to hell.'

But I had never thought I would leave Dada. He was the man I knew while I was growing up, while Abbu was away earning a living for the family. He was the man about whom I complained to the whole world, and he was the man I looked up to and idolised.

He was harsh with me, no doubt, and possessive about me. But he had a reason that was beyond my understanding then as a kid.

Perhaps it was the guilt from an accident. Even if it was no fault of his.

I had an older brother. One afternoon, while Abbu was away in Gopalganj, my brother was playing with Dada. Dada fell asleep for a moment and the child sneaked out, perhaps chasing a ball that Abbu had bought for him. When Dada woke up, he realised that the toddler wasn't there. A frantic search led to a red shirt floating in the pond next to our house. It was him. With his goddamn toy floating right next to him.

Perhaps that was why Dada didn't let me out of his sight. Maybe he had other reasons too for shielding me so zealously. There were numerous stories of young boys being lured into sexual acts by older ones, the complexities of which I came to understand only when I grew up. That SoAndSo fucked SoAndSo when they were playing hide-and-seek. Or on a pakdi tree while he was teaching him how to climb. We giggled when faced with the victim – in our ignorance, we saw the molesters in our stories as brave and macho, and the victims as girlish and weak.

Or perhaps he feared that a friend might sneak me out of the house in the middle of the night to watch (lewd) qawali or dance troupes – we villagers called it arkestra – where, often, the women were men dressed up in female clothes. The young men from the village watched it all night, threw money at the dancers and passed dirty comments about them.

I never got a chance to attend an arkestra.

Maghrib, the evening prayer time, was my curfew. I was not allowed out after sunset, no matter what, unless Dada or another family member was with me. Or unless it was really urgent – for example, if someone called from Saudi Arabia on our phone, I had to run and inform his family, so they could come and talk to him when he called back in a few minutes.

A neighbour's kid once tried to teach me how to lift a dog by its tongue. He said, 'It's like what your Dada does with your ears.'

Not true. He never did that to me. Although he did beat me a few times when I couldn't recall his lessons, especially in Riyazi, Mathematics. The subject was beyond me, more so land measurement. 'If a farmer doesn't remember these simple measurements, how is he going to survive?' he fumed, and thrashed me.

Nine inches equal one bita
Two bita equal one haath
One haath equals 1.5 feet
Six haath equal one laggi
One laggi equals one dhoor.
And
Twenty dhoor equal one kattha

Twenty kattha equal one bigha.

Once he did set upon me, I must admit, with his slippers. I had wandered outside at night to play with my friends because the mohalla was all lit up with a generator for a wedding party. When Dada realised I was missing, he sent Aamir Bhayya for me. I came back home to find Dada waiting outside with a slipper in hand.

The older kids in the village often asked me the English words for things that interested them. They would say, 'Okay, you are good at your studies. So tell us the English for *that* thing.' That thing! I looked silly, knowing nothing of boy-talk.

Just licking books doesn't make you a man.

I made sure that next time they asked, I would surprise them all with my deep knowledge of the subject.

Breast.

Penis.

Penis? It sounds like peni. Baalti ka peni. The base of a bucket. Hahahaha.

And, and, what about that? That. Hahahaha.

Achha, with Bh or B?

But all this happened away from Dada's eyes and ears. I usually went out to play when he was away: at the market, in Gopalganj for bank work, visiting relatives, in the fields or at the Panchayat. In the evenings, he would go to Pakhopali or Sukulwan market for vegetables. That's when the heavens descended for me.

Pakhopali is the first major village you cross if you take the pucca road from Thawe to our village. It's a small but growing market centre now, with a private school, coaching centre, local bank, a few doctors and medical stores, a madrasa, masjid, phone recharge shop, telecom tower, a few sweet-and-snack shops and a few general stores.

Pakhopali melts into Inderwan Abdullah, and that into Inderwan Sakir. My village, Inderwan Bairam, comes after. There are four villages, big and small, called Inderwan. It's believed that there were four brothers in the Inderwan family who settled here, and their settlements eventually grew into the villages we now know.

Also adjacent to my village is Sukulwan, which was once famous for its yearly cattle market. In its modern avatar, it has a private and a government school, a post office, a coaching centre, a mandir, a medical store, a local bank, a recharge point, a telecom tower, some sweet and snack shops and a few general stores.

Dada would often go to one of these markets in the evenings, and stay on to have tea and snacks with his friends. He was considered a wise man, and was known for settling disputes in the village and its surrounds. His ideal of a just ruler was the second caliph Farooque and the Mughal emperor Jahangir.

I had read about Caliph Farooque's virtues but didn't know what Adl-e-Jahangiri meant; it was something I'd heard him say often. When I asked Dada, he told me to consult my loghat, the Urdu dictionary.

Alif, alif, alif, alif ...

No, not Alif, it starts with Ain, he corrected me.

Ain, the twenty-fourth of the thirty-eight letters in the Urdu alphabet. Alif is the first.

Ain, ain, ain, ain ...

Daal, daal, daal ...

Laam.

Ain, Daal, Laam ... which makes it ... hmm ... adl.

Got it. Justice, it says.

Okay. So what happens when you put the two words together?

Jahangir's justice.

The famous story of Adl-e-Jahangiri goes like this, Dada said. Once, the wife of Jahangir, Nur Jahan, was out hunting, and her arrow accidentally hit a washerman near a pond. The washerman died and his distraught wife came with a complaint to the emperor's durbar. Such was Jahangir's justice that he told the lady to shoot the same arrow into the husband of the one who had killed her husband.

Dada tried to follow these principles of impartiality in his Panchayat hearings. One time, two neighbours in Inderwan Abdullah had approached him with a long-standing dispute over their land, so old and entangled that no one was expecting settlement anytime soon. Brothers had failed, neighbours had failed, the local Panchayat had failed, the courts had failed. So Dada was invited to settle the matter. During the Panchayat, one party offered him a cup of tea. Drinking this tea could well be seen as taking a favour from one side, so Dada asked the other party to get another cup of tea for him. Then he asked another unrelated person to bring an empty cup. He poured in half the tea from each cup and drank the mixture – part milk tea, part black tea.

He would say that not only should justice be done, it should be seen to be done. And that judges need to be respected by both parties. The dispute was settled peacefully. My village didn't have a madrasa. The imam of the village mosque would take classes only occasionally. So Dada decided to engage a maulana to teach us religion. The villagers in Pakhopali allowed him to appoint a maulana of his choice from their madrasa.

Dada wanted to ensure that the one he chose shared his own ideology. He interviewed each maulana at length.

Did he have a basic understanding of Islam? Which sect and ideology did he belong to? Where did he come from?

What madrasa had he graduated from?

Was he an Aalim, Faazil or Haafiz? Graduate, Master or one who had learnt the whole Quran.

The maulana was to stay at our place full-time, like a family guest, and teach us in the mornings (before school) and evenings (after school), and on our off-days. Quran and hadees and akhlaq. Other families in the village were free to send their kids if they wished to, and Maulana sahab was free to earn a few bucks from them if he wished to. All the talib-ilm – my siblings, cousins and kids from the village – would gather in our veranda. It turned into a kind of chartered madrasa with (personal) jute mats for each student and religious books spread on their (personal) rihal tables. Some read the Quran, some learnt Urdu and others received Maulana sahab's whole-hearted thrashings for not remembering what he had taught.

Once in a while, Maulana sahab would also give lessons on huqooq-e-niswan, women's rights, to my elder sister and cousins, who stood behind the (curtained) window or (curtained) door of the veranda.

I learnt the Quran from Maulana sahab and also the duas that you need in daily life. Like the dua you recite before starting to read:

Rabbi zidni ilma.

My Lord, grow me in knowledge.

Or the dua you recite before eating:

Bismillah wa ala barkatillah.

In the name of Allah and with the blessings of Allah I begin (eating).

Or before sleeping:

Allahumma bismika amouta ahya.

O Allah, with your name I live and die.

I also learnt how to read the call to prayer, the Azaan, with proper tone and tenor.

God is Great.

I acknowledge that there is no God but God.

I acknowledge that Muhammad is the messenger of God.

Hasten to worship.

Hasten to success.

God is Great.

There is no God but God.

You must remember to add, in the morning Azaan, 'Prayer is better than sleep.'

When Maulana sahab certified that I had learnt it properly, Dada took me once to read the Azaan over the village mosque's loudspeaker. My friends told me I was audible even outside the village, right up to the eidgah. The only problem was that I fumbled once. 'But just once. Not more,' they assured me.

While Maulana sahab taught me about God and godliness, Dada taught me about the world and worldliness.

What to read.

Where to go, where not to go.

How to behave. Sit down before you drink water. Eat with your right hand. Stand up when someone older approaches and offer him salam. If you don't know him, say adab.

Adab. Respect.

And Assalam-o-Alaikum. Peace be upon you.

There are many variants of the dua Assalam-o-Alaikum, and a slight change of letter could distort its meaning, the maulana had cautioned me.

Saam-o-alaikum. May Allah destroy you. Assam-o-alaikum. May Allah give you death.

Assa-e-alaikum. May Allah make you thirsty for happiness.

Sala-le-kum. May Allah curse you.

I addressed one variant to my sister once when she had (in my opinion) extorted more than her fair share of our pocket money. So I showered her with my choicest adjectives: kaali, bhains, moti, bauni, kameeni, kutti, nakchadhi.

And then I said, Assam-o-Alaikum. Death be upon you. That was the first and last time I used those words on anyone. Instantly, there came a loud shout from Dada and angry enquiries about where I had learnt such a stupid, ungodly thing.

Nauzubillah. I seek refuge in Allah.

Scared, I spilled (half) the beans. 'Dada, Maulana sahab told me about it. That people use it against the enemy.' And I recited to him all the variants I knew.

That very evening, the maulana was asked to pack up and leave. He was given no chance to explain his well-intentioned sharing of information.

Now that I wanted to say salam and Khuda Hafiz – May God keep you safe – to Dada, I was not able to, because of the stupid rush everywhere. Forget getting seats, even standing inside the bogey seemed impossible. The train moved with a jerk. People on the platform started moving backwards. Cries of Namaste-Salamalekum-Namaskar-Khuda Hafiz rose above the din. I couldn't see Dada. Had I known it would go like this, I would have said salam and Khuda Hafiz to him before I boarded. Nobody told me it would be *this* crowded.

I want to say salam to Dada. I want to talk to him.

The train gathered speed slowly, steadily, and the world outside ran away from me. The crowd was still to settle down. We squatted at the airy, scenic doorway, and put our bags on the rack meant for the pantry. Bhuttu Bhayya told me that if the TTE came, he and Aamir Bhayya would take a stroll, or would hide inside the toilet to avoid getting fined for riding in a reserved bogey with a general ticket. I was supposed to occupy the place in their absence. Before they could put their plan into action, a TTE arrived out of nowhere. He asked if everyone had tickets for the reserved coach. 'Yes, we do,' lied my cousin, confidently. 'Except this kid.' Except this kid. So, the TTE fined This Kid for travelling unreserved in the reserved bogey. It was a calculated move by Bhuttu Bhayya. Now I had a licence to stay in the reserved coach and watch the luggage while Bhuttu Bhayya and Aamir Bhayya vanished each time the TTE arrived, without any worries that the place would be encroached upon by other passengers. That's called farsightedness!

There was a washbasin close to where we sat, with a mirror above it. I had the privilege of watching people spitting gutkha and paan in the basin, their spittle flying in all directions in the tempest of the running train. People came, looked in the spit-stained mirror, appreciated their beauty and left. And I cursed them, fearing another assault on the freelance spittoon.

Once in a while, an adventurous soul would appear at the door. He would crane his neck, and ignoring the existence of the basin, spit outside. He would leave only after reassuring himself that the train was running with all its bogies intact, with engine properly placed in front and guardroom at the back.

Sitting at the door, I watched the fast-backward motion picture outside.

Trees passed by.

Villages passed by.

Cows and goats passed by.

Poles, wires and the birds on them sped by.

Rivers, streams and bridges passed beneath us. On bridges, the driver would sound a loud whistle. On manned bridges, old men stood with red and green flags, both clutched in one hand. I wondered how the driver made out if the signal was meant to be green or red. Farmers crouched in their rice fields. And then a fountain of water came in from nowhere to hit my face. Someone was washing his hands at a window in the bogie ahead of us. Or spitting after rinsing out his mouth.

When the train made a long stop at an unscheduled local station, Aamir Bhayya got down and bought me groundnuts (shelled, roasted, salted and mixed with green chillies).

The wind blew hot, heavy air into my face. The lowest rack of the luggage box near the door was broken; I would fit in there to sleep during the night. As the crowd settled,

Aamir Bhayya and Bhuttu Bhayya came and sat at the door. Blocking the wind from blowing directly at me. Through the evening and the night. Cursing the train's slowness, watching the scenery outside and talking to keep awake as they sat with their feet dangling outside.

The journey smelled of train. And iron when the train stopped, or burning if it stopped because the emergency chain had been pulled.

In the constant noise of chhakchhukthakthuk, I thought of home. And Ammi. And my brothers and sisters.

I was sad, but the world I saw was new. The old world I was leaving behind was slowly turning into memory.

Memories of studying in a circle around a lantern. In the semi-darkness of its dim light, no one outside the circle could tell that we were playing a passing-the-chit game. Until it turned ugly, which was usually because someone in the circle adjusted the lantern and the shadow of its stand would fall on your book. 'It's so dark, how am I going to see what's in the book?'

Baaji was always blamed for taking advantage of being older. And I accused her of trying to monopolise the lantern because she had won it for a speech one Independence Day. Anyway, ehsan, taking credit for doing a favour, is never good manners. Just as the argument was hotting up, Ayaz would whisk away the lantern, and whirl it to see if the kerosene oil spilt.

Jaah, tel gir gaya. Damn, you spilt the oil.

And then everyone's attention would shift to him.

Jaah, jaah, jaah. Maar nalayak ko. Pakad ise. Catch the rascal, beat him.

He would throw the lantern down and run for his life. Ayaz was always excused, but when I tried it once, Baaji happened to see it. I got a good shouting from Ammi. Baaji slapped me. Because I was not a child anymore and I was not supposed to behave like a child. Or jahil. Uneducated.

I so wanted to slap her back but didn't. Remember, when the man he defeated spat at him, Hazrat Ali had let him go? So I made it clear to her in straightforward terms that she shouldn't underestimate me because I was a kid but know the reason why I didn't slap her back.

We buried the hatchet a few days later; she gifted me the brand-new diary that she had won for being class topper. That diary was now packed in the bag that I used as a pillow in the train.

The train moved at an Indian train's pace. The passing trees reminded me of the jamun and goolar and aam at home. The glow of bulbs and lanterns in the evenings. Beards at railway crossings and platforms reminded me of Dada. He used a scooter but that day he would have had to pedal the cycle home from Thawe after we left. What if it had rained? And who would bring Dadi her paan?

Dadi would always keep her paandani close to her bed, so she could spit out the paan when she was done. Below the bed, she would hide a matka in which was hidden the household's sugar. Her secret had somehow found its way out – one of Dadi's confidantes, Ammi or Chhoti Ammi, had defected. The wily old lady noticed that her sugar was steadily decreasing and devised a way to catch the thief. She procured a plastic sheet, which made a loud crackling noise the moment you touched it, and placed it on the sugar in the matka.

So, when we next tried to steal the sugar, unaware of the trap that had been laid, we were caught red-handed. And then followed a litany of complaints to Ammi and Dada. What irritated Dadi was that no one took it seriously.

Everyone laughed at this heinous crime – *at a time when nothing grows in our fields, everything has to be bought and everything is so costly*.

Dada laughed.

Ammi laughed.

Chhoti Ammi laughed.

We all laughed.

Even Nabijan laughed.

2

Breaking News!

19 SEPTEMBER 2008, FRIDAY; 18 Ramazan 1429, Jum'a.

A normal day. I was in the final year of my undergrad. As usual, I had overslept and was running late for lab session. This time I had an excuse: sehri, the pre-dawn ritual breakfast during the month of Ramazan. I normally went to bed well past midnight, which made waking up early very difficult. So, to avoid missing the sehri (which would mean fasting without any food at all until sunset), I would go to sleep only after eating, just before sunrise. Like most young people in Jamia Nagar.

It was a student's lifestyle: staying up the whole night, studying (or pretending to), chatting, hanging around at tea stalls and then going to sleep in the early hours. During the holy month, the sun rose for us youngsters every evening with the iftari, the breaking of our fast, and it set with the sehri. You could say, it was a month-long night out on the town (completely halal, of course).

Ramazan in Jamia Nagar was a feast for the senses. The creamy colour of sevaiyan. At sehri, the smell of biryani and home-made haleem. At iftar, seekh kebabs simmered on coals under a tiny table fan. And Rooh Afza reddened the evenings. Lassi danced from pot to pot after Taraweeh, the special prayer during Ramazan.

Kurta-kurti shops sprang up in the market. Special clothes for Eid, special discounts on regular clothes. As the month progressed, mehndi appliers occupied strategic corners on chowks.

Believers thronged the mosques in Jamia Nagar and invited others to join them. Like every pious Muslim should. The holy month also induced an extra ounce of piousness among greedy believers like me. While you are supposed to follow the religion in letter and spirit throughout the year, there is more incentive to do so during Ramazan, when God is extra generous. He rewards you seventy times more for every good thing you do in this month, so goes the belief. So, during Ramazan, one would offer namaz punctually. Give alms generously. Avoid lying or hurting anyone.

Once in a while, I would even go to the masjid to offer namaz. That morning, on 19 September, I had waited for Fajr before going to sleep.

I woke up late and, eyes hardly open, rushed to get ready for college. A cousin from Bihar was visiting Delhi in search of a job that would take him to the Gulf. He was staying with me.

When people from the village visited Delhi, they often stayed with me. Because they were guests, I was supposed to respect them and help them in whatever way possible, which I did. But if, say, I had showed them around the city, they would go back and say, 'When does he study? He has seen the whole city.' And if I didn't, they would say, 'He is a fool. He knows nothing about the city.' These were the older ones, of course. The younger ones preferred my place simply because I lived alone and that offered them unlimited freedom.

My cousin was still sleeping when it got time for me to leave. I couldn't wake him, which meant that I had to leave the door unlocked – although I was worried because all our belongings were lying around in open bags.

The university is walking distance from home if I walk northwest through the short-cut lanes of Ghafoor Nagar, but I took a rickshaw because I was running late. The rickshawallah tried to pedal fast – half-crouching, humming some Bengali song. We rode from Muradi Road to the main road leading to Jamia and the rest of Delhi.

It was about 10.30 or 11 a.m.

Still drowsy, I entered my department, and immediately realised that something was amiss. There were crowds gathered outside, and yet it was calmer and quieter than a crowded college ought to be. I rushed towards the chemistry lab; it was empty.

My classmates were huddled outside with exam-time faces. The lab assistant appeared to be lecturing them about something. Had they been thrown out of class for coming late? Or not doing some assignment? I was sure to join them in either case.

As I reached them, my classmate Alim broke away from the huddle and announced, 'Encounter! Encounter!'

'What encounter?' I asked, confused.

'Where are you, man? There is an encounter underway near your house. Near Khalilullah. Police have killed someone there.'

'What? Oh! Is that why I heard police sirens as I was passing the Batla House bus stand?'

I had noticed a lot of traffic at the bus stand, but that was hardly unusual and I didn't give it any thought. Even the many police vans and sirens caught my attention only momentarily. I mean, this is Delhi, right? It could be an accident or a fire or simply some VIP visiting. I had (nonchalantly) asked the rickshawallah if something had happened around here. He (nonchalantly) replied that there had been some kind of shooting near Khalilullah Masjid.

The masjid route is the one I usually took, because the Muradi Road exit was often clogged with gutter water. Thank god I didn't take it this time. But why the shooting? There used to be a court ban on construction on the Yamuna riverbed, which didn't allow for even the repair of houses. Officially. A temporary relaxation of the order allowed repair work, and this had triggered nothing less than a construction boom. For those who could afford to, you know, repair. The people who benefited the most from the relaxation were the property dealers. I had imagined the shooting must involve property dealers taking the fight up a level.

'It's all over TV. They are saying these guys were involved in the Delhi blasts,' Alim said.

Serial blasts in Delhi had killed thirty people a week ago. These blasts, following others across the country, had jolted the capital city. Parliamentary and Assembly elections in Delhi were due in less than a year. The government was on the backfoot, and the opposition unrelenting in its criticism. It accused the government of being soft on internal security, of encouraging the patrons of terror and of directing all its energy to the nuclear deal with the US. The then Gujarat chief minister, Narendra Modi, had reportedly warned then prime minister Manmohan Singh just a few days before the blast that Delhi was on the target list of the terrorists.

Home Minister Shivraj Patil, most of all, faced the ire of the public, opposition and media alike. On the day of the blast, he had appeared in public in three different suits within the space of a few hours. Patil was widely mocked. One news channel asked, '*Desh bada ya* look?' Do you put the country first, or your looks?

The intelligence apparatus had failed. Now, the Special Cell of the Delhi Police, which functions under the Home Ministry, was called in for damage control. Very soon after the blasts, they had raided a few places in Delhi, including some in Jamia Nagar; questioned and detained many suspects; issued sketches based on witness accounts.

The encounter in Jamia Nagar took place on the morning of the sixth day after the last blast.

Two men were killed in a fourth-floor flat, just two minutes from my place. A police inspector was said to be injured. It was, reportedly, a fierce encounter.

By noon, the chief of police made an announcement. With the killing of the young men, he claimed, the police had solved the puzzle of the serial blasts in Delhi, as well as those in Ahmedabad, Jaipur, Faizabad, Varanasi and Bangalore over the last few months. He said the bombs in all these blasts were of a similar make, which meant they were the handiwork of the same group – Indian Mujahideen – and the masterminds had just been killed in the Batla House Encounter.

Alim was right. It was all over television news. India was relieved to hear the news that the terrorists had been eliminated. And why not? The blasts had killed so many people. It was another matter that, within days of the encounter, there was another blast outside the Mehrauli dargah in Delhi,[5] followed by blasts in Malegaon in Maharashtra[6] and Modassa in Gujarat,[7] both minority- dominant settlements.

But, on the ground, there was something that the parachuted eyes of the reporters could not see: the silent rage of the people of Jamia Nagar.

The residents of Jamia Nagar didn't much trust Them, the police.

The police didn't much trust Them, the residents of Jamia Nagar, either.

Each had othered the Other long ago.

Over time, the police would change their version and alter the details of the encounter again and again. The media would faithfully relay each version – with few questions asked, few eyebrows raised.

On television, the encounter looked dramatic, but that wasn't how eyewitnesses described it to us. Many of my neighbours were scared and avoided talking to the media (they whispered, mumbled, grumbled and went indoors); privately, they contested the police's claim.

Only a few were vocal in public.

Like the tall, bearded, skull-capped man who was all over the news channels. He lived next to the EncounterBuilding. His son, Asjad, was my classmate in school. Our English teacher had given me the task of making sure Asjad fared well in his exams, at least in her subject. We still occasionally bumped into each other in Khalilullah Masjid. His father was an obnoxious official in the university whom we had to beg to process even the slightest bit of paperwork; the only thing that stopped us from showering him with invectives was respect for his long beard.

There was also the kid who happened to be in the parking lot of an apartment close to the EncounterBuilding. He spoke to the TV cameras on an impulse soon after the encounter and his face was everywhere. As the story unfolded, he realised he had made a mistake and soon vanished. He would go back to where he had come from, to poverty in faraway Bihar.

There were others who said they hadn't seen any movement to anticipate trouble. And some said they had noticed unknown men in the street early that morning when they woke up for sehri. A senior in college said that there had been an unusually large police presence at the local thana around midnight while he was passing it to pack biryani for sehri.

It was so close to home. The most dreaded of our professors lived close by, only three or four buildings away. He would bump into me at the masjid occasionally and flash a sarcastic smile. Alim lived just a few houses from the professor's flat. Two of my classmates from school lived in a gully just behind the building. My friends and I used to drink tea and eat samosas and jalebis not far from it. We often passed the building during our walks to the banks of the Yamuna on evenings when long power outages drove us out of our homes.

It was too close. Too close for comfort.

The facts were getting confusing as time passed and residents' accounts and rebuttals floated around. None of us had seen or heard anything or met anyone who could have been even remotely connected to such a serious thing as a bomb blast. Once in a while, you met someone who supported the Pakistani cricket team. There were people who were angry about Babri Masjid and Gujarat. There was America-bashing over Palestine, Iraq and Afghanistan, or even support for Sharia-style governance (secretly) and the dictator Saddam Hussain (openly) – but bombing our own country? That was unheard of. Such people existed, of course, but they certainly didn't live among us. They inhabited faraway lands with which we had no connection.

Jamia Nagar knew what it was guilty of. And it was certainly not the bomb blasts.

But that's not what the TV channels and police were saying.

It was an attack on peaceful Muslim youth, Jamia Nagar felt. A narrative took shape gradually: first the police hounded bearded men from madrasas, now they are persecuting college kids. Jamia Nagar was used to reading about these things, now it was at the centre of the discussion.

I was fasting, but I went straight from college to Azmat's paratha joint to watch the news. During Ramazan, Azmat would often cover his television with a beautiful homemade cover, which led to the joke that it observed purdah during the holy month. That day, his TV was naked, shouting out the breaking news.

Do atankwadi marey gaye. Dilli ke Jamia Nagar mein.

Two terrorists killed. In Delhi's Jamia Nagar.

An anchor on one news channel said, 'Abu Bashar provided information about terrorists hiding in the area.' Abu Bashar is a cleric from Azamgarh, an accused in the Ahmedabad blasts. He was arrested from his village by the Gujarat Police on 14 August 2008. His family alleged that the policemen had come to his home on the pretext of meeting a prospective groom, one of Bashar's brothers. After the meeting, Bashar went to see the guests off to the outskirts of the village from where they whisked him away. He was brought to Delhi from Ahmedabad a day before the encounter, the news channel claimed. The reporter on the ground was shouting hysterically. He said that Abu Bashar had travelled to Delhi and stayed with a friend named Danish in Jamia Nagar the day the Ahmedabad blasts happened: 26 July 2008. 'The area is being searched as there might be more terrorists hiding there.'

He declared that the Delhi Police had confirmed it had killed one terrorist, but they 'don't know his name and organisation yet'. And that there had been heavy crossfire and a huge cache of ammunition had been recovered.

The studio anchor asked him for more details.

The reporter said, 'The police received information that a terrorist would be coming to Batla House. The police found this terrorist near Batla House. They tried to stop him, tried to arrest him, but cross-firing happened and the terrorist took four bullets. He was taken to AIIMS where doctors declared him dead.'

The anchor asked if all the policemen were safe.

'In such combing operations, police wear bullet-proof jackets. The police say one or two Special Cell officers have been hit by shrapnel. But there is nothing to worry about.' The anchor explained that the Jamia region is considered quite sensitive, and that the police had suspected there might be terrorists hiding in this area. He asked the reporter about the locality: 'What's the reason that SIMI is active in Jamia Nagar and Zakir Nagar? What's the demographic condition? What kind of locality is Jamia Nagar where terrorists get the opportunity to proliferate? Tell us about the locality.' The reporter responded that SIMI – Students Islamic Movement of India – was headquartered in the Zakir Nagar neighbourhood of Jamia Nagar. The organisation had been banned in 2001. 'This is a hub of SIMI terrorists.

The police and Intelligence Bureau believe that there are still many SIMI terrorists hiding in the locality.'

The anchor from the studio asked, 'It has happened near the Khalilullah Masjid. What section of people lives there? How did the terrorists get a chance to make it their hideout?'

The reporter was talking so fast that he ate half his sentences. 'Zakir Nagar is a sensitive area. The masjids there are such ...' and then he changed tack, 'I have told you earlier as well, whether it's home minister or Delhi police commissioner, whether it's local ... whether it's IB's information, there has been revelation that in such incidents which are happening the locals are involved.'

Another correspondent joined in. He said that there were lots of sleeper cells in the country.

The anchor repeated the earlier question in different words: 'After all, what is so unique that Zakir Nagar, Jamia Nagar is a prominent hideout of terrorists?' The reporter, instead, explained what a sleeper cell was. Then he said the terrorist network operating under the sleeper cell tried to infiltrate the community among which they lived, 'the sections which are sympathetic'. He elaborated, 'As you know, this is a Muslim-dominated area, they certainly try to assemble people who are their supporters, who could advocate for them, those who can join them.'

The cafe owner began switching channels. One channel claimed that the encounter had happened in Khalilullah Masjid. Yet another said that the news was false. It was all very confusing. No one on campus had mentioned any fighting in the masjid. Terrorists in Khalilullah?

It was my favourite masjid. For one, it was where I had offered my first namaz in Delhi. Besides, it also scheduled namaz later than the other masjids in the neighbourhood, which worked best for me, especially for Jum'a, the weekly Friday prayers, the only one that most of us attended. And though I wasn't particular about sects, the imam was known to have Sufi leanings, much like my own family.

As I watched the news, the neighbourhood in which I had grown up began to look scary. The descriptions on TV were alien and disturbing. I had never met, or even heard about, anyone who was planning a bomb blast. Or was as scary as the people they were describing on TV.

I decided to go see the spot for myself.

3

Hopes Arrive in New Delhi

THE MORNING THAT WELCOMED me to Delhi was hot and humid.

A pile of big sacks had appeared overnight next to the train door where we sat, and a crowd had lined up for the toilet in front of it. No one knew who the sacks belonged to – parcel post, passenger, pantry. One of the toilets was filthy, the other was Western-style. People saw the filthy toilet, turned to the Western one and returned to the other, mumbling to themselves. Men monkey-jumped over the crowd sleeping in the aisle to reach the toilet or the washbasin; children and women found that feat difficult. I woke up early and was sitting behind my cousin, watching the world outside. The young sun was preparing to shine ruthlessly into the evening. You would feel the imprint until midnight – by which time I would certainly be home. My new home.

Dilli. Dehli. Delhi.

The city that would, I was assured, lead me to a new world of possibilities. And when I went back home, I would take stories of this great city to my friends and family. From the city of my dreams. Small big dreams.

Inherited dreams. Readjusted dreams. Repackaged dreams. Re-remembered dreams. Of returning an educated man, a bada admi.

Delhi welcomed me in the morning, standing, walking, squatting along the track, looking less impressive than anything I had imagined. It was sad and struggling, not rich and shiny. It seemed to be full of people who had escaped flood-prone districts like mine to live along the main roads of small towns.

In jhuggis. Structures you could barely call home.

In Gopalganj, along the Thawe–Gopalganj main road, or along the irrigation canal that ran through the district, they had ghaas phoos to shelter them; here they had polythene. Blue and black. Bricks on top held the sheets down against the wind. They lived their lives along the tracks – carried water in white and blue jerrycans for their ablutions, bathed in the open and cooked not far from there.

I sipped my morning tea, looking out at a view of rusty metal, uneven concrete, chimneys and smoke.

Factories.

Like the sugar mill in Gopalganj. It was smaller, but it was still a nuisance for the people who lived around them. When the sugarcane season arrived, trucks and tractors descended on the mill, jamming and destroying the meagre roads. Then the mill owners would release water, flooding the fields around the factories. As if the yearly floods were not enough. But what to do? How do you hate them? All that existed in the district in the name of industry were a few sugar mills. They provided bread and butter – such as it was – to many. Dada had worked in one of these sugar mills until both his sons were settled in good jobs, and eventually built a concrete house in stages, bought land, bought a tractor (second-hand) and a scooter (first-hand). Few people in the village had the luxury of a regularly paying job. Dada got a few more villagers jobs in the mill where he worked. As a mark of respect, these men deliberately slowed down their bicycles for Dada to lead them when they left for the mill for their shifts.

As we entered Delhi, I saw the morning sadness of workers who waited to cross the tracks. The walls beside the tracks had hundreds of advertisements painted on them. Mostly for hakims who treated something called gupt rog. 'On Monday, Wednesday and Saturday, 100% cure guaranteed.'

The platform appeared.

New Delhi, in three languages. 214 metres above sea level.

The railway station was as crowded as the train. There was a cola and juice stall. A blue box, like a suitcase, had a Pepsi logo on it. The shop also had a fridge with a transparent door, stacked with many types of Pepsis and Frootis. Black, Orange, Green. Also a few glass bottles with a ball in their necks – I learnt later that it's called banta. The lesser man's cold drink, of soda water made in local factories.

The station looked a lot like Siwan station, only that Delhi was bigger, more crowded and had more stalls. There was a bookstall that sold newspapers, magazines and books in Hindi and English. None in Urdu.

Beggars were everywhere here, as they were in Siwan. The garbage pickers were of my age or a little younger. One of them almost snatched the water bottle Aamir Bhayya had bought for me. I stared at him, he stared back. Then he bared his teeth, ridiculing me, and ran away before I could alert my cousins.

We exited from the Paharganj side. Delhi was disappointing – chaotic, crowded, ancient and sort of like Gopalganj, only with bigger buildings. And louder. Chhoti Ammi had described it as beautiful and all-new and clean ... like they show you in films.

Our bus arrived. Bhuttu bhayya asked us to get ready to run and occupy seats. 'Be careful, take the seats only on your right.' 894-A: Na Di Rey Station Paharganj – Escort Holy Family Jullena 894-A. The driver started negotiating a U-turn without even stopping to let passengers off. Bhuttu Bhayya jostled his way in through the crowd making its way off the bus. We took seats on the right side of the bus, as they were general seats; those on the left side were meant for women, handicapped, senior citizens and conductors.

There were instructions to this effect written on the insides of the bus above the windows. No passes. No staff. Above the front and rear seats on the left, Conductor. The seats between these, Women in English and hilayein in Hindi (the 'Ma' before it scratched out). *Saaf bra ki zimmedari apki hai.* The responsibility for keeping the bra clean is yours. The Hindi letter Sa of 'bus' had been strategically amended to read 'bra'.

Blue cushions had blackened; and Delhiites had butt-pressed them into thin sheets of dirt. People stood in the aisle, and swayed back (when the bus moved forward) and forth (when the bus slowed down). In a non-synchronised chorus, with curses on vocals. The conductor stood outside, shouting almost unintelligibly: OkhleyOkhley, JamiaJamJamJamia, Jullena, Maharani Bagh, Ashram AshramAshamAsham, Hajrat Nijamuddin, DargahDargaDarga, Okhley, OkhleyOkhleyOkhley.

The driver pressed the accelerator repeatedly but didn't move. The collective cursing of the passengers was what finally moved it. The bus was already crowded when it left the station but the conductor kept stuffing people in at every stop. A few hung from the doors, a few stood on the steps. I had no idea the buses in Delhi got this crowded. As crowded as in Bihar. *And they call Bihar a backward state.*

The conductor came in shouting: ticket ticketicketicketic tick tick ticket. They didn't have a system of tickets where I come from; the conductors took the money and remembered your beautiful face.

'Three tickets? Twelve rupees.'

'No,' said Bhuttu Bhayya. 'One full and a half. I am staff.' Staff meant either you were from the bus fraternity or a student of some university or college. In this case, Jamia. The conductor asked to see his I-card.

'Here.' Like Abbu's passport.

That was impressive. The conductor didn't ask any more questions. We gave him a fifty-rupee note and he pulled out tickets for me and Aamir Bhayya. He took out a pen plugged between his ear and temple and wrote '44' on a ticket before giving it to us.

It was a cheque of sorts for Rs 44 that would be honoured when the conductor had enough change in his bank. Bhuttu Bhayya told me to remind him to take the money before we got down. 'These guys are very smart. They don't return the money unless you ask for it.'

The conductor, however, remembered. After returning the money, he took the ticket and tore it a bit in the middle – proof that the cheque had been encashed by his bank. As the bus travelled, my early disappointment receded.

Delhi seemed to be exactly what Chhoti Ammi said it was. Beautiful, glittering, grand, clean.

Big, shiny buildings. All of them newly built and newly painted. Much bigger than my house in the village and way taller.

There were traffic lights and zebra crossings that looked exactly like the pictures in my English books. And footpaths for people to walk on. The edges of the footpaths and road dividers were all painted black and yellow.

It was amazing. Even the roads were painted here. As soon as the signal turned green, people accelerated, as if they were running back home after school.

I knew we had to go to Zakir Nagar, where Bhuttu Bhayya lived. Near Jamia Millia Islamia. Bhuttu Bhayya told me that Jamia means university, so you don't need to add university at the end of its name.

Bhuttu Bhayya studied there. Everyone knew he was a brilliant student and he looked like Shah Rukh Khan. And like Shah Rukh Khan, he would join Jamia's Mass Communication course after graduation. Who doesn't know that Jamia is the best college in Asia for heroes? Surely, Bhuttu Bhayya will get a job that pays one lakh rupees as soon as he graduates, and he will also get a Maruti. Then he will become Shah Rukh Khan.

Bhuttu Bhayya would be my local guardian. I was to stay with him in the rented accommodation that he shared with two other students from Gopalganj.

My bus stopped only at bus stands and red lights.

Traffic intersections. Wow, a Mercedes!

'It runs completely stuck to the road,' proclaimed Bhuttu Bhayya knowledgeably. It means, he said, your vehicle won't overturn at bends even when you're driving very fast. I exchanged a smile with Aamir Bhayya. We remembered the morning he was teaching me how to ride. We took our scooter to the village graveyard, part of which had no graves (or they had sunk into the earth) and was our playing ground. He had told me that day that scooters run 'stuck to the ground' unlike motorcycles. Soon, I had rammed the scooter right into an old grave. We laughed for hours that the scooter had been so stuck to the ground that it ran straight to a grave.

Ah, this building has glass all over. That's good; they don't need to paint it. But how do they clean the glass? Doesn't it break or fall off? Aamir Bhayya explained, 'They hang from the top with the help of other workers to clean the glass.' That reminded me of a joke we told in the village. Once upon a time, there was a scientist who visited a village. He stood staring at a wall for hours. Then he asked the villagers, pointing towards the cow-dung cakes pasted on the walls to dry, how did the cattle climb up the walls to shit there?

A few intersections and the conductor announced that Chidiya Ghar was approaching. I could not see the zoo from my side. A crumbling building – mosque? – was all I could see. I wanted to visit the zoo, and now that I would be in Delhi, I could go any time.

The conductor announced Hazrat Nizamuddin Dargah. Some people wearing skullcaps and kurtas, standing in the aisle next to our seat, struggled to get down with their bags (and survived). The conductor continued singing: Okhley Okhley Jamia Jamia Jullena Escort Ashram Ashram Jamia Jakir Nagar Batla.

A board on the right indicated that the street went to the dargah and to the markaz – the centre of Tableeghi Jamat. Two sets of differing ideologies, merely a few metres apart. In the street leading up to the dargah, beggars sat with bowls in their hands – exactly like Dadi had described it when telling us about her visit to the dargah years ago.

Four fakirs, wearing green kurtas and green pagdis, held a green chadar by its four corners. Such fakirs visited our village every year around the time of Eid-e-Milad-un-Nabi, the anniversary of Prophet Mohammad's birth. They walked together, holding the chadar and singing, visible more than audible from the bus. Devotees were supposed to put their alms, sadqa, in the sheet.

The bus crossed a flyover and turned left on Mahatma Gandhi Marg. The name of the road was written in English, Hindi, Urdu and another language – Punjabi, I was told. *Oh, they have written it wrong here. You don't write Mahatma like this in Urdu. And why does it say Marg both in English and Urdu? Not road or sadak?*

The bus turned right on to a road named after a scientist: C.V. Raman Marg.

C.V. Raman was the first Indian scientist to win a Nobel Prize. The Nobel Prize was started in memory of Alfred Nobel, in 1901. Alfred Nobel invented dynamite. He invented it, not discovered it. Discovered is when something already exists. Invention is when you create something new. Like a radio or a bulb.

I wanted to be a scientist now, no longer an astronomer, which was one of my early childhood dreams. We'd be sleeping on the terrace and then, suddenly, it would rain in the middle of the night, with not even a cloud to warn us. It was most annoying! The only thing that could help, I had learnt, was Astronomy. I would then be able to predict rains and storms, and help Dada plan his planting and harvesting.

But what ruined it for me was Dada's jantari, an annual booklet that predicted the weather, as well as sunrise and sunset timings and namaz timings. What was the point of studying Astronomy then?

So, Astronomy is useless. Science is best. Scientists invented the aeroplane, radio, scooter and tractor.

Edison was my favourite scientist. Thomas Alva Edison, the man who invented the bulb. I loved stories of Edison feeding his maid with insects or sitting on bulbs. I was no Edison but I, too, had experimented with bulbs many times. Electricity was like a guest in our village. When it visited, it was often angry-red – more voltage than the bulbs, wires and switchboards could take. The thin wire inside the bulb had always fascinated me; how did it light up the whole room? One afternoon, when everyone in the house was napping after lunch, I took a chair from Dada's room, placed it on my bed and took down a bulb. I observed it from all angles. There was nothing special about it. I shook it and nothing happened. I shook it again and found out that the filament was not as strong as it looked when lit.

Damn!

If I got caught, I would be blamed for every bulb that had ever blown a fuse in the house. I put the bulb back in the holder, dragged the chair back to its place and pretended to be sleeping.

Days later, when electricity made one of its brief appearances, Dada wondered why even the Philips bulb he had bought only a few days ago had broken down.

Only this little scientist knew the secret.

C.V. Raman Marg took us to the bus stand near the gurudwara in New Friends Colony.

Guru Nanak was the first guru of the Sikhs. Dada, whose beard was exactly like the guru's, long and white, had told me stories about him.

'So, have you read the story about Guru Nanak sahab in your Urdu book?'

Silence.

'Tell me?'

I have.

'Guru Nanak's father once gave him money and asked him to go Lahore to attend to some business. On the way, Guru Nanak saw some hungry fakirs. He arranged food for them with the money his father had given him and returned home empty-handed. You know that, right? Besides being achhe mizaj ke, he was good at Maths and Farsi too. What about you?'

Persian. This is precisely why I didn't want to talk about Guru Nanak. I could hardly go beyond ... Aamdam Aamdi Aamad Aamdeem Aamdeed Aamdand ... The basic grammar they made you memorise before starting to learn Persian.

It meant: I came You came He came We came You came They came.

I don't like this nonsense Persian grammar thing. I know all these important words, isn't it enough? Like biradar means brother. Pidar, father. Madar, mother.

And also, pidar-e-buzurg, that's Dada. What else does he want?

We got down at the bus stand in New Friends Colony and took a rickshaw.

The rickshawallah wore an almost-dead shirt, and sped as if his life depended on it – overtaking other rickshaws, crisscrossing through the well-paved roads, and almost through pedestrians and kids who waited for their school buses in (new) school uniforms, (new) bags and (new) shoes. Fancy cars lined the road, parked outside beautiful homes, partly on the footpath, partly on the road. All the buildings had watchmen.

Bhuttu Bhayya pointed to a red building. 'See, this is Priyanka Gandhi's house.' The board on the house said 'Vadras'. We could see flowers, guards at the gate, a ceiling fan on the first-floor veranda.

A little ahead, he pointed again, '… and this is Ashoka Park.' Manicured grass and plants. Fountains!

People ran and walked inside, some of them with dogs. Uncles and aunties jumped up and down, parading like they were in school. Many women were in half-pants.

Such a big woman is wearing a half-pant. Even I wear a full one. Qayamat is very close. And see this man; he has tied his hair like a woman.

'On the other side of this colony is Jamia,' said Bhuttu Bhayya, pointing to his right.

Jamia Millia Islamia. Everyone knows it's a very big university. This is why I am here. Please, God, let me clear the entrance test.

I soon found out that Bhuttu Bhayya had told my family only half the truth. There was a student strike on, and no entrance examinations as long as it continued. Students were demanding reinstatement of the 10 per cent quota for Urdu-medium students, which the High Court of Delhi had struck down. The quota had helped Urdu-medium students, apparently a euphemism for Muslims, get admission. *Qaum ke ladke.*

The removal of the quota would soon strengthen the demand to declare Jamia a minority institution. About a decade later, this would become a reality.

A board in Urdu, Hindi and English announced that we had descended – literally, by a few feet – into Zakir Nagar. The road that came from New Friends Colony sloped down, adjusting for the Yamuna's river bank, and turned into a cluttered street. Further inside, road turned into footpath, footpath into road. There were no sparrows here, or crows. No plants and trees. Or fancy cars and big homes. The rickshawallah raced through puddles of water that had spilled from the gutters. The buildings were all cramped together. Some had tiles on the walls, others naked brick. Houses had signboards with their owner's name and address painted or engraved. In English and Urdu, or Urdu and English.

A general store was stocking bread from a truck and blocking traffic. This, of course, invited enthusiastic honking. Perhaps the owners had no idea that there is a hadees that asks you to be a good citizen, wherever you are.

The shop responsible for that jam had 786 inscribed on its board. The numbers stand for Bismillah-ir-rahman-ir-rahim: In God's name who is most benevolent and merciful.

The representation of Bismillah-ir-rahman-ir-rahim as 786 comes from an Arabic numeral system in which each letter of the alphabet is assigned a numeric value. The first letter of Arabic, alif, is given a value of 1, the second, bey, is given 2, and similarly, ya is assigned 10, qa is assigned 100 and so on. When all the numerical values of the letters in Bismillah-ir-rahman-ir-rahim are added, you get 786.

Sometimes, the numeral 92 is also written along with 786. 92 represents Muhammad. Sallalahu Alaihi wasallam.

May Allah Grant Him Peace; you say this when you read or hear Prophet Muhammad's name.

This Arabic system of numerology is also used to choose names for children. It's called tareekhi naam, names that allow you to calculate a person's date of birth from the alphabets of the name. Dada's annual almanac listed the date-names for every day of that year. He used the jantari to name all the kids in my family.

Except me.

My elder brother who drowned as a little child was named Farooque (without an extra E). Dada had named him after one of his two favourite historical personalities who were famous for their justice, Emperor Jahangir and Caliph Farooque. Dada admired Omar Farooque's courage in facing down any obstacle in the cause of truth and justice. Once the caliph's son had committed a misdeed but was shown favour by a governor in Egypt. When Farooque got to know of the incident, he wrote to the governor that his son be sent back to Medina so that he could be punished impartially for his sins.

Hazrat Omar was one of the Prophet's closest companions. He became caliph after Abu Bakar, the first caliph. Centuries later, the ruin of this same caliphate became a matter of contention between great powers. The British wanted to abolish the caliphate, then in Turkey, which Muslims widely opposed, even though its value was no more than symbolic. In India, that resistance was known as the Khilafat Movement, which Mahatma Gandhi supported too. The movement was led by the Ali brothers, Mohammad Ali Jauhar and Shaukat Ali Jauhar, who were among the founders of Jamia Millia Islamia (where I would study, Insha Allah).

So, when I was born, I was named Farooquee – a variation of my lost brother's name. How Neyaz Ahmad was added to my name is another story.

Soon after my birth, Ammi had a dream in which a man, who seemed like a pious man or a saint, appeared and gave her two silver eggs. He told her many good things about the two silver eggs – which were never shared with me – and addressed one of them as Neyaz Ahmad.

Ammi narrated the dream to Dada, who had read books on dreams and would interpret them. Often, we heard him saying something unpleasant was going to happen, and it would. Once he had anticipated something would fail him, and his scooter didn't start when he had to take Baaji for her class 12 exam. Someone else had to rush her to the exam centre on a bicycle. Another time, he had warned that something bad was going to happen, and my younger sister fell ill and had to be rushed to a doctor. He foretold misfortune, and unseasonal rains ruined our crops.

He interpreted the two silver eggs as two sons, one already born and the other who would come into this world a few years later. That's how Neyaz Ahmad got added to Farooquee, a disproportionately large name for my size – longitude- or latitude-wise.

Somehow, he didn't interpret one of the silver eggs as a daughter – Baaji – and the other as me. Though, in his defence, he had named Baaji 'Rahmat', blessings. And then the other granddaughters, my sisters and cousins, Musarrat, happiness; Tabassum, smile; Tarannum, singing in rhyme; Firdausi, the highest of the heavens, and so on.

He would often recite the hadees that says that if a boy brings one Rahmat, blessing, to the house, a girl brings ten.

In all, including my cousins, my home has two male blessings, 110 female blessings.

Zakir Nagar looked like an incomplete city of posters, banners and unlit restaurants. The sky was a mesh of wires. Even mosquitoes must worry about getting electrocuted. The roads were dug up here and there.

On the painted board of a juice shop, a blushing Shah Rukh Khan held a glass of juice in one hand. The owner was from Bihar, I learnt later. There were many restaurants on both sides of the road. Some of them served kebab and paratha, cooked on stoves that extended into the road. 'Here. These hotels,' Bhuttu Bhayya pointed out. 'You will come here for your lunch and dinner. Can you see that one? Lane no. 20. Mumtaz Hotel. It's the best hotel around here.'

A banner in Urdu fought with time for survival. It had asymmetrical holes in it to minimise the force of the wind. It announced the sale of Muradabadi biryani – sirf sabut masaley ka, only unground spices used – and declared that the shop sold both chicken and badey ka. Beef.

Hamara koi branch *nahin hai*.

Colourful posters dotted the walls, especially near the masjid's gate. Upcoming netas – with their pictures at the bottom of the posters – congratulated established netas on their nomination or election to one post or another.

General Secretary of Okhla Congress Unit. President of Saifi Muslim Society.

National party president of some godforsaken party no one had ever heard of.

In the procession of posters, there was one by a neta announcing that he had got the Zakir Nagar road repaired. A poster for a coaching institute claimed its students had cleared B.Tech and Diploma in Engg. in Jamia, with black-and-white portraits of the students. It stated that the institute also prepared students for AMU and IIT entrance tests.

Should I take coaching classes for my test? I asked my roommates later. No, they said. 'They fool you,' one pronounced. The other said, 'I know the teachers in those coaching centres. They can't even read properly, forget teaching you.'

The rickshaw turned left, from Rashid Hotel on the main road into a narrower street. About a hundred metres, and two streets later, it turned into another street, narrower still. Lane no. 6, my new abode, a few metres from Zakir Nagar's main mosque, the nearest landmark.

4

Primetime Bulletin

KHALILULLAH MASJID WAS BARRICADED on all sides when I reached it on the noon of the encounter. Police and onlookers packed every inch of space outside the mosque. Hordes of media vans stood there too, with wires extending deep into the crowd. There were vans of channels I had never heard of. Mediapersons screamed into their mikes, and cameras vied for the best shot. Men in skullcaps made for a good shot and if they were shouting slogans, even better.

I couldn't bring myself to go closer. There were lots of policemen, more than I had ever seen, in all sorts of uniforms, with all sorts of sophisticated guns. It was not reassuring to see such a large number of armed men in a locality that rarely saw much police presence (except on election days, when the area found itself categorised as 'sensitive' by the Election Commission).

An innocuous story, but just a few days ago, some mischievous juniors from Jamia had a minor run-in with the police. On their way to the university library, they were passing the Batla House bus stand where a few policewallahs sat vigil that evening. One of the young boys felt frisky, and said, looking at the policemen, 'What are so many thulle doing here?' Thulla, a stereotypical slow-moving policeman with a potbelly. One of the thullas glared at him. Another young man from the group said, in a loud voice, 'Come on. Don't call them thulle. They are mama-log.' Mama. Maternal uncle, slang for a policeman.

A policewallah ran towards them, but they had all vanished – except one, the studious, earnest man in the group. The bechara had to do uthak-baithak on behalf of all the culprits, and then promise that he wouldn't call any policewallah a mama.

Okay?

Okay, sir.

And not even thulla. Okay?

Okay, sir.

But here this morning, it was way more serious. An encounter. A real encounter with shots fired and two men killed and another injured. The men in uniform here were not the human forms we saw in thanas. These were commandoes in blue, khaki and white, sporting bandanas. Wearing bullet-proof vests. Heavily armed.

They carried AK-47s, Sten guns, MP5s and, of course, pistols. I had never seen such sophisticated weapons close up. In our group at college, Kafil was the one who was interested in weapons, technology, aircraft, automobiles – 'it's auto*mobeel*, not auto*mobyle*'. He would ruin our movie-watching with whisper-tutorials on guns, tanks, fighter planes, engines. He was usually a quiet chap, but these things really got him going. And the next moment you were learning all the stupid differences between an MP5 and an AK-47, a four-stroke engine and a five-stroke engine, a MIG and a Sukhoi.

Just a few days ago, the bunch of us were on a conference call – thanks to the telecom operator's offer of free calls during the late-night hours – continuing our daytime bakchodi. One of us jokingly threatened to lodge a bullet in another's bottom. The others mocked the would-be assaulter; did he even have a functioning gun? And if he had (let's assume he had, for the sake of argument), was it potent enough? Soon there was a verbal scuffle over metaphorical guns and bullets, and the matter was referred to Kafil as the expert on the (real) stuff.

He elaborated on the diversity of guns and bullets. Close combat, bullet-proof vests, hand guns.

'AK-47 (which of us have AK-47s?).'

'Neyaz?'

'Huh. Neyaz would have no more than a pistol. He is a midget.'

'Asbah?'

'Come on. He is so beautiful, a gun wouldn't suit him.'

'Perwez?'

'Oh, please. He must have a Sten gun.'

'Why?'

'Because it was used in World War II.'

We often teased Perwez about ageing because he was going bald. I used to say that Perwez was so old that he had seen the extinction of dinosaurs. He would, in return, mock my thinness and, ahem, medium height, and say that I had skipped adulthood. 'Shut up, you archaebacteria.' Archaebacteria are among the oldest creatures on earth.

That afternoon, Kafil and Perwez were also at the site. They heard the reporters shouting into their mikes that the young men who had been killed had been tracked for days and that many phones were under surveillance in Delhi.

Kafil was scared. He knew what tracking meant. And it scared him that he had talked on the phone for hours about guns, bullets, bombs, tanks, fighter planes and whatnot. He saw the lethal weapons in the security men's hands and vanished to his home in Mathura without a word. Not even a call.

Perwez, too, returned home to Jullena without a visit to our headquarters – my home, so close to the EncounterSite. I had nowhere to run. This was my locality, my address.

I had lived in Jamia Nagar for more than a decade now, about half my life. I had moved at least eleven times before finally settling into this house that my parents had bought by selling some land back home. I had been living here for six years.

Strolling around the locality, I tried to make sense of things. The street in front of the four-storey building where the encounter took place was barricaded. The street to the back was open, though, and the police didn't stop the crowd from going up to the building. There were many journalists on the terrace of a neighbouring two-storey house, valiantly trying to close in on the EncounterFlat, two floors above them.

I later learnt that an acquaintance of mine lived on the ground floor of that building. Like most of us, he too had gone to bed after sehri and was fast asleep when the encounter happened. The noise woke him but he ignored it, thinking it was construction work nearby.

It was a panicky phone call from his parents that alerted him. At first, he tried to ignore their calls and slumber on, but when they kept calling, he picked up. He was anticipating a lecture from his parents on sleeping late, instead they asked frantically: *Are you okay?*

His parents, working in the Gulf, had heard the address in news bulletins. Two young men killed in the building where their two sons lived. For a few minutes, when he didn't take their call, they imagined the worst.

But both their sons were safe. Alhamdulillah.

After talking to his parents, he opened the door of his flat and saw policewallahs moving around calmly in the stairway. He asked them if something was wrong, and they said, 'No, it's all okay.' He tried to go back to sleep but his parents kept calling him, insisting that he leave the place. He switched on the TV to check what was happening and realised that it was not all okay.

His home was everywhere, on every channel. Suddenly, opening the front door seemed dangerous.

He opened the back door and saw people crowding the street. He left the place quickly, never to return. The flat remained vacant for months before it was rented out to students who had not been around at the time of the encounter and so had no memories to haunt them.

That afternoon, the crowds around the building were agitated. They were as upset with the media as they were with the police. They never trusted the police much to begin with, but now the media was failing them too. The crowd was shouting into the microphones of journalists, 'We know you won't telecast our version. You all are biased.' The locals said over and over that the men killed were no terrorists. They were young men in search of education and livelihood and dignity. In the background, the sound of slogans reverberated in the air.

Naara-e-Takbeer. Shout that God is great.

Allah-o-Akbar. God is great.

I met the chaiwallah who had a stall just next to Khalilullah Masjid. We would often go to his stall in the evenings on our way to the Yamuna riverbank. He would shout for his helper, a kid barely in his teens, calling him Bihari. The chaiwallah's own accent, of course, gave away that he too was a Bihari. The Bihari accent has its own beauty.

Bihadi, he would say. In many parts of Bihar, R and D are used interchangeably. *Adey bhai ganwa band kad do. Ajaan ho daha hai.*

His shop had little business going during the fasting hours. So, he had joined the onlookers-cum-protesters gathered around the building, and gleefully told me that the crowd had roughed up one of the media guys. The journalist had been telling his studio that the encounter happened in Khalilullah Masjid where the Terrorists were hiding.

'*Thok diye saley ko. Jadoodi tha pelna. Jo mann me ata hai bol ke khisak leta hai sab.*' We thrashed the bugger. It was necessary. They just say whatever they feel like and vanish.

This was satisfying to hear. To many ears.

There were some who tried to report other stories. They tried to get the angry and scared locals to speak to them. I saw the old uncle who lived in a neighbouring lane talking to a young media person. He sounded like a helpless father protesting his son's innocence: '*Maar diya unpe jhoota ilzam laga ke. Aur upar se aap log bol rahe hain ki masjid mein dahshatgard maarey gaye hain.*' They were falsely accused and killed. And on top of that you people are saying terrorists have been killed in the mosque.

In the background, a crowd kept up the sloganeering, wearing brave faces as if they were not afraid of the police. But when the police decided enough was enough and came forward to shoo them away, they ran. Ran backwards, tumbling over each other.

Some of them bumped into the cameraman and the reporter who was interviewing the old man. They almost fell into an embrace. After a brief awkwardness, the interview resumed. '*Beta, apke umar ke thhe woh bachche.*' Son, they were as old as you are.

Meanwhile ...

It started raining (half-heartedly).

It rained for a while.

It stopped raining (half-heartedly).

The weather became pleasant.

But the atmosphere did not.

I didn't offer Jum'a prayers that day. It was tough for a Muslim to hide on campus if he was not offering Friday prayers. On the few occasions that I didn't go for Jum'a, I hung out with Shyam. He had the undivided attention of the girls on Friday afternoons because most boys were in the masjid. Ah! Flirt jihad. We envied him.

On EncounterDay, I was home during prayer time. Those who were on campus offered prayers at the masjid there. They told me the imam held an unusually long dua session after the namaz. I had been going to that mosque since I was in school, and knew that long duas were the norm for him, but that day, everyone agreed it was long even for him.

When I was in school, I would try to go to the masjid with Ashhar every Friday. He was considered a good boy, and one of the toppers in class. We would sit at the back, in the park outside the masjid, and hurry away as soon the imam finished, before he began reading the non-obligatory prayers. Even before the prayers, though, imam sahib would test our patience with his long lecture and duas – on piousness, life, the afterlife, Ramazan, on anything that was in the air about which Islam had something to say. Then he would read the sermon in Arabic, chewing each word slowly. And then, still slower, he would lead the namaz. And, finally, his never-ending duas.

Quam ke liye. Millat ke liye. For Community. For Nation.

For the healthy. For the diseased.

For the dead.

For after-death.

For justice.

To bring the cruel to the right path.

Asking patience for the innocents.

He prayed for sinners and non-sinners alike.

That Friday noon, he wept during his dua, my friends said. He pleaded to God to give justice to the innocent. Ameen, said the followers, in unison.

'If the young men were indeed involved, they must be punished' – the 'ameen' from the rest reverberated in the imam's microphone.

He asked God to give everyone sabr, patience. 'God knows best and He will indeed give justice.' Ameen.

Summa-ameen.

A few steps from the masjid, the Jamia Community Radio appealed to residents to stay calm. Some distance away, officials of the university were gathered to answer students' questions, especially the big one: were the two young men who had been killed students of Jamia? The media said they were, but the university authorities said, no, they were not.

This was satisfying to hear.

The long day ended in a flash. Evening descended, and it was iftar time. Jamia Nagar was filled with security forces that the residents skirted around as they visited the stalls selling iftar items. More police would fill the streets after iftar, once news of Inspector Sharma's death was announced. Many masjids, along with the call to prayer, asked the residents to stay calm. 'It's the month of prayers and compassion and mercy. God sees everything. And He is just.'

That evening, it was a quiet iftar at my home. Perwez, Kafil, Furquan and Asbah didn't turn up. And they wouldn't, for many rozas to come.

For days, weeks to come. Even after Ramazan.

5

Tana Tan Sunni and 24 Number

18 JULY 1997, THAT was the day I reached Delhi.

By then, Bill Clinton had become president of the US. (Source: All India Radio) And Tony Blair, prime minister of England. (Source: *Competition Science Refresher*) More than 300 people had died in an accident during Haj in Saudi Arabia. (Source: BBC Urdu Bulletin) In the coming days and months, K.R. Narayanan would become president of India. (Source: *Hindustan Times*) Princess Diana would die. (Source: Roommates) And Mother Teresa would soon follow. (Source: *Hindustan Times*)

The third Friday of the month.

Even before I could settle in, my roommate Hafizji dropped a bomb: there might not be enough water as it was a Friday, the day usually reserved for cleaning and washing. We should bathe early.

Hafizji and our other roommate Raju Bhai bathed hurriedly. Bhuttu Bhayya followed. But before I could make it to the bathroom, one of our neighbours occupied it. Hafizji smiled and said, 'Now that Buffalo is inside, you might have to go to the masjid without taking a bath.' He was right. Even when the tap started making scratchy noises, a sure sign that the water supply would soon stop, he didn't emerge. Fortunately, even after Buffalo was done, we managed to fill a bucket each for Aamir Bhayya and me in the trickle that continued.

Bathing with just one bucket of water (or even the idea of water-shortage) would have been unthinkable back home. The water even smelt funny. Bhuttu Bhayya said it was chlorine, which killed germs.

Bhuttu Bhayya went to the neighbourhood masjid, a majestic building with a big courtyard, after his bath. Hafizji and Raju Bhai waited for Aamir Bhayya and me. They preferred to offer namaz in Qadri Masjid, which followed the Barelvi sect of Sufi Islam. By the time we reached, the Jamat – the main namaz led by the imam – was over. So they decided to offer namaz in Batla House's Khalilullah Masjid, which was scheduled for the latest possible time, 2.30 p.m. This masjid, too, adhered to Barelvi-Sufi Islam, which was also the sect my family subscribed to.

It didn't surprise me that, instead of going to a masjid 100 metres away, we went to one a kilometre away. I'd seen these divisions at home too. The Barelvis mocked other sects like the Wahabis and Jamatis, making fun of, for example, their short pajamas, and calling them chaubees number – twenty-four being the numerical code used for Jamati and Wahabi, just as 786 represents Bismillah. In return, the chaubees numbari called us Barelvis TTS – Tana Tan Sunni. Cracking followers of sunnat.

The two groups disagree, among other things, on the question of Prophet Muhammad's immortality – the Barelvis consider him immortal, while those of the Jamati and Wahabi camps claim he was like any human in life and death, except higher on morality and piousness.

The Wahabi camp, which preaches a relatively purist and literal version of Islam, mocks the often non-literal and liberal interpretations of the Sufis and others. The Sufis revere saints like Ajmer's Chishti, or his disciple Nizamuddin in Delhi, as they believe the saints had achieved closeness to God through their piety. The literalists ferociously denounce the Sufi followers' practice of visiting the dargahs of saints as un-Islamic.

Buses full of devotees used to go from my village to the Nizamuddin Dargah and Ajmer Dargah. It was the poor man's Haj. Slowly this changed. Fewer and fewer people went and those who did were largely seen as deviant. Somewhere down the line, visiting a dargah became biddat – deviation from the faith.

Such irony! It were the Sufi saints who attracted large numbers of people in India to Islam. Their synthesis of Islam and the practices and beliefs of local cultures drew droves of followers from the subcontinent to the faith.

They rejected less, assimilated more. Not what one could say about the increasingly exclusionary versions we have come to know.

Often there are squabbles in hungry, nondescript corners of the country – and the world – over what is True Islam. Over the Sufis' interpretation of Islam, and Wahabism or Salafism and whatnot. People have intense disagreements and fights over these esoteric matters, even though the basic needs of life elude them.

Small gatherings, whether for celebration or the sharing of sorrow, have come to be defined from a narrow prism.

This is not Islam. That is not Islam.

Only my version is Islam. The rest of you will go to hell.

There is less and less acknowledgement of, and respect for, other versions.

There used to be milads in our village, organised on festive occasions, or at the time of life-cycle rituals.

A wedding, birth or death, a house-warming dawat, circumcision of a male child.

Tents would be brought in, mattresses spread for attendees to sit on, and generators hired to light the place in our electricity-starved region. The flickering tubelights brought a certain feeling of happiness and curiosity among both kids and insects. Before the maulanas arrived, the mikes would get a chance to commit a few sins; they would blare out a few Bollywood songs or Bollywoodised qawalis, angering the elders, who preferred naat, poems sung without accompaniment in praise of Muhammad. The maulanas would usually start with a recitation of Hamd, a poem in praise of God. Then the lectures, the monotony of which was occasionally broken by a naat. In the end, everyone stood up and sang 'Salam', a qawwali praising the Prophet. Then the chhuhare or khurma would be distributed, which was why we kids stuck on till the end. Or sneaked back in towards the end.

Even back then, these well-meaning gatherings would often turn into an opportunity for the maulanas to diss other traditions. And now, the Salam – which was once read in many masjids after the morning prayers – has come to be considered a non-Islamic addition.

After the Salam was purged from the morning prayers and milad, it was the turn of the milad itself to be condemned as an un-Islamic addition. So, in many places, milad isn't dignified anymore.

If, on the one hand, the puritans interpreted Islam too literally, the Barelvis became reactionary, often turning away from the core sentiments of Sufism.

The Salafis, for example, allow women to offer namaz in the mosque, though not to lead men in prayer. Barelvis or Sufis, at least where I come from, don't subscribe to the idea of women going to mosques. Their reaction is often as extreme as that of the purists who denounce everything not mentioned in the Quran and hadees as un-Islamic.

Once, a Tableeghi Jamat group visited my village and stayed in the masjid for a few days. Many villagers, including Dada, protested. They said that no one could be prevented from praying at a mosque, and Jamatis were welcome to come in and offer their prayers, but that it was not a place to stay in. They offered the Jamat members a place to stay outside the mosque.

The village couldn't agree on the matter and the group stayed in the mosque. When they left, the other faction, which included Dada, washed the mosque.

Only a few months later, before tempers had been soothed, another Jamat group visited. The arguments were so bitter this time that many stopped going to the mosque – a place that they, and their forefathers, had enthusiastically contributed to building. Dada too stopped going. He began to offer namaz at home, and for the weekly Friday prayers (which, it is recommended, be offered in a mosque), he would go to a mosque in the neighbouring village.

When the villagers requested him to forget past squabbles and come back, he went to the mosque again – just that once. This is a masjid for which he had spent years leading the collection of funds, approaching people row by row during the Jum'a and Eid prayers, going house to house and convincing people who were working in the Gulf to donate more, and planning the shape and size of the minaret, the pedestal, the colour each particular decoration should have. Choosing the cement, the bricks, the mason himself. Ensuring that not a single grain of sand was misused, not a single penny wasted. It was God's house.

I remember when one part of our house was being constructed, we were short of a rod for the lintel, about a metre short. The village mistry, who had also helped build the mosque, suggested that Dada should send me to get a rod that lay unused at the mosque.

Dada was infuriated. 'No way. Never,' he said.

A worker was sent to the nearby market to procure the rod. Meanwhile, the mason and I had to listen to the story of an egoistic king whose great kingdom was destroyed by God, simply because a bird had picked up a straw from a mosque and dropped it in the fort while it was being constructed. 'That small unaccounted straw from the masjid, God's house, destroyed the kingdom of a great king, so who am I?' he asked.

We had no answer.

A few months after the squabble over the mosque, Dada met with an accident that almost ruined God's plan to end his life with cancer a few years later. One monsoon night, he slipped on the bamboo stairs going up to the roof and injured his head, arm and ribs. This near-fatal mishap caused him to further withdraw from village affairs. So, no masjid, no Panchayat, nothing. He offered namaz mostly at home for the rest of his life.

He didn't force any of us to follow him, so we continued to visit the village mosque. Here in Delhi, I went to Khalilullah because that's where my friends went. Khalilullah wasn't as majestic as the masjid in our Zakir Nagar, but it had a bigger courtyard than the mosque in my village, and taps for ablutions.

That first day, the masjid was already full, and people were lined up at the taps. There was no place inside, so namazis had spread their mats on the road and gullies outside. But even these spaces were packed. We had not brought mats, and had to wait around, hoping someone would offer us some space on theirs. Hafizji sneaked onto a corner of someone's mat. Someone else offered Raju Bhai half his mat. Aamir Bhayya also found a bit of space to pray.

One gentleman, seeing a lost kid, asked me to squeeze into the space between two people standing on a narrow mat. People had put their shoes and sandals in front of their mats. I couldn't bring myself to keep my footwear next to where I would bend for the sajdah. So I put them next to a wall. It was only after the namaz that I realised why people kept their footwear in front of them – I walked back home barefoot.

The imam went through the prayers quite fast, probably because so many people were offering namaz outside in the summer heat. As soon as he finished, people started leaving, without offering dua. Back in the village, no one moved until the imam had finished the dua, when namazis appealed to God to grant their wishes.

I went inside the masjid to offer the rest of the namaz. First dua with the imam, then sunnat and nafil prayers. Sunnat, which Prophet Muhammad used to offer besides the farz, the obligatory one. Nafil, the non-obligatory, for brownie points.

After the dua, the imam sought forgiveness for all the worshippers.

God forgive our sins.

Aameen.

We are the sinners and God will show us the right path. God knows best, only He can forgive us sinners, only He can show us the true path.

Aameen.

O God, make our death easy, our stay in the grave easy.

Aameen.

O God, make easy the day of judgement.

Aameen.

God, give us all health.

Aameen.

Then he prayed for the safety of God's houses wherever they were.

Aameen.

And safety for the entire ummah, wherever they were.

Aameen.

Aameen. Summa Aameen.

Allah humma rabbana atina fid duniya hasanata wa fil akhirate hasanata wa qina azaban naar. O Allah! All glory is due to You, I praise You, Your name is the Most Blessed, Your Majesty is highly exalted and there is none worthy of worship but You.

The dua ended. People offered sunnat and nafil and left. Outside, beggars lined the street, sitting crouched, standing hunched, with bowls in their hands. Women in burqas. Old men on mats.

The temporary biryani stall did brisk business. One gentleman sold attar, skullcaps and handkerchiefs. Another sold mausambi juice from his cart.

And I searched for my chappals. In vain.

6

Shut Your Doors and Windows

I WAS SCARED THAT night, too scared to really sleep. This was true, I am sure, of people across Jamia Nagar. The coming nights and days would bring no relief. More so for young people like us, who were living away from our families. As hope, as keepers of unfulfilled dreams. Of returning as doctors engineers managers civil servants rich and powerful.

Asjad, my classmate from middle school, kept vigil to the sound of patrolling around his house. Alim didn't sleep at home, going to stay with a cousin instead. Our friend's bhabhi, who lived near the EncounterBuilding, tossed and turned all night in her newly bought flat.

The kid who had been all over television explaining what he had seen and heard that morning was packing to leave for home. I had no idea where Mama, my classmate from Azamgarh, was. (Because he always sucked up to the girls, we teasingly called him Mama.)

Kafil, Perwez and Furquan, regulars at my place, didn't turn up either.

My parents, a thousand kilometres away, regretted buying this house in Batla House six years ago. But, of course, they still couldn't afford to buy anything elsewhere in the city, in places where the chances of a police encounter would be smaller.

I didn't have a TV, but I did subscribe to an English newspaper. And for many mornings after EncounterDay, I bought other papers too. I always bought more newspapers when something significant happened – the World Trade Centre attacks, the US invasion of Afghanistan and Iraq, the joint session of Parliament to introduce the Prevention of Terrorism Act, the bus to Pakistan, terror attacks in the country, election results, the cricket world cup.

In the days following the encounter, there was an information deluge – from newspapers, TV, the internet, neighbours, friends and flying rumours. Though morning after morning, the newspapers appeared to all say the same thing, a close reading revealed wild contradictions, almost as if the reports were about different incidents. To be fair, Jamia Nagar would have hardly noticed these contradictions had we not been the subject of discussion.

Us, educated Muslims.

In the capital of India.

With the means and resources to fight.

Or at least cry hoarse.

Media reports seemed to disagree on the very basic facts of the encounter: when the operation took place, how many rounds were fired, how many police went inside, how many – and how – the suspects escaped, how the police got their clues, whether it was a planned operation, and who among the Terrorists played what role. Even the names of the accused and the items recovered varied. In fact, the documents that the police later filed in court too would use different names for the accused.[6]

There was no clarity about who killed Inspector Sharma, how the Terrorists ran away when, as the police chief said, the building was secured from all sides. If there was anything at all that remained constant, it was this: the flip-flop by the authorities.

You could say that these were small discrepancies, and we too would have forgotten them in the grind of daily life. But then the police chief claimed that, with this encounter, his team had solved all the major blast cases across the country. The young men, he said, were the masterminds of the blasts in Jaipur, Uttar Pradesh, Ahmedabad and Delhi. These same newspapers, however, had reported that other masterminds had been caught for those blasts. For the blasts at Sankat Mochan, Varanasi, a cleric named Mohammed Walilullah was convicted by a fast-track court and sentenced to ten years. It was said that three men from Bangladesh had given him the bomb.[7] For the 2007 UP blasts, Khalid Mujahid and Mohammed Tariq had been arrested. (Khalid died mysteriously in police custody on his way back to jail from court.)[8] For the Jaipur blasts, Munawwar Hussain Qureshi had been arrested. Qureshi and the ten men arrested with him were released in 2011, after three and half years in jail. It was only then that the country realised that they had been charged with being members of SIMI, even though the media had reported they were accused in the Jaipur blasts.[9]

For the July 2008 blasts in Gujarat, the cleric Abu Bashar from Azamgarh had been arrested. After his arrest, the police claimed to have busted SIMI's pan-India network similar to what they had said after the encounter at Batla House. Many reports said that Abu Bashar had been brought to Delhi from Ahmedabad and had tipped the police off about the Terrorists' hideout, though he himself had been in police custody since August 14. But then the police commissioner claimed that finding the men in Batla House was entirely the work of the Special Cell, and that none of it had anything to do with Abu Bashar's presence in Delhi. 'In fact, Bashir didn't have any link with Abu Bashar,' reported *The Hindu*, quoting an anonymous police source. (Many early reports named the main accused, Atif, who was killed in the encounter, as Bashir.)

Initial reports said the police had gone to the flat because they had information about a dreaded terrorist hiding out there. Later, the media said that the police had merely gone there for reconnaissance and armed terrorists had taken them by surprise. Still later, other versions were added. (One account published in a magazine said it was a friendly fire between the policemen that killed Sharma.[10] There were reports that an X-ray report at the hospital where he was admitted didn't show any foreign object inside his body, and we don't know if the bullets were recovered from the EncounterSite for forensics.[11]) In the end, though, most reports claimed that the Terrorists had been under surveillance for some time. They did not say how these men had managed to bomb the city when they were under surveillance, or why it took six days for the police to reach their flat after the blasts.

Before the encounter, the Delhi Police had raided and detained at least ten people in Delhi, mainly from Jamia Nagar, in connection with the blasts.[12] It was not clear why they were arrested if the 'real terrorists' were under surveillance. It was also baffling that the Terrorists chose to stay on in the flat even though it was common news that the police were raiding places in Jamia Nagar.

None of this is to say that the accused men were innocent or that they were involved in the blast – neither has been proven beyond reasonable doubt yet. But all these contradictions cemented the suspicions that we had in Jamia Nagar about the genuineness of the encounter. No one trusted the police anyway, and people's collective memory remembered the lack of proper investigation in every major case of injustice against Muslims in the past: Nellie, Bhagalpur, Muradabad, Meerut, Ayodhya, Mumbai, Gujarat.

The police had issued four sketches of suspects after the Delhi blasts. Four sketches for three men. One of them wore a skullcap, the others had trimmed beards. None of these sketches matched the portraits that the newspapers published of those killed in the encounter.

In the coming days and weeks, sceptics pointed out that the dead men had all presented authentic documents for SIM-card verification. The police responded that they had been overconfident, implying that the Terrorists had disguised themselves as Normal Human Beings – as students, as working men.

Normal Human Beings.

Of all the many claims that the police made, this was the scariest. In one stroke, it brought every youth in Jamia Nagar under the scanner of suspicion. How was a truly normal person expected to behave? And what distinguished him or her from someone who is merely normal-looking? How was one supposed to identify someone who was disguised as a Normal Human Being? Am I normal? Are you?

This ostensibly harmless statement made us all – brave, cowards, closet cowards, everyone – paranoid, if you will. I thought about fleeing Delhi. But then I remembered the police claim that two of the Terrorists had fled. What if they said I was one of them? Already a major news channel was broadcasting a programme warning people about the absconding men: 'Shut your doors and windows, they could be hiding anywhere.' I abandoned that plan.

But staying in Delhi presented its own challenges. On the day of the encounter, the police had picked up five or six schoolkids who lived in the EncounterBuilding.[13] They were released late in the evening that day after some senior lawyers intervened, but it was scary. If schoolkids were being picked up, college students were not safe at all. A school boy from another colony was dragged out by plainclothesmen from his home. I heard they had asked for his elder brother and were told that he wasn't home; so they dragged away the younger boy.

I heard that a young man was picked up from Lajawab tea stall near Batla House chowk and taken away in a For-You-With-You-Always van.

We stopped going out after sunset. No Bismillah tea stall, no Lajawab, no nightlife of Jamia Nagar. We were scared of the police. I recalled the old village wisdom Dada often quoted: Never grow a ber ka ped at your door, never befriend a policeman. Ammi told me to be careful and avoid stepping out unless it was really important.

She had good reason to fear. The most educated person in her maternal family, her cousin, had been killed by the police in the Mumbai riots following the demolition of Babri Masjid in 1992, and our joyous visits to Ammi's maternal home always held the undertone of a missing uncle, a widowed aunt and orphaned cousins.

My uncle was a maulana who taught at a madrasa-cum-masjid in Mumbai. At around 10.30 a.m., while he was doing his ablutions before reading the Quran, a troupe of policemen entered his madrasa from the rooftop of a bakery next door. They asked for the head maulana – Maulana Qasim, my uncle.

His son, barely in his teens, and scared and confused, directed them towards his Abbu. But his Abbu knew what the police action meant in that communally charged city. He shouted to his students: 'Monsters have come; start reading darood.' Darood, a common dua that is read in daily life in praise of Prophet Muhammad, and that many consider good to read for a dying soul.

My cousin witnessed it all. They shot his Abbu, but his eyes were still open. They dragged him down the stairs from the upper floors. Then they kicked his Abbu towards the railing. Still alive, he clung to the railing, while his polio-stricken leg dangled in the air. Then they shot more bullets and his Abbu finally fell to the street below.

His Abbu asked them for water. But they put their shoes in his mouth.

His Abbu lay there while they killed others.

The boy saw blood flowing from his Abbu's mouth. His front tooth was broken – the tooth that had been replaced a few years ago. He had asked his Abbu where he got a new tooth from, and Abbu had joked that 'I stole your tooth when you were asleep and that's why your front tooth is missing.'

That day, the thirteen-year-old watched as his Abbu slowly died, a man gagging him to prevent him from crying out.

The street was red with his Abbu's blood.

Some policemen ordered the kids in the madrasa to form a queue. But another policeman pleaded, 'What have the kids done? Leave them.'

Good people are everywhere, you know.

It was 9 January 1993.

When the curfew was lifted, my cousin went to the mortuary with a relative to retrieve his Abbu's body. The face was swollen beyond recognition but his handicapped foot was unmistakable – the disability that had, as a child, made him less suited for worldly affairs, and had caused his parents to send him into God's service.

He washed his Abbu's body as per the rituals, wrapped it in a shroud and placed it in a coffin. Then he offered funeral prayers and buried his Abbu. By now, curfew had been imposed again and they had to complete the rituals quietly.

Besides those in the graves (new and old), there were only three people in the graveyard.

The relative who had accompanied my cousin.

My cousin.

And his Abbu. Dead Abbu.

Maulana Qasim had taught Ammi all the duas and hadees that she later taught me when I was a kid.

To the outside world, the case is known as Suleman Usman Bakery firing – in which, besides the maulana, eight more were sent to heaven.

The B.N. Srikrishna Commission, set up to investigate the Mumbai riot cases, said in Volume 1, Chapter 2 of its 1998 report:[14]

> Police suspected terrorists to be holed up on the terrace of Suleman Usman Bakery in Pydhonie jurisdiction. Operation launched against the alleged terrorists by the Special Operation Squad (SOS) under the direction of joint commissioner of police, R.D. Tyagi, and extensive firing by the SOS resulted in deaths of nine Muslims. The police failed to apprehend even a

> single so-called terrorist, nor did they seize any firearms, sophisticated or otherwise, from which firing was done at them, as claimed.

It was eight years after the murder of the maulana that the first FIR against the policemen was registered. But the unarmed men inside the madrasa and the nearby bakery were made riot-accused soon after the shooting. The accused policemen are yet to be punished; the main accused became the chief of Mumbai Police and eventually retired. Only in 2015 was a trial ordered against them.[15]

Meanwhile, here in Jamia Nagar ...

News of the police raids – in police clothes or plain clothes – spread like wildfire. Given the media's incoherent scare-mongering, rumours had become the most trustworthy source of news. Most of them turned out to be true in the next day's newspapers. In slightly different language, though. Plainclothesmen were termed as police, picked up and kidnapped as detained.

Along with many young men, the caretaker of the flat in which the encounter took place was arrested too. It was later, when the Jamia Teachers' Solidarity Association published its fact-finding report, that more details emerged. We knew then for certain that we were right to be scared. On the day of the encounter, the caretaker had gone to the local police thana, but there were no policemen there, so he went to the office of a television news channel. There, he showed the tenant verification form of the men living in the flat. His son, Zia Ur Rahman, was friends with the dead men, as they all hailed from Azamgarh, and Zia had reportedly introduced them to his father as prospective tenants for the flat. The caretaker claimed he had accompanied Atif to the local police thana for verification.

They were not terrorists, he stated.

The next day, he went back to the police station. The police claimed that the verification forms were fake and arrested him and his son. They charged Zia as one of the bombers. They termed the rent agreement as fake, even though it was the address the tenants used for their SIM-card verification, which requires physical verification by the telecom company.[16]

There was even a rumour that the flat owner went to the local police station, paid a few lakhs and secured his patriotism. So went the rumours.

Like Zia and his father, a student named Zeeshan – who had been a flatmate of one of the dead men, Atif, and also a resident of Azamgarh – went to a TV channel to profess his own innocence publicly. He was appearing for his MBA exam when the encounter took place. As soon as he came out of the studio, he was arrested. I knew a Zeeshan too, a senior in college, who was also from Azamgarh. In the confusion, I thought, if they had Zeeshan, they could come for me too. Not wanting to take any chances, I deleted his number from my phone. It turned out the man they arrested was a different Zeeshan.

Most newspapers reported that Zeeshan had been nabbed from central Delhi's Jhandewala locality, without mentioning that it was outside a television studio. A few papers even said that he had been arrested in a night raid in Jamia Nagar.

My classmate Mama was from Azamgarh too. He was an idiot, and I had faced off with him in my first weeks in college to be elected class representative, but I couldn't imagine he was involved in anything more than blabbering. Still, who knows? Why take chances? I deleted his phone number and the numbers and messages of all the classmates who used to hang out with him. I also deleted the numbers of all the others in my contact list who were from Azamgarh or were close to anyone from the district. I knew many others who, like me, deleted the contacts and text messages of their acquaintances from Azamgarh. Saquib Nisar, another friend of Atif's, was working in a firm in Delhi and had graduated in Economics from Jamia. Like others, he too went to the same news channel to profess his and Atif's innocence.[17] He too was arrested the next day.

Another young man from Azamgarh, Mohammed Shakil, was arrested from Sangam Vihar, a big colony predominantly populated by migrants, labourers and daily-wagers. I had lived there, in the Jamia Hamdard University campus, while I was preparing for my MBBS entrance before starting college in Jamia. I was on a scholarship from a society of the university that provided coaching to minorities and other weaker sections of society at subsidised fees.

These were coincidences, but now everything seemed ominous. I would have no explanation if, God forbid, I got arrested. In fact, what seemed like a trivial coincidence could look like eerie design … as if God had colluded with the police.

A day after these young men were arrested, having protested their innocence on television, all the major newspapers published a photo on the front page – featuring the arrested young men, surrounded by jubilant policemen. The young men's faces were wrapped in kaffiyehs, the scarf worn by many Muslim men in the Arab world. It was not a black hood or a random piece of cloth that's generally used to mask the face of criminals, but something that evoked a specific religious and communal identity. The use of kaffiyeh left no doubt about what the police was trying to convey. There was not even a pretence of subtlety.

Confused and disenchanted, I wanted to erase every trace of the connections and events that could remotely cause any suspicion to fall on me.

So …

7

Who Do I Play With?

My first home in Delhi was a two-room flat on the ground floor – not quite the basement, even if it was actually two feet below ground-level. A common passage opened out into two square rooms on the right. On the left was a toilet, a bathroom and an open kitchen that faced our room.

The first room was occupied by three young men from Darbhanga, Bihar. The oldest worked in some private firm. His younger brother had finally taken up work as a security guard after all attempts to find a 'respectable job' failed. The third one had been searching for a job for months. The one offer that he got required him to travel daily to Gurgaon, about 40 km from Jamia Nagar, to which there was – still is – no direct bus. The indirect routes took some courage, and investment – of money and time.

Our room, at the rear of the house, was one Bhuttu Bhayya shared with two other students from Gopalganj. Hafizji and Raju Bhai. Aamir Bhayya would also stay with us until I settled in.

The morning we reached, it was dark inside, and my new roommates still slept. There was a folding cot to the left, with straps that hung loose from its iron frame. Hafizji slouched in it. The door to the room was obstructed by a cot placed perpendicular to the other one. This was Bhuttu Bhayya's bed. On the floor was a mattress where Raju Bhai slept.

My mattress was assigned a space next to Raju Bhai's. This was something we did for fun back home, making our beds on the floor. In winters, when our cousins came to visit, we would spread rice hay on the floor of our spare rooms to sleep on. We looked forward to the opportunity it provided for mischief. But the hay would also slip away at some point, bringing us in contact with the midnight cold of the floor. We never complained, though, for fear of forfeiting the right to sleep with our cousins and hearing their renditions of Bollywoodised naats – and making hell the lives of lizards, spiders and sparrows.

In my new room in Delhi, I felt out of place among these college-going men. I spent most of the time alone, lying on my mattress, watching the struggling fan and fluttering spider webs above me. I could see the underside of the beds and the bulges left by my roommates' butts. A Quran, on a glass shelf, was decorated with dust on top, but looked clean from below. The walls were flaking white-blue at the bottom, dry blue at the top.

Hafizji and Raju Bhai were friendly enough, but they were busy with their friends. And they called me Chhotu, little one, which I didn't like. Once in a while, in good-natured banter, they made fun of my Bihari accent.

Bhuttu Bhayya was studying political science at Jamia. Raju Bhai was studying something called Sykology there. Hafizji was a real hafiz – he could recite the entire Quran from memory. Almost 78,000 words. He was studying commerce at Delhi University.

Jamia was on strike when I arrived, so I was enrolled in a local school for the time being. English medium. That would have been something to be proud of back home – except, here I was demoted two classes.

I went to school in the morning and returned at noon, when there was no one to talk to, no one to hang out with, no one to ask if I would like to have lunch and no one to bear my tantrums – IDon'tWantThis, IWon'tEatThat. My roommates only returned in the evening, that's if they didn't stay late in the library or at a friend's place. I had nowhere else to go.

The room had no windows but my roommates kept the door shut, partly to shut out noise from the street and partly because the toilet stank. Besides, when our neighbours cooked in the kitchen, they ended up smoking us in. They paid more rent, so they had a window in their room and the right to use the kitchen (and smoke up our room too). It was suffocating. I had lived in a huge house – at least compared to my new address – airy, with big windows, doors and ventilators. No doors in our home were shut during the day. So, when my roommates were out, I would open the door of the room as far as it could go, which brought me a slight (and false) sense of freedom.

There were some kids who played cricket in the street outside but I didn't know them. And I feared they would mock me for my Bihari accent. They also used bad language. Very bad. About mothers and sisters. Dada never allowed me to play with such kids in the village. So I couldn't play.

I couldn't eat much either.

On my first day, I went to have dinner in the hotel that Bhuttu Bhayya said was the best in the locality.

Khak best. Its bestness was on full display outside the hotel itself.

A man sat outside kneading flour in front of a furnace. He wore a greyish baniyan, and was dripping from his forehead, nose, chin. His arms, right up to his elbows, were inside the dough, and his hairy armpits not too far from it.

I was revolted. And it was no different in the other hotels either, I soon realised.

The rotis they made were thick like tractor tyres. If they were served hot, they were so crunchy that there was nothing to eat. When cold, they were like rubber. Dunlop roti I called them.

That was not all. Most of these hotels sold only buffalo meat. Qorma, kadhai gosht, qeema, bheja, stew, paya, nihari. All buffalo. And worse, they called it 'badey ka'. Beef. What badey ka? I had never heard of buffalo being called badey ka.

These Delhiites will eat anything.

I complained to my roommates about it. One of them said, 'Exactly! That's why the girls in Delhi have everything so huge,' forming semi-spheres with his hands. They both laughed and laughed. Then they whispered to each other, 'No, no, don't talk like this, he is just a kid.'

As if I didn't know what they were talking about.

I had never imagined, not even in my wildest dreams, that dal would become my favourite food.

Dal and roti at dinner. Biryani at lunch. It was all I could bear to eat.

The smallest and youngest in that crowd in the hotel, I would shout and wave for the waiter, navigating bellies and arms. I knew what I was going to order but before I could say anything, the waiter would come and start reciting the menu – korma kadhai gosht qeema bheja ishtu dal paya nahari aloo gosht dal fry chapati tandoori – breathlessly. When he finished, I would ask for one dal fry and a roti.

A jaw-exercise it used to be, and then came the most insulting part. One time, I went to pay, and the cashier asked me what I had eaten. When I told him, he gave me a suspicious look.

'That's it? Only a dal and a roti?' he asked. He caught the waiter's eye to assure himself I was not lying. Then, in a pitying tone, 'Okay. Five rupees.'

Jahil sala! He thinks I am lying for one roti.

Home, food, friends, family ... the nostalgia grew and grew.

I called home to relieve some of the loneliness. But on the phone, I had to sound brave. I would not cry; that would mean upsetting Ammi, Dada and everyone else.

Yaqeen mohkam, amal paiham, mohabbat fatah-e-alam,
Jihad-e-zindagani me hain ye mardon ki shamsheerein.

Firm belief, actions and love conquer the world,
These are the swords of men in the holy war of life.

About two years before I came to Delhi, I had been sent away to a hostel in Gopalganj so that I could study at a better school. A few weeks later, when Dada came with bhuja and new clothes for me, I started crying the moment I saw him. I was brought back home.

I would not repeat that cowardice.

Mobiles were still a rich man's device. And students and migrants who didn't have proper addresses could not get their own landline connections either. So, phone booths were our connection with home, and these booths gave a discount for calls made during non-busy hours. It would be half the daytime rate after 8 p.m., and quarter rate after 11.30 p.m. Half-rate all day on Sundays.

So phone booths were busiest on Sundays. Besides being cheaper, it was also easier to get through to home during the late-night slot, as there were few customers waiting up so late to make a long-distance call. Since telephone penetration was still low, often the calls had to be made to a neighbour's home in the dark, electricity-starved villages of the time.

I called after 8 p.m., late by village standards. Dada, Ammi and Baaji were still awake to offer the Isha namaz.

Dada would pick up the phone and I would ask if all was well, then hurriedly I'd reply to their questions. In concise, precise words.

I am well.

The room is good.

Yes, I eat on time.

Yes, the food is good.

Yes, I have my school uniform and new bag and new books.

Now I will have to disconnect.

I didn't tell them, but I had a litany of complaints.

I am missing home.

I have no one to play with.

I have no one to race a bicycle with.

There is no bicycle for me here.

I don't like the food here.

I have to wash my clothes myself.

It's very hot in Delhi and I have rashes all over my body.

The room is small and my roommates keep it shut all the time.

The toilet smells all the time and the smell fills my room. I want to come back home.

Back in the room after the call, lonely as usual, I lay in bed and sulked. The excitement of Delhi had started to run out even before I had properly settled in.

I fell ill within a week ...

... and an old man, on hearing the news some thousand kilometres away, hopped on to the first train he could, to come and see his grandson, leaving the harvesting of his farms midway in the hands of God.

Parindey Ki Fariyad – A Bird's Complaint
Muhammad Iqbal

Ata hai yaad mujh ko guzra hua zamana
Woh bagh ki baharein, woh sab ka chehchahana
Azadiyan kahan woh ab apne ghonsley ki
Apni khushi se ana, apni khushi se jana
Lagti hai chot dil par, ata hai yad jis dam
Shabnam ke ansuon par kaliyon ka muskurana
Woh pyari pyari surat, woh kamini si murat
Abad jis ke dam se tha mera ashiyana
Ati nahi sada'en uski mere qafas mein
Hoti meri rihai ae kash mere bas mein!
Kya badnaseeb hun main ghar ko taras raha hun
Sathi to hai watan mein, main qaid mein para hun
Ayi bahar, kaliyan phulon ki hans rahi hain
Main iss andherey ghar mein qismat ko ro raha hun
Iss qaid ka elahi! Dukhda kise sunaun
Darr hai yaheen qafas mein main gham se marr na jaun
Jab se chaman chhoota hai, ye hal ho gaya hai
Dil gham ko kha raha hai, gham dil ko kha raha hai

Gana isey samajh kar khush ho'n na sunne wale
Dukhe huwe dilon ki faryad ye sada hai
Azad mujh ko kar de, O qaid karne wale!
Main bezuban hun qaidi, tu chhor kar dua le

I constantly think of the times gone by
Those springs in the garden, that chorus of chirping
Gone is the freedom of my own nest
Where I could come and go as I pleased
My heart aches when I think
Of the smiles of those buds, of the dew's tears
That beautiful figure, that enchanting form
Which was the source of all happiness in my nest
I do not hear those lovely sounds in my cage
O that I could have my freedom now!
How unfortunate I am, longing for my home
My companions are in the homeland, I am in prison
Spring has arrived, the flower buds laugh
In this dark house, on my misfortune I wail
O God, to whom shall I relate my tale of woe?
I fear I shall die of grief in this cage!
Since my separation from the garden my condition is such
My heart feeds on sorrow, sorrow eats my heart
O listeners, do not mistake this for a song and be happy
This call is the wailing of my wounded heart
O you who have confined me, set me free
A silent prisoner am I, earn my blessings by letting me go.

8

Like a Normal Human Being

So ...

Confused and disenchanted, I wanted to erase traces of every connection that could even remotely cause suspicion to fall on me.

I logged into my Orkut account (Facebook was yet to become popular in India) and deleted all the 'friends' I didn't really know but had added only to show off my fat friends' list. College-level greed, nothing more. But this imprudent vanity had led to connections with unknown people and it had started looking scary.

I un-joined all the communities that might cast me as a Terrorist disguised as a Normal Human Being.

I un-joined the community of Zakir Naik, the tele-evangelist who spouts passages from all the major holy bestsellers like a (condescending) robot. I un-joined the page on Muhammad Iqbal, the poet credited with originating the two-nation theory that led to India's Partition, even though I was not interested in the ideological zeal of his later years, only his poems.

Tarana-e-Hindi: Song of India

Sare jahan se achha Hindustan hamara
Hum bulbulein hain iski, ye gulsitan hamara
Mazhab nahin sikhata apas mein bair rakhna
Hindi hain hum, watan hai Hindustan hamara.

The best in the entire world is our India
We are its nightingales, and it is our garden
Religion doesn't teach us to hate each other
We are Indians, our homeland is India.

Bachchon ki Dua: Children's Prayer

Ho mere dam se mere watan ki yun'hi zeenat
Jis tarah phool se hoti hai chaman ki zeenat.

May my soul embellish the homeland
As a flower embellishes the garden.

Ek Pahaad aur Gilehri: A Mountain and a Squirrel

Nahi hai cheez nikammi koi zamaane mein
Koi bada nahi qudrat ke is kaarkhane mein.

There is nothing that's worthless in this world
All are equal in God's empire.

Jugnu: Glow-worm

Chhote se chand mein hai zulmat bhi roshni bhi
Nikla kabhi gahen se, aaya kabhi gahen mein.

This little moon has light as well as darkness
At times it emerges from an eclipse, at times it hides.

Hamdardi: Empathy

Hain log wahi jahan me achhe
Aate hain jo kaam dusron ke.

Good are only those people
Who help others in the world.

And many more.

I un-joined the community on Maulana Abul Kalam Azad, just in case. Also the one named for Sir Syed Ahmed Khan, who established Aligarh Muslim University. He advocated that Muslims should support the British Raj, and urged the community to take up Western and scientific education. He invoked the tradition of Islam that used rationalism to interpret the Quran.

I un-joined every community that I thought might even remotely appear like a jihadi influence: Islam, Quran, Urdu poetry.

I un-joined the community on poet and nationalist Shibli Nomani whose work I had known since my school days. I had even spoken about him in school functions. Dada often quoted from his biography of Muhammad Sahab, and cited the poems on Adl-e-Jahangiri and Adl-e-Farooqui as the inspiration for his dealings as village elder. Shibli mocked the Muslim League. He had been taught by a rationalist maulana whose students included nationalists like Muhammad Ali Jauhar – one of the founders of Jamia Millia Islamia.

Still, I un-joined the Orkut community named for him. He was from Azamgarh. Most of the men who had been arrested were from Azamgarh. The notorious underworld don Abu Salem hailed from that district too, but it was the encounter that tranformed Azamgarh into Atankgarh, the fortress of terror.

I had many friends from Azamgarh, and casually knew many more.

My first friend from St Giri School in Delhi was from there. He too had studied in a Hindi-medium back home, so we had faced the same difficulties in this English-medium school. Azmi Bhai, who had graduated a few years before but would often visit the campus, was from Azamgarh.

He had started a voluntary group to collect and distribute donations for the victims of the Bihar flood that year. Only days before the encounter, I was with him, collecting donations and planning to go to the state for distribution. Zeeshan Bhai, our senior in college, was from Azamgarh. And, of course, my classmate Mama. What if he was arrested, I wondered. It would lead directly to me. To all of us – me and my friends.

If that happens, God forbid, who would defend us? Our parents were not here. Even Jamia had not been willing to own its students in the beginning. They had announced that no student from the university was involved. The media told a different story. It was clear we were orphans.

Educated orphans. Disguised as Normal Human Beings. Many of us clean-shaven. Smart and confident. And tech-savvy. With high aspirations.

The encounter had come too close for comfort. Too close. I heard many people saying that one of the Terrorists had studied in Jamia School in my batch. If the police were to say I was friends with him, how would I deny it? I had very few friends in school, but who would believe that?

The past and future flashed before my eyes. The past seemed worrisome – you can alter your future, but how do you change your past?

Things big and small that were almost lost to memory now surfaced, ominous and worrying.

I had lost a cellphone – my first ever – when I was returning from the airport after seeing off Chhote Abbu. Someone had picked my pocket in the rush of a crowded DTC bus. I had not filed an FIR because there was no way the phone would ever be retrieved, a fact every Indian knows. Now, years later, I feared its possible misuse and rued not having reported its loss.

I had once left my school ID card behind at a photocopy-cum-telephone shop. I didn't bother to go back and pick it up because the ID was more or less useless now. Years later, its loss seemed heavy.

My best friend from senior secondary school days, Salik, shared a flat with Razi, another friend, in nearby Ghafoor Nagar. Salik studied Engineering at Jamia, and Razi was in the Economics Department, and they came from the same district in Bihar. Two of the arrested Terrorists were connected with the Economics Department – one had graduated in 2007 and another was to graduate in the ongoing session. For that, and no other reason, Razi was scared, and by extension Salik too. They didn't know whether to go back home or to stay put in Delhi and risk arrest.

Salik tried to call me for advice. I didn't take his call and deleted his phone number too. Unsurprisingly, we ceased to be best friends. Even today, I doubt I've been able to make it up to him.

Years ago, in the Ramazan of 2000, when I was visiting my village, an encounter had happened one Friday morning on Batla House colony's Muradi Road, just days before Eid. I had read about it in the *Hindustan Times*, the only English paper that once in a while reached my village. It said the police had killed a Kashmiri man in the same block where my rented accommodation was, and that they had arrested an internet cafe owner. Apparently, he had been involved in the Red Fort attack of 2000. The building where that encounter had taken place had an internet cafe and a telephone booth on the ground floor. I used to go there often to call home or use the internet. In the end, I didn't tell my parents about it for fear of worrying them. When I returned to Delhi, I learnt that a different internet cafe, one in Ghafoor Nagar, was the one involved. That cafe was in the building where Salik and Razi now lived, oblivious to the fact that the building was once tainted. And I heard an entirely other story about the encounter from friends in the neighbourhood.

One of the boys in my neighbourhood said that there was no encounter, and that the police had sealed the area so no one could see what was going on. They climbed the stairs, firing away, and entered the empty flat where they put the corpse of a man they had killed elsewhere. There was no retaliatory fire, according to this boy.[18]

We tended to listen to him more attentively than to others – his sister was very beautiful.

That encounter was eight years ago. Everyone went silent. Who knows? He was Kashmiri; he might well have been a terrorist.

Now, eight years later, it was a different matter. This was *us*. Normal Human Beings.

My mind buzzed with questions. What if they arrest Razi? What if they arrest Mama? And what about Perwez, with whom I spent most of my time in college? His cousin's friend was a classmate of one of the arrested Terrorists. Perwez was from West Bengal's Islampur, bordering Bangladesh. We had often joked that he was a Bangladeshi and had sneaked into our country by bribing the border security forces with a goat.

A Bangladeshi. Studying biology. Preparing for bio-warfare?

My own details would not read too differently; I was a biology student. And I had recently visited Barakhamba Road, one of the sites of the blasts, where the regional office of Saudi Airlines was based, to reconfirm Abbu's ticket back to Saudi Arabia after Eid. Newspaper reports said that the Terrorists had recced the blast site before placing the bombs.

I could well be a Terrorist doing a recce of the blast site at Barakhamba.

Seen in front of the Saudi Airlines office.

And also at Delhi's International Airport, just days before that, receiving a bearded person.

Now this too had to be feared, the Saudi connection that had fed that bearded man and his family for years. It was the connection that had allowed his ageing father to quit his sugar-mill job and finally live a life. And his sons and daughters no longer needed to wear just the one patched-up garment to school or college for a whole year, as he had had to in his day. Or to drop out of college as he had had to, to feed the family and marry off sisters. Or run a wheat-grinding machine like he had had to when his employers in the Gulf threw him out. Abbu had contracted tuberculosis, perhaps inhaling the dust from the machine, running it day and night, with no money for treatment, overworking the machine for a few extra bucks, until he wore that machine down too.

It was always that Saudi, or the Gulf, connection that had bailed him – and us – out.

The day the encounter took place, Chhote Abbu called to ask if I was okay. He too lived in Saudi Arabia, and watched the news on satellite TV. 'What's going on there, beta?' he asked. 'I saw it on TV. You are safe, na? They are from your college? Isn't the place close to our house?' There was already a rumour that phones in Jamia Nagar were being tapped. Here I was receiving a call from my uncle in Saudi Arabia, and he was talking about my locality and college when the loyalties of both were being questioned. I didn't know what to do. I couldn't tell him on the phone to not talk about all these things. I tried to keep my answers concise: Hmmm.

Alhamdulillah, all okay.

Hmm.

Hmm.

Ummm ... hmm ... you don't worry.

He didn't say it outright but he had phoned to satisfy himself that his nephew had not fallen in with bad company. *He is living alone; who knows if he has befriended the wrong people.* His nephew assured him he hadn't.

The awkward call ended with a pocket-sized sermon about where to go and where not to, to be home by sunset, to be careful and whatnot.

Perwez with his Bangladeshi connection, I with my Saudi one. Both in the same university, the same class, and spending most of our time together. Another potential accomplice was Furquan. He and Perwez had enrolled at a coaching class in Connaught Place. They would take the bus home from Barakhamba Road, one of the blast sites. What if someone were to say they too were doing a recce?

They stopped going to the coaching class after the encounter.

Everyone in Jamia Nagar was vulnerable, but I was scared for myself. In my mind, there were many connections that led to me.

One of those arrested was reportedly my schoolmate. So, him to Neyaz. Another of the arrested men was introduced to Perwez's cousin as his classmate, from Perwez to Neyaz. Saqib and Shakeel to Razi to Neyaz. Mama to Neyaz. Zeeshan Bhai to Neyaz. Asjad to Neyaz.

They all lived in the same locality. They studied in the same university. They had the same hangouts. They prayed in the same masjids.

And they all looked like Normal Human Beings. How do I explain that Jamia Nagar is a small ghetto, packed with people like sticks in a matchbox? That the world for most of us in Jamia Nagar revolves around a few hangouts, a few masjids, a university, and about half-a-dozen haphazard colonies of confounding legal status, anywhere between authorised and unauthorised. That it's such a mess you don't know where one colony ends, where another begins. That the entire ghetto is only a few square kilometres in area, crushed between middle-class Delhi and the Yamuna. That in such a small place, everything is connected to everything else, everyone to everyone else. You run into one another, you meet someone and he is someone's someone. You have no idea who all you have been seen with. Often you don't know the names, but you know the faces. Or you know the names and are confused about the faces.

Jamia Nagar creates a jumble of names, faces and identities, and possibly faulty memories. That memory could be yours, or someone else's, and if that someone else is, let's say, a Terror Suspect disguised as a Normal Human Being, you have no idea how his memory is going to behave.

It was an alarming thought and it made everyone untrustworthy. Friends, close friends, acquaintances, strangers, everyone.

Being an 'internal student' of the university, I knew a lot of people around the campus and in the locality. My friends joked that I shook hands with so many people that the fortune lines on my palms would wear off, and then even God would not know what he had written into my fate. Knowing lots of people had served me well so far. But now I was scared to shake hands with anyone.

It kills me to admit to this, but I had even become suspicious of close friends – Salik, Perwez, Furquan, Asbah, Alim, Kafil, Rameez. With whom I used to spend all my days. Who had become my family away from my family. With whom I shared my joys and secrets, and fought and cribbed. And jointly hit on girls.

I didn't trust them, I don't know if they trusted me; the topic was never broached. I don't know if Shyam, my classmate, and also among my best friends, trusted me. He would still meet and hang out with us, but he avoided talking about the encounter. If the topic came up somehow, he remained quiet and didn't crack any of his trademark desi jokes.

Asbah kept to himself. Kafil fled to his home in Mathura. Furquan fell ill and was planning to find a way to leave for home.

Rameez stayed with his uncle in Jamia Nagar but seldom stepped out. He was scared for another reason. Our classmate Shivam Sharma used to live on rent in another flat in the same building, which belonged to Rameez's uncle. Shivam was a friendly guy and, like Mama, was close to the teachers and to the girls in class. He had all the gossip and secrets that never reached my group otherwise due to our general hostility towards people outside the group. He was our favourite friend outside the group, especially during exams. He had gone to school in AMU and had joined Jamia for a graduate degree, and so was well aware of the cultural nuances of Muslim society. He had imbibed Urdu poetry in his AMU days. In conversation, he would often throw in couplets that most of us didn't know. Perwez – who had done his final years of schooling in AMU – knew a few couplets and he would recite these in response to any couplet Shivam threw down. And a poetic banter would start between them.

But after the encounter, all of Shivam's familiarity with Muslim culture suddenly began to seem odd. It was rare for a Hindu student to go to school in a Muslim institution like AMU and then come to another, Jamia. (He would go to BHU and then JNU, where he would campaign for ABVP.) And he was staying in Jamia Nagar, even though he was a strict vegetarian. I mean, the locality was not exactly a haven for vegetarians! All the other Hindu students stayed outside.

Was he a khabri? He didn't seem worried or at all affected by the encounter.

The great gift of the encounter was that, in less than a week, everyone had become a suspect. Friends suspected best friends, acquaintances reassessed each other, landlords threw out students, shops downed shutters early, hangouts were deserted, streets empty by sunset.

And young men withdrew into their shells. They lost everything there was to lose: hope, pride, their carefree lives. They didn't know if it was a virtue or a vice to be: smart, confident, clean-shaven, bearded, working, jobless. Like Normal Human Beings.

9

Aaj Karey So Kal Kar, Kal Karey So Parson

HERE I WAS IN Delhi, temporarily enrolled in a local private school because Jamia was on strike. St Giri School, in nearby Joga Bai, seemed right; close by, and not too costly. The best thing, as everyone said, it was an English-medium school. I was known to be very good at English back home.

My family was sure I would do well here. Of course, I had no idea my fall from grace would come so quickly, that I had been but a one-eyed king in the land of the blind.

The school had weekly tests and I failed most of them in the very first week – even though I had joined class 4, two levels below the class I had been in, back in the village. To begin with, I had missed many classes as the term had already begun when I was admitted. Besides, this was the first time that all my books, except the Hindi textbook, were in English. (There was no Urdu.) Back home, all the texts were in Hindi – they even taught English in Hindustani. I had never seen an entire book in English, and had never spoken English beyond a few rehearsed sentences.

My Name is Neyaz.

My father's name is Afaque Manzer.

My village's name is Inderwan Bairam.

Post office is Sukulwan and police station is Thawe. I study in class 4.

Or memorising things like go-went-gone, learn-learnt-learnt, subject-verb-object.

I knew many of the answers to the questions my teachers asked, but could not respond properly in a language that I had never really spoken. And because they taught everything in English, I couldn't understand all they said either.

Soon enough, I found myself in the illustrious company of those who always stood outside the class, or were made to stand with hands raised throughout the session, or made to do murga, or even beaten with sticks. For the first time in my life, I was punished for being dull. Wasting your parents' money. Fooling yourself, not your parents.

I started sitting on the back benches, something I had never done before. Backbenchers are trouble-makers, not good students. I befriended a student who sat on the last bench. He was new too, and had come from Azamgarh. Gulf money had roused in his family this aspiration for an English-medium school. There was no immediate solution for us, except to put up with the insults and become shameless.

As I had missed a few classes before my admission, I borrowed a notebook from a classmate who didn't look like a bully. Next school day, his parents arrived and complained to the teacher that someone had stolen their son's notebook. I told the teacher that I had his notebook and that he had lent it to me, but no one seemed to trust me. I was new, I was a bad student. The boy from Azamgarh was witness to the fact that I had borrowed the notebook, but he too was new and dull.

I was in the school only for a few weeks, through all of which I had to live with the knowledge that my classmates thought I was thief and a liar.

Hadees: Lying is a sin. You lie only if you have to save someone's life.

When Independence Day arrived, I was surprised to hear that the school was celebrating it on 14 August, the day Pakistan celebrates its independence. I realised later that it was so no one would have to come to school on 15 August, a holiday. Then there was no *Lab Pe Ati Hai Dua Ban Ke Tamanna Meri* in morning assemblies. It was something in Hindi and English that I had never heard before. Girls tapped their feet, as if dancing, to the songs in the assembly. They even danced during school functions; unheard of where I had come from. No girl from a respectable family would ever do such a thing.

What I was going through in class bothered me much more than all this, though. What if I failed the final exam? It would upset everyone. How could Farooquee fail? He had been a topper all along.

The family's academic flag-bearer was definitely failing, though. And he had not a clue what to do about it. Topper *babu taayein taayein phiss*.

I asked my roommates what I should do to improve my English. Both Hafizji and Raju Bhai advised me to subscribe to an English newspaper. *Hindustan Times* sounded like a familiar name, so I subscribed to it. Soon I switched to *The Hindu* – it's the newspaper all the Indian Administrative Service (IAS) aspirants read, I was told. But it turned out that merely subscribing to an English newspaper wasn't enough. You have to read your course books as well.

I didn't understand things, so I didn't feel like studying. Because I didn't study, I didn't understand things. I slipped further. Soon, I was bunking classes on one pretext or another. I often fell 'ill'. Away from home, no one was watching me every moment – no Dada, no Ammi. That's when I discovered my infinite potential for wasting time.

Bhuttu Bhayya used to sleep early but my other roommates were up till late at night; so I stayed up too. Not that I was studying then. I wasted time with my roommates, playing ludo and chess, and listening to their college gossip, often adult stuff, with many code words and much winking of eyes.

As I woke up late, I often reached school late and was punished regularly. Of course I was sleepy in class. Bhuttu Bhayya realised that staying up late was not a good idea for a school-going kid. He asked me to sleep early, so I pretended to go to sleep. The moment he fell into his bed, I was back on my feet.

If he woke up in the middle of the night, I would pretend to be studying for my tests. Raju Bhai and Hafizji would snigger, turning their faces away.

When a teacher asked me to get my diary signed by my parent or guardian, I would coax Hafizji or Raju Bhai to sign it so Bhuttu Bhayya wouldn't scold me. They often obliged.

Bhuttu found out one day when he happened to notice my diary, which was lying open next to my pillow.

Doom.

Thereafter, the scoundrel hovered over me all the time after college like a Malkulmaut, the angel of Death. You are dumb. You don't study. You waste a lot of time. You sleep a lot. You stay awake all night and sleep all day.

No one had ever shouted at me, except Dada. And I was not used to being insulted.

I don't like this Bhuttu Puttu. He is mean.

He asks me to go and get bread in the rain.

He can't even read Urdu. He asks me to read it to him while preparing for his Urdu exam.

He acts over-smart.

He doesn't even go outside in slippers, as if he is a prince.

He shaves twice a day. Idiot. Somebody told him he looks like Shah Rukh Khan and he believes it.

I will complain to Dada about him.

Nindak niyarey raakhiye, aangan kuti chhawaye
Bin paani, sabun bina, nirmal karey subahye.

Keep your critics close to you,
They clean your conscience for no fee.

The strike in Jamia ended in a few weeks and finally the entrance test was held. I was one among six selected from over a thousand. No one could have been more ecstatic – this allowed me an escape from the humiliation at the English-medium school, and now no one would need to know that I had failed.

Here, in Jamia Middle School, I was back among the toppers in class 6. The classes had continued, unaffected by the strike in the university. By the time my admission formalities were completed, I had already missed an entire quarterly session and the term exams. Still, by the grace of God, I fared better than most at the end of the year, simply because I could understand what I was being taught. It was all in Urdu. I hadn't studied in an Urdu-medium school but I knew the language quite well.

Barqui tawanai. Electrical energy. Ghiza'. Food.

Ata'ard. Mercury.

A'shariya. Decimal.

I was back to being a hero in a matter of days, and one of the teachers' favourites. Everyone wanted my notes and my company, everyone wanted to sit next to me during tests. A teacher even asked me to groom classmates who were weak. Among them, Asjad – who, years later, I would wish I hadn't known because he lived just next to the building where the encounter happened.

After a few months, I left Bhuttu Bhayya's place, because he had graduated and was ready to leave, and shifted in with a few seniors from Gopalganj. Now that I had unlimited freedom, I mastered the art of sitting idle endlessly. That, I guess, was my undoing.

It would take no more than two years to derail my course to becoming a bada admi. I had become the antithesis of what Dada had taught me. He would often recite these lines from Kabir's poetry:

> *Kal karey so aaj kar, aaj karey so ab*
> *Pal mein parlay hoyegi, bahuri karoge kab.*
>
> Do tomorrow's work today, today's work now,
> This world might end in a moment, when will you do it all.

I had become the parody of this doha that I recited to friends: *Aaj kare so kal kar, kal karey so parson, itni bhi jaldi kya hai, jeena hai abhi barson.* Do today's work tomorrow, tomorrow's the day after, what's the hurry, I have long to live.

If St Giri was much tougher than I had expected it to be, Jamia seemed to be the opposite. For various reasons: the medium of instruction, Urdu, which has lost favour with the powers that be in modern India; the economic status of my classmates; the government-style functioning of the teachers; and because most students were first-generation learners – there was a lack of competition. Though I never showed my scorn, I pitied the students who couldn't pronounce, for example, Czechoslovakia, or didn't know the English of 'hubbul-watani', or know that cricket is also an insect, or couldn't translate 'Gaya Gaya gaya' (Gaya is both a person and the name of a place, so Gaya has gone to Gaya).

They also didn't know that Ethiopia's capital is Adis Ababa. I knew this because Abbu had gone there when he could not find a job in Saudi Arabia. Hardly anyone in my class knew about the country called Philippines. Philips is different from Philippines; Philips is the radio that Abbu had bought for Dada, Philippines is the country from which several of Abbu's colleagues came. He had also worked in Kuwait. It's a country but only as big as Gopalganj. And Iraq is close to where Abbu worked in Saudi Arabia; they bombed the city where he worked but saved the labour camp where he lived. It was called the Gulf War.

The praise all around made me high, cocksure. I took my studies lightly and, within two years, I had slid from the merit list to the lower end of the middle. My teachers and classmates, initially surprised, eventually got used to it. There was something about this school. It lured good students by the thousands, from distant villages and towns of India, to provide it the satisfaction of ruining them. The promise of the internal-student quota for college admissions was a very attractive proposition for students and their parents. Or perhaps it was just the unlimited freedom that students enjoyed away from their families, which destroyed them and the dreams they came with.

The results of my class 8 exam should have been the first clue for my parents and Dada. But they kept faith in me. When the results were declared, I was at home for the summer vacations. Baaji's husband, Shafiullah Bhai, who was now my local guardian, got to know that the results were out. Believing his ward would be among the toppers, he went to school to collect the mark sheet. But my name wasn't on top. There was, however, one Farooque Ahmad, who was second in the merit list. Shafiullah Bhai was content with that, and angry that some negligent official had printed the wrong name.

The meritorious student was indeed Farooque Ahmad, from the neighbouring district of Siwan. His own Farooquee was among the bottom-dwellers.

When I returned to Delhi, he met me armed with fury, and reminded me of the faith my family had in me. But I was prepared. When he cornered me, I made excuses to defer his fury: that there must be something wrong, that I would get the copies rechecked. He was in no mood to relent. As a last resort, I played my master card: a cherry-picked hadees.

> *Jo bhi hota hai woh khuda ki marzi se hota hai aur achhe ke liye hi hota hai.*

Whatever happens, it is God's will, and for one's good.

Though this aggravated him further, he could not find a good enough response. His face contorted in anger, he went quiet.

Shafiullah Bhai never again asked for my results. It was his small revenge. Or God's – for misusing His name. I was left alone to choose how I would ruin myself: idleness, procrastination, shamelessness, obfuscation, lies.

Dada, Ammi and Abbu were away. I could lie to them easily, and convincingly, while conveniently ignoring another hadees: *God knows everything and he certainly knows who is lying.*

I had always been advised against making too many friends, even when I was in the village. Now, this was stressed upon even more. 'Remember, even Muhammad Sahab had only one best friend. He was courteous to all, but he was good friends with only one person. Abu Bakar Sahab. You can't have more than one true friend,' Dada would say. 'It won't be a real friendship that you can bank on.'

I tried to follow his directions, but there was always the urge to be like the other boys in my colony. They would hang about the street in stylish clothes and shoes, hair well groomed. They stayed out late into the night and played video games in the neighbourhood parlours. They stood at gully corners to ogle at girls and identify the ones they liked. '*Teri bhabhi hai yeh.*' Dude, she is my girl, your sister-in-law.

Sometimes they even fought among themselves over a girl, even though she had no idea whatsoever about their unflinching love.

In school, though I didn't take part in all this, I listened with great interest to the stories of others' mischief. That so-and-so put a log of wood on the doorbell of some neighbour in the middle of the night and ran away. Or fire-crackers in the switch box of the doorbell to blow it off. That some guy climbed over the wall to watch the hostel warden sleeping with his wife. That another chap emptied his toothpaste in someone's pants while the victim was fast asleep. That someone beat up a teacher who was strict with him. The teacher was going home on a scooter, and as he slowed down at a turn, the student pushed him down and thrashed him. That so-and-so drinks and does drugs with seniors in college.

It was like an American attorney said: I have never killed anyone, but I have read some obituary notices with great satisfaction.

Somehow, the ideas that had been drilled into my head in my early childhood kept me from joining these boys. It didn't keep me from feeling bursts of envy, though.

Kabira khada bazar mein, mange sabki khair
Na kahu se dosti, na kahu se bair.

Kabir stands here before all, wishing everyone well,
If he is not friends with anyone, he is no one's enemy either.

I usually came directly back to my room after school. And although I didn't study, I did read everything outside of the curriculum. I read the *Hindustan Times*, *Cricket Samrat*, *Sportstar*, *Competitive Science Refresher*, *Manorama Year Book*, *Payam-e-taleem*, *Science* (Urdu), *Wisdom*, *Nai Duniya* and *Champak* (mostly in Hindi, with a few attempts in English).

I didn't have TV. *It ruins kids.*

But I had a radio and listened to the FM programmes on All India Radio. I liked the evening programme on sports, and the broadcasts of songs and quizzes on Sundays. Though

I always intended to write to them and take part in the contests, I never did send in a letter. I still have a list of the names of those programmes and the addresses that were spelt out at the end of the show.

The BBC too had travelled with me from home, where Dada would religiously listen to the morning and evening news bulletins. He would also tune in to the Urdu or Hindi broadcasts of Voice of America and other international channels. Many of Dadi's complaints – about our misbehaviour or to do with the harvest – went unheard while Dada was glued to his radio, decoding the smaller details of the larger world. He would listen to the Hindi or Urdu bulletin, and when English blared out, he changed the channel or munched his food.

The BBC used to telecast a show on learning English. In Delhi, I would tune in to listen to the show before going to school. Medium wave didn't catch in my house, short wave did after some noisy protest.

I learnt many new things in Delhi – through English and Urdu newspapers and magazines, through people around me, through posters and banners in Jamia Nagar and, later, through the internet (in internet cafes).

All this challenged what I had known about Islam and Muslims. About Palestine, Kashmir, Taliban, Babri Masjid and All That. There were so many things that I had never known before. I would often be saddened by what I read, and responded in the language that I had known since childhood – poetry. Many of those couplets are lost as I shifted house numerous times, but some have survived.

Back in my village, I had learnt that Palestine had one of the holiest sites of Islam, Masjid-e-Aqsa. It is believed that the prophet Isa – Jesus – would descend there and lead prayers from this mosque before the world ended. (In Islamic traditions, it is believed He ascended to the sky, not crucified.) Here, in Delhi, I came to know that the Yahudis, Jews, had occupied Masjid-e-Aqsa and their security forces had entered the mosque in shoes.

Afghanistan used to mean Rabindranath Tagore's story 'Kabuliwala'. And Taliban was merely the plural of talib-ilm. Student. Students. The maulana at home often addressed us as talib-ilm. It was not so in Delhi. Here, after the Taliban takeover of Afghanistan, it was a curse word.

I had come here with the hope that I would return as an IAS officer and make Dada proud. But I gathered from friends that Muslims were discriminated against in the IAS exams. Merely two or three in a hundred got selected.

And what about Babri Masjid? We all know what happened to it.

So, I wrote my response to what troubled me.

Ae Musalmanon, darte kyun ho, Allah hamare sath hai
Gar kar liya yakin is pe to Babri kya Hindustan bhi hamare hath hai.

O Muslims, God is with us, Why fear?
If you believe this, why only Babri, all of India is ours.

And,

Ae Musalmanon, kya fayda hai in kafiron se darne ka, Khuda se daro
Ke akhir ek din to jana hi hai apne is tehnasheen haveli mein.

O Muslims, why fear these infidels, fear God,

After all, we all are destined to go to our graves.

From Dada, I had heard the couplet that Amir Khusrau had supposedly composed, and Emperor Jahangir had used to describe Kashmir:

Gar firdaus bar-rue zami ast
Hami ast, hami ast, hami ast.

If there is any heaven on earth,
It's here, it's here, it's here.

Here, in Delhi's Jamia Nagar, I heard that Muslim women got raped in Kashmir, young men got kidnapped, tortured and killed regularly.

I was sad. I was confused.

It was 1999, when India and Pakistan were at war over Kashmir. I had read Iqbal's poems on the Himalayas, the mountain range where the two countries were fighting. Iqbal, in his poem 'Sare Jahan Se Achha', called the mountain range 'pasban' and 'santari' – protector and watchman.

Reacting to the war in Kargil, I wrote 'Zameen Ka Dukhda' (Earth's Complaint):

Asman ne jab zameen ko dekha rota baar baar
Poochha zameen se roney ki wajah hai kya zar-o-qatar.
Kya bataun tujhe zameen ne kaha ho ke ashk-o-bar
Sunaya asman se apna dukhda ho ke beqarar.
Ki jinhe Khuda ne mujh pe paida kiya hai woh hain insani bazar
Ki kuchh ho gaye hain unme be-iman wa shaitan se bhi bekaar.

Jinhone bana diya hai pak Ganga ko misl-e kooda-dan
Aur hamarey pasban woh santari ko ladai ka maidan.
Jinhe khuda ne bakhsha hai duniye hi mein jannat-o-mukarram
Bajaye banane ke firdos lage hain bananey par jahannum.
Sunn ke sada zameen ki asman ne kaha yun
Ki suna do apne muqeemo ko meri naseehat hai yun.
Ke rahein woh mil kar sidq dil se bhai ki tarah
Ki misaal hain aaqae do jahan, rahein unki tarah.

When the sky saw the earth wailing
It asked the earth what she was ailing from
What should I tell you, said the earth, crying
And then she narrated her complaint, despairingly.
God has created on me a bazar of human beings
Some of them are so dishonest, more wicked than Satan
They have turned the sacred Ganga into a dumping yard
And our watchman and protector into a battlefield
God bestowed Heaven on them in this world
Instead of turning it into the best of the heavens, they are busy turning it into a hell
Hearing the earth's complaints, said the sky
It's my teaching to them, tell your inhabitants
That they should live like true brothers, and
Look up to Prophet Muhammad as the example to follow.

Though I had mastered the art of endless idleness, I guess I realised that what I was doing wasn't praiseworthy, because I wrote:

Badi pareshaniyan ati hai hum Musalmanon ke samne,
Ke is daur-e-mehnat me hamein aram ne kaahil bana diya hai.

Muslims have to face a lot of problems,
In the age of striving, our indifference has made us lazy.

Once a fellow tenant told me that what I was reading was not ilm, study, it was merely a hunar – a skill, to earn a living. Ilm is the Quran and hadees, and that's what you should read and follow. It began to worry me that we don't think much about our afterlife, which is eternal, unlike the finite life we are living. I remembered how we used to play in the graveyard at home.

Hum to raundte hue nikalte hain badi shan se
Ke ek din hamari bhi rukh hogi is hameshagah ki taraf.

We go romping on the graveyard
After all, we are destined to go there as well.

It worried me how I would face God's angels Munkir and Nakir. After your death, Munkir and Nakir – the denied and denier – visit your grave. They ask you questions, and if you fail to answer, your punishment starts then and there. Only the pious can answer their questions.

They ask you, 'Who is your Lord? What is your religion? Who is your prophet?'

If your answers are right, you are set till the Day of Judgement. Then on the Day of Judgement, all God's creations since the beginning of life will be summoned to answer Him. The ones who did good deeds will find their way to heaven, the ones who didn't follow God's path will burn in hell.

I pondered the years gone by, and I wrote:

Bachpan to guzar di humne is imtehan-gah mein
Pata nahi guzregi kahan hamari woh naujawani.

I have spent my childhood in this exam centre,
I don't know where I will find myself in my youth.

When I heard about students who drank and took drugs, I wrote:

Ae sarparasto zara nazar utha kar idhar bhi to dekho
Ki kin ke sath rehte hain woh tere naujawan bachche.

Take a look here as well, O' parents
In what company your young children live.

I realised that a lot of poems had been composed about alcohol, but I had never heard such poems from Dada. I read a bit and found out that Ghalib was the biggest culprit. For example, his famous couplet said:

Zahid sharab peene de masjid mein baith kar
Ya woh jagah bata de jahan par Khuda na ho.

Let me drink in God's house, O devout one
Or else tell me the place where there is no God.

I used Ghalib as a metaphor for the poet-class and wrote:

Ghalib ne jo kahi sher zayadati nasha woh sharab ki
Ho gaye mash'hoor is sharabi duniya me maslan rawani-e-aab ki.

Since Ghalib composed verses on intoxication
He got famous in this drunken world, like a fast-flowing river.

I often turned to poetry while trying to comprehend the world. For instance, there was this time that I read a story in *Payam-e-Taleem*, an Urdu magazine that Jamia had been publishing since the university's early days. I liked it, and turned it into a poem in English titled 'Politics', which I have edited slightly here:

I will read you a rhyme
Once upon a time
There was a boy named Jain, Indian true,
He was curious to know about politics too.
So, he asked his father what to do.

His father said, 'Do as I tell you.'

Ordered him to climb a tree
Asked him to jump down free.
The boy was very scared
'Jump, son, I am asking you to dare.'
But Jain was full of fear

> Father asked again of his son so dear
> 'Jump, son, I will catch you,'
> 'Trust me, do as I tell you.'

Then Jain jumped down and fell

> And Father asked, 'All is well?'
> When his son groaned in pain
> Father said, 'That's politics, Jain.'

They joke: if you go to Aligarh Muslim University, you lose your deen, faith. If you go to Deoband, you lose your duniya, world. And if you go to Jamia, you lose both deen and duniya.

I had lived up to the stereotype, and it was entirely my fault.

In classes 11 and 12, I failed to achieve a good enough grade to get into the Science stream, which in my part of the world means that you are a failure; Commerce and Arts are streams reserved for losers.

Dada, though, wanted me to take Arts because he thought that most IAS people came from that background. Amir Subhani, from our neighbouring district, who topped the IAS examination in this year, studied Persian. One gentleman a few villages away also studied Arts and became an IAS officer. A distant cousin in the village, who was preparing for the civil services, too, studied Arts.

But I had set my sights on medicine. It took some time, but I finally managed to convince Dada that, even after studying medicine, I could appear for the civil services exam. What made my case compelling was a death in the family.

Chhoti Ammi's death.

It was the year 2000, the worst year for my family. And the month she died remains the worst in my memory, the month of unabating sorrow.

That year, Abbu's and Chhote Abbu's Eid vacations had coincided for the first time since they had moved to the Gulf, and the brothers were happy that they would be celebrating Eid together after years. Even my winter vacations in school had coincided with their visit. And Baaji too was back from her in-laws. Her husband was to join us soon.

But on the first Thursday of that Ramazan, an elder cousin, from Badey Dada's family, died soon after giving birth to her first child.

Inna lillahi wa inna ilaehe rajiuun.

Surely we belong to God and to Him we shall return.

She was in the best hospital they knew in Patna, but nothing could save her. I was in Delhi and left for home as soon as school closed. Her infant child died within the week, and on the noon I reached home, his dead body reached home from the hospital too. Before evening, our family was at the qabristan, burying him.

It was the second deadly Thursday of that Ramazan. And then, on the very next Thursday, it was my Chhoti Ammi's turn to die. She felt intense pain in her chest in the middle of the night, and was rushed to the government hospital in Gopalganj, the only hospital open at that hour.

It was sudden, so sudden that Chhote Abbu, who ran to get the prescribed medicines from a shop just outside, couldn't return in time.

Surprisingly, there were doctors in the hospital that night, a rarity at that hour. And while she was being rushed here, the guard at the railway intersection in Thawe had opened the gate as soon as he could. Even Badey Dada's temperamental Ambassador car had started in one attempt in spite of the December cold, and didn't require pushing or revving, as it normally did.

Throughout the last few days, the car had brought only bad news; only gloomy faces stepped out of it. No one, except God, knew what was happening or why.

We humans did our best but what could you do when god was hell-bent on taking all the credit? Who do you blame? Who do you beg before? Those who were dying, their time had not come. What the next Thursday would bring, no one knew.

It was Eid. *The* Eid. But on *that* Eid day, our cow fell ill. Dadi said she had drawn the ill fortune to her and averted another crisis.

People didn't come to greet us Eid Mubarak; they came to say we feel your pain. No adult in the family wore new clothes. No sevaiyan was made. Eidis remained waiting in the pockets of our elders. The neighbours too scaled down their celebrations.

Badey Dada's family was to soon fall apart. They blamed each other for his granddaughter's and great-grandson's death, with Badey Dada helplessly watching them, almost bed-ridden.

Chhote Abbu had been in the Gulf for most of the years his four daughters had known; the youngest of them was seven. In the absence of their mother, he had a tough time negotiating Eid day with them. Within a few weeks, he had chain-smoked himself to hypertension and eventually heart complications.

Abbu watched his brother's helplessness. Ammi couldn't fill the void of the mother who was no more. Dada and Dadi sat around a ghur, still, all day and night, watching their granddaughters and bereaved son, perhaps cursing the failure of the god-established tradition in which the young are supposed to see their old die, not the other way around. Doctors said it was a heart attack. Oblivious to the complexity of the medical sciences, I said to Dada that, if there had been a doctor in our family to attend to her immediately, she might have survived. And one more life could have been saved – that of Baaji's first son, who had died a few months ago.

Dada must have remembered the abandoned dreams of others in the family. Baaji had wanted to be a doctor but couldn't succeed. Then his younger son had wanted to be one but couldn't – he did practice as a doctor in the village after finishing college, but one fine morning, the government decided to call him what he was, a jhola-chhap doctor, the crooked doctor, and his services were no longer favoured and respected. He decided to go to Saudi Arabia to earn a living.

Perhaps I could finally repair that dream? A village-level aspiration, not much.

Changing my field of interest was an honest attempt on my part to respond to what the family was going through. I realised only later how hard it was to get into Medicine. By matriculation, I feared my plan would boomerang publicly any day. To keep up the shroud of secrecy, or lies, I had maintained around my grades, I appeared for a

Supplementary Improvement Exam in maths without telling my friends and relatives. I wanted to get a good enough grade to enrol in the science stream.

I did qualify by a whisker. By the time results were declared and I got admission, classes had already begun. And I was back in a familiar position: I had missed the early, foundational lectures, so I was struggling to get through. That should not have been a cause for worry as I had enrolled in a coaching class for the MBBS entrance exam. But that was it, only enrolment. I was at the bottom of the class here too. I hid my score cards before they could fall into anyone's hands. I kept weaving a dream that I knew, in my heart, would not come true.

To Dada and my parents, I was still the studious kid who would most certainly crack the entrance exam in the very first attempt. To them I was different from all those pretenders who camped in Patna for years on the pretext of preparing for entrance tests. I was not honest with them; I couldn't bear to break their hearts.

Hadees: Those who lie go to hell.

Back in school, I failed the first sessional exam. To avoid the inevitable failure that was coming, I persuaded Dada and my parents to allow me to take my class 12 exam from some school in Bihar, where in those years, it was normal to take admission and not attend classes. I gave the excuse that I needed time to prepare for my MBBS entrance exam. School and coaching together was becoming too much.

They allowed it, but I still couldn't get enough marks to qualify for the MBBS entrance exam. I had to reappear to get the qualifying marks.

I finally appeared for the MBBS entrance exams and, needless to say, didn't qualify for even a single college.

'Don't worry,' Dada said. 'Next time.' That was all the more difficult for me.

He added, 'You tried and couldn't succeed. At least you tried. Don't lose heart. Trying honestly is more important than anything else.'

Honestly, of course!

Then he let off one of his favourites:

Girte hain sheh-sawar hi maidan-e-jung mein,
Woh tifl kya gire jo ghutno ke bal chale.

Only soldiers fall from their horses in the battlefield,
How would a toddler fall who walks on his knees?

What sheh-sawar and what maidan-e-jung? His soldier was an idiot who had deserted the battlefield already. Only, the commander didn't know this. He wouldn't know either. He would die soon after, saying his last words to Ammi, who was present at his bedside:

You should not worry about Farooquee.

He will take his time.

But he will eventually succeed.

He has my duas.

And then he left us forever ...

... with his sons in the Arabian desert, his grandsons and eldest granddaughter in Delhi. His daughters, daughter-in-law and granddaughters were the only ones to bid him farewell.

Part Two

10

The Hideout

I HAD LIVED IN almost every major colony in Jamia Nagar Zakir Nagar, Joga Bai, Batla House, Noor Nagar – when, in 2002, I finally settled into my own house. My own house! My younger brother Ayaz had come to Delhi too, in search of good schooling and better company. Abbu thought it was worth buying a house so that we would not have to waste time running around trying to find accommodation at the whims and fancies of landlords. Dada was reluctant. He had heard stories of goons squatting on properties in Delhi, and didn't want to take a chance with his grandsons living there. Also, it meant selling some ancestral land – the most important treasure a farmer owns.

But Abbu persisted. Ancestral property is important, very important, but not as important as the education of your children. And why else was he wasting his life in a desert far from home if not for his children's education? Besides, my family reasoned, a house in Delhi would also help relatives who visited Delhi for medical treatment or to fly to the Gulf on work.

So they sold some land in the village and took a loan from relatives and friends to buy a house, a modest one compared to others in the locality.

It was between the mohallas on Muradi Road and Khalilullah Masjid. Muradi Road runs parallel to the Batla House–Zakir Nagar main road. Older men, who had witnessed a nondescript village on the outskirts of Delhi turn into a crowded ghetto, claimed that they used to fish in the vicinity of Muradi Road when the river Yamuna ran close to it. Older women said they used to wash clothes there in the days when they were young brides newly arrived in the locality.

The river, if her story were to be heard, would have a sorry tale to tell. Once her beauty had delighted the hearts of the Mughal queens as they sat on the ramparts of the Red Fort. She had provided the means for residents of Dehli to swim, fish and irrigate their fields. Upstream she was blessed by the Gods in Yamunotri, downstream from Delhi she proudly hosted the symbol of (royal) love, the Taj Mahal, before sacrificing her identity to the Ganga further down in Allahabad.

Her good days are done. Now, her banks mostly house (polluting) industries and (polluting) ghettos. Like Yamuna Pushta – which used to house a lakh-odd people but was demolished in 2004 during the drive to beautify Delhi for the Commonwealth Games – and Jamia Nagar.

In Jamia Nagar, she has receded to make way for buildings, including my house. Then further down, for the mohalla around Khalilullah Masjid. Still further, through the lane in front of the EncounterBuilding, one reaches the locality where the better-off people of the ghetto have their flats – with prices often running into crores of rupees – close to the Yamuna's (new) bank. The rich people's river-view stinks. Oops.

It had been planned that a road would run along the river bank, but the governments of Uttar Pradesh and Delhi have been wrestling in courts forever about who has jurisdiction over the land that once belonged to the river. For the time being, a dhobi ghat spreads along the stretch next to the Batla House and Zakir Nagar ghettos. The dhobi ghat disappears every now and then to accommodate the waters of the Yamuna (in the monsoon), the high- handedness of the police (season-neutral) and the mood swings of the municipality (season-neutral). It appears and disappears and then reappears, in a cruelly regular game played between the Yamuna, officialdom, property dealers and the (helpless) poor.

Facing Khalilullah Masjid, on its right, is the UP government's sprawling guest house, decorated with tiled walls and secured with barbed-wire fences all along what is known as Sailing Club Road, which ends at the Yamuna. An NCC camp occupies the bank further down the road. Since British times, the areas around the camp had been used as a picnic spot, and residents of Old Delhi would visit the place on their leisure days. On the other side of the camp runs a (dying) Raj-era canal that still makes the extravagant claim of flowing to Agra, as if no one knows how much water it contains.

The canal cleaves Jamia Nagar into two disproportionate halves. On the larger side lie the university, Batla House, Joga Bai, Ghafoor Nagar, Zakir Nagar, Ghaffar Manzil, Haji Colony, Noor Nagar, Johri Farm, Okhla Vihar, Okhla village, and on the other side, the UP government officers' quarters, Abul Fazal Enclave and Shaheen Bagh, sandwiched between the canal and the curving Yamuna. Between the small nallah and the big nallah. Between a stagnant residue of stink and a flowing mass of stink.

The Shaheen Bagh side of Jamia Nagar ends in a highway that connects Delhi to the suburb of Noida in UP, across the Yamuna. On the Jamia side, the locality ends in two hospitals – Holy Family and Escorts Heart, an old church and the village Sarai Jullena, a prosperous old hamlet of Jats, who earn well from renting out their houses to Jamia students and nurses working in the nearby hospitals. On the Zakir Nagar side is the posh New Friends Colony.

Between Shaheen Bagh and Jamia lie Okhla Vihar, Johri Farm and Haji Colony. Okhla Vihar abuts Jasola, a newly built centre of prosperity, with planned houses and a playground (access by membership only), while Haji Colony is next to semi-posh Sukhdev Vihar. There is a smelly waste recycling plant recently started by the Jindals in the centre of these colonies. Haji Colony houses mainly migrants and the lower down-the-hierarchy staff of Jamia. Many Kashmiri Muslims who fled the conflict in the valley are also settled in Johri Farm, which on the one side opens into a low-lying ridge that once provided relatively fresh air to the migrants. Now, they can savour the smelly fart of Jindal Inc. (in association with the Delhi government), sharing the stink with three major hospitals, a university, many schools and many other colonies – posh and non-posh. Jamia Nagar was once a village of farmers and potters on the outskirts of Delhi, known as Okhla Gaon. In the 1920s, something happened about 150 kilometres from the village that changed its fortunes. Nationalist fervour against British colonialism was at its height and Aligarh Muslim University was an intellectual centre for Muslims. The British recognised both

AMU as well as the newly set up Banaras Hindu University (BHU) in the 1920s, granting them state patronage. A section of AMU nationalists was uncomfortable with that, and on Gandhi's call to boycott British-run or supported educational institutes, these thought-rebels decided to break away from AMU. On the one side, there were those who would later justify the formation of Pakistan, and on the other were those who opposed the partition of India and lived and died here: Maulana Abul Kalam Azad, Dr Zakir Hussain, Maulana Mohammad Ali Jauhar, M.A. Ansari, Hakim Ajmal Khan and others.

They named their idea Jamia Millia Islamia. The National Islamic University.

To give it shape, they built a small campus just outside AMU with Hakim Ajmal Khan's generous contributions. They had Gandhi's blessings. When they considered dropping Islamia from the name, as it was becoming difficult to get donations, Gandhi said, 'Jamia has to run. If you are worried about its finances, I will go about with a begging bowl.'

He did, in a way. When there was a funding crunch after the death of Hakim Ajmal Khan, Gandhi asked the Tatas, Birlas and others to donate. He even wrote to the head of the Hindu Mahasabha for support, saying that the institution was open to all.

In the year 1925, Jamia moved to Delhi's Karol Bagh, one of the colonies that would, just over two decades later, house Hindu and Sikh refugees from the newly formed Pakistan.

But the institution needed more space. Finally, in 1935, it found a home in the area that would later become Jamia Nagar (the university town), between Okhla Gaon and village Sarai Jullena (named after a Portuguese woman called

Juliana whom the Mughal emperor Akbar had appointed as doctor to his harem).

The thought-rebels bought some land here, and generous patrons contributed some. The local villagers donated land too. There is no one left in the village today from the generation that witnessed the arrival of Jamia, but sons remember their fathers speaking of how they willingly donated their lands to what they called the madrasa. Here, on what was the outskirts of a city, there was no worthy centre of learning, and so they welcomed the 'madrasa' wholeheartedly. With the 'madrasa' came national attention Jinnah, Iqbal, Nehru, Premchand, Sarojini Naidu and other prominent intellectuals visited the campus.

Early on, at the instance of Gandhi, Iqbal had been offered vice chancellorship of the university, but the poet declined. Nehru called the institution an oasis in the Sahara. Another scholar visiting India said it was the only Gandhian institute in the country. Tagore called it 'one of the most progressive institutes in India'. And someone else wrote to Jinnah before Partition claiming that the institution was a centre for Hinduisation that would leave its students Muslim in name but Hindu in outlook.

Following Partition, the Karol Bagh campus was ransacked and looted, and the Jamia Nagar campus faced the threat of being burnt down. Students and teachers kept vigil. When rations ran out, a generous teacher brought supplies from his church in nearby Masih Garh.

While all this was going on, Zakir Hussain and others pledged to serve the institution their whole lives. Due to the funding crunch, they served on meagre salaries, which they took only after ensuring that everyone else in the institution had been paid.

The selflessness and the vision of its founders turned this 'madrasa' into a deemed university soon after independence. In the late 1980s it was given the status of a central university. This was a time when the Babri Masjid demolition movement was peaking. The emerging Bharatiya Janata Party and the dying Congress were vying to fool voters, one in God's name, the other not in God's name.

Soon after, Hindu militants demolished the Babri mosque. Numerous riots followed, big and small, which continued to establish the supremacy of politics over humanity. In small towns like Meerut, Bhagalpur and Surat, in big cities like Mumbai, Ahmedabad and Kanpur.

And then followed commissions to investigate the obvious.

Commission after commission.

Extension after extension.

Trial after trial. Year after year.

But nothing came out of it all. Nothing worth recalling. And rarely anything healing.

The injustice, often repeated, and the denial of people's pain in far-flung areas reached other far-flung areas. Not everything was unjust but the SampleCases were being witnessed, noted and stacked meticulously in the corner of the brain that never seems to forget.

Around this time, India's economy was liberalised, and all Indians were promised a shiny new future. In a newly hopeful country, many more turned to cities in their search for a better life. Muslims from poor and middle-class families in villages and towns followed the trend and moved to Delhi and other cities. But what place in the metropolis would be welcoming as well as accommodative of your dreams and hopes, of your safety and dignity? And also be affordable?

The answer for many was Jamia Nagar. It offered a (physically and mentally) safe haven. Proximity to opportunities. A sense of security. An educational institution nearby.

And of course, Musalmani mahaul. A Muslim environment.

With time, the locality turned out to be a great leveller. Young and old, poor and rich, villagers and city-dwellers, Delhiites and non-Delhiites, religious and non-religious, Ashraf (high-born) and Ajlaf (low-born), good Muslim and bad Muslim, capitalist and communist, modern and orthodox, all came together in the cramped, stinky, overflowing lanes of Jamia Nagar.

The deluge of people brought with it memories, nostalgia, alienation, victimhood and insecurity.

And an assertion of identity.

Jamia Nagar provided a healing touch. Everyone's secrets stayed within Jamia Nagar – only to spill out if something like an encounter happened.

The ghettoisation intensified in the year following the Gujarat riots of 2002, a decade after the Babri demolition. These were the first major communal riots after the opening up of cable TV in India, which broadcast scary images from the state. The pictures affected everyone in the country – cold-hearted, brave-hearted, heartless. It shattered many a naive dream of a shining India. It gave ghettoisation a new meaning – Muslim ghettoisation as well as its inverse, Hindu ghettoisation. But there was, however, a world of difference between forced ghettoisation and by-choice ghettoisation – it was determined by the lopsided concentration of power. More than ever, when Delhi-bound Muslims were in search of a sense of security, they turned to Jamia Nagar.

There is a saying here: India comes to Delhi, Muslims come to Jamia Nagar.

I had come when the ghetto was still young. In the years that followed, Jamia Nagar changed tremendously.

The electricity began going off less often. Factories that stitched clothes, quilts and aprons withdrew to sites closer to the Yamuna. Furnaces producing bakery items became fewer. Cars took over the narrow streets. Coaching centres, toddlers' schools and property dealers dotted the colonies. The maximum height of buildings officially increased from three to four storeys, and unofficially from four to five. Electric transformers appeared on the sides of roads, eating into the already narrow lanes. Kebab and biryani shops grew in number (and taste). Designer sherwani and lehenga shops opened, and slowly built up a brisk business. Gyms and fitness centres opened and shut down and reopened. Telecom operators got smart, and seized the business opportunities offered by festivals, languages and identities. Banners, often advertising in Urdu, offered talk-times of 786 minutes and special Eid packages.

A new middle class emerged and searched for spaces to spend their money. They looked around and found, for example, the community centre in nearby New Friends Colony. Soon, the community centre became Jamia Nagar's, more or less. New Friends Colony's residents withdrew, more or less. No one said anything, no one needed to.

While all this happened, the locality, the university in its neighbourhood began to be viewed with reluctant pride – not modern enough for Modernists, not conservative enough for Conservatives. Both sides, though, took pride in its historical splendour.

Over the years, especially in the 1990s, the university saw an exponential rise in the number of students from different strata – Muslims, non-Muslims, liberals, conservatives, from the neighbourhood, from faraway places in Delhi and outside. This was to forever change Jamia. The change, good or bad, still continues.

Conferences, lectures, extra-curricular activities got their due. New centres of learning opened. The infrastructure improved. Guitars, if they are a sign of anything, are not uncommon on campus anymore. Neither are parties or drugs. Jeans and T-shirts have long ceased to be taboo for girls. Now they coexist with dupattas and, increasingly, burqas and scarves, but also with skirts, dancing, basketball and mischief in the girls' common room (I have heard this). The change, good or bad, has spilt over into Jamia Nagar.

Jamia Nagar, where I live.

Where my friends live.

Where Terrorists lived.

Where Normal Human Beings live.

Jamia Nagar: where shops, restaurants and overflowing gutters rub against masjids and chaos. It has no parks for children (except one or two small ones, buried in garbage), no playground (except the unused space in the graveyard), no footpaths (where these exist, they have surrendered to hawkers, small shops, parked cars).

It has everything in it for a specialist doctor of malaria and gastronomical troubles to flourish, but until recently, there was only one small private hospital. Now one more, with slightly better facilities, run by the Jamat-e-Islami, fills the vacuum.

One State Bank of India branch is located where Zakir Nagar ends and Delhi's New Friends Colony begins. Another bank shifted its operations to the colony when they were asked to move out of the university. There are two branches of a local bank no one trusts. Recently the J&K Bank opened a branch in Batla House.

After the encounter, ATMs came up to assure the residents: don't worry, banks exist on the periphery of your colony. But banks still hesitate to give loans to the residents of Jamia Nagar. And the Election Commission almost always classifies the area as a 'sensitive zone', even though there have not been reports of any mischief.

When I came here in 1997, the colony was already close to saturation. Now it's over-saturated, and the numbers keep increasing. The drainage is not equipped to handle the pressure. Cars line the barely single-lane streets. Streets too narrow to be one-ways work as two-ways. People know the shortcuts, they escape one jam through lanes and bylanes to land in another. What can I say, it's a common form of timepass in these parts.

Jamia Nagar is fast turning into another Old Delhi in terms of chaos, sans the old city's historical past and architecture – a new Old Delhi, if you please, with unplanned buildings and chaos.

Typical India, but with a different memory: that of riots, of discrimination, of victimhood, of paranoia, real and imagined, assembled from across the country.

Somewhere in these chaotic lanes, between Muradi Road and Khalilullah Masjid, is my little home. It has only basic facilities, and one open hall rather than rooms – a legacy of its previous occupant, a factory where (hopeful) traders had garments stitched for export.

When we moved in, we inserted a plywood partition of about a man's height across the middle of the hall; the inner half became like a bedroom, with some privacy. The house has a small kitchen and a bath-cum-toilet. As you enter, a naked stairway on your left goes up to the first-floor terrace that is hemmed in on all sides by taller structures, sort of like a well. In summers, when there were frequent power outages at night, the well was my bedroom. On winter afternoons, it gave me ample space to pretend I was studying and impress a few neighbours. Below the stairs is the bathroom-toilet, and next to this is the kitchen. The kitchen ceiling could just about accommodate an Amitabh Bachchan standing, and above the kitchen was a small water tank (which somehow kept its contents cool in summer, not too cold in winter).

The house hasn't changed much since we bought it in 2002. I have maintained its heritage value, so to speak; my friends say it ought to be declared a protected monument. Next to a small tin door is a large window that has netting to keep mosquitoes away, but no window frame, and no way to shut it. It welcomes into the house the winter cold, the summer dust, the noise of the neighbourhood.

A mattress with a thin quilt used to lie to the right of the door. A noisy cooler stood on the floor, level with the mattress. When my friends assembled in the house, lulled by its noise, we believed no one outside could hear us. Unknowingly, we must have given the neighbours several lessons on topics we knew little about: biology, cricket, politics, sex.

The toilet enthusiastically overflowed when the gutter outside was jammed or if it rained wholeheartedly. In the monsoons, yellowish-brackish water entered the home, quietly slipping under the front door, filthy and odorous. It turned the house into a shallow swimming pool that shone dusty-golden in the dim light.

I lost a laptop to these intrusive waters once. I woke up that morning to realise it was drizzling. Since the weather was pleasant, I figured I would sneak in a nap. It was noisy outside, with beggars singing their pleading songs and duas while monkey-jumping from brick to brick. *Allah aapko maghfirat de. Allah apko nek aulaad de. Allah apko imtehaan mein pass kara de.* May Allah grant you forgiveness. May Allah grant you virtuous children. May Allah grant that you pass your exams.

They sang duas for everyone but themselves. And they didn't seem likely to let up. So, annoyed and half-asleep, I went inside, behind the plywood enclosure, to sleep on the chauki, the low wooden bed, there.

I dreamt of my favourite weather. Rains, endless rains. I would have also liked to have situated the dream in a forest (the hero is always adventurous), but it was still lovely. Then some beggar or kid fell into the water outside and began to create a ruckus. Irritated, I got up to shout at them to fuck off from in front of my house. But with the first step I realised I was marooned. Yellow scum floating in golden water. In the outer room – room? – my mattress was floating about, and with it, my laptop.

The bathroom had a bucket and a mug and a (reluctant) shower. A soap-holder in the corner, tied to a nail in the wall with a thin plastic rope. A few sachets of different shampoos, mostly empty, a Lifebuoy soap. I kept the detergent powder for washing clothes in the kitchen. Somehow, it didn't seem stupid then.

My kitchen was always fragrant with stale food. It was PETA-friendly too – cockroaches and rodents were equal partners. Sunlight never reached the inside of our building, which made the house intensely hospitable for the cockroaches. Rodents too loved to sneak in from the gutters outside, through a hole at the base of the door that had been made to tap an illegal connection from a newly laid water pipeline. The rats were cute in their own right but so big they intimidated even the neighbourhood cats. Just outside the bathroom, there was a washbasin – sky-bluish (when clean), blue-grey-brown (usually). It was the first thing you noticed as you entered the door. The tap like a uvula hanging in an open mouth. Below it were a few buckets, and a few utensils waiting to be (amateurishly) washed. Washing was as infrequent as cooking for me, and the utensils eventually resigned themselves to the pleasure of water dripping from the washbasin above and the company of a healthy family of fungi.

An old rack partly stood, partly leant against the plywood divider. Ayaz had got it from a sweet-shop owner who was replacing it with a new one. The rack had two shelves. I kept my books in one, and Ayaz kept his favourite things in another: screwdriver, pliers, small motors, copper wire, nails, grease, duct tape, soldering iron. Dusty editions of *The Hindu*, *Hindustan Times*, *The Times of India*, *Asian Age* and newspaper-clippings competed for space on the rack. I could never bring myself to sell my treasured papers to scrap dealers.

When the pile was high enough, my friends would take the papers away on the pretext of cleaning the house and use the money to throw a little party.

Parties. Our parties were simple. They were held either at al-Bake restaurant in the New Friends Colony community centre, or at home. One day, I was fast asleep when my friends 'cleaned' the house. That day they bought delicious kebabs and parathas from Azmat Café, the restaurant on Muradi Road that had a temperamental owner who shut shop whenever he felt like it. The party was inaugurated with champagne: for us that was Pepsi or Coke (the soft drink one). A little shaking of the cola bottle does the job. And if you put a bit of salt in it, it works even better than champagne. Champagne rained on me and I woke up to realise my treasure-trove was gone. I had no choice but to enjoy the party, or the eatables would all be soon gone.

From hooks screwed into the walls and plywood hung jeans and shirts. Somewhere in there lurked my vests and underwear. On the plywood partition was also a slogan written with a permanent marker: 'If you can't convince, at least confuse.' Perhaps it had seemed cool when I wrote it. On the opposite wall, hung a calendar with a photo of Masjid-e-Nabwi on it, with a few verses written in Arabic, and a saying in Urdu: *Namaz se mat kaho kaam hai. Kaam se kaho namaz hai.* Don't say you are too busy for prayers. Say to your work that you have to offer prayers.

Another poster in Urdu hung on the same nail. The poster read:

The person who doesn't offer Fajr prayers
the lustre of his face is taken away.
The person who doesn't offer Zuhar prayers
the blessings of his earnings are taken away.
The person who doesn't offer Asar prayers
the strength from his body is taken away.
The person who doesn't offer Maghrib prayers

the success of his children is taken away.
The person who doesn't offer Isha prayers
the peace of his night's sleep is taken away.

Behind the plywood partition was another wooden rack with books and notebooks, selected newspaper-clippings, and a few certificates and marksheets. There were pocket- sized biographies of Isaac (urf Is'haaq) Newton, muchhad Albert Einstein, Leonardo Da Vinci (da Pincy) and others that I had bought at a book fair in Delhi (10 per cent discount! Choose any book!). There were two volumes of an encyclopaedia of science, bought as and when I could afford them. There were few issues of *Payam-e-Taleem*, *Huda*, *Wisdom*, *Competition Science Refresher*, a year book, a torn Oxford dictionary that I had won for topping a test in school – the last time I had done anything worthy. On top of the rack were candles, a few Abu-Fas painkiller spray cans, a dwarf pencil, a few dead pilot pens, and other flotsam and jetsam.

The farther right corner of the house had the limping chauki, held together by its diseased skeleton. The bedsheet had miraculously changed colour, from blue-white to black-grey. It was so old (allegedly) that no one remembered when exactly it had been first spread over the bed. I (allegedly) never washed the bedsheet and if I were to do such a thing, I would need to replace the (allegedly) old bedsheet with a new one.

Next to the chauki were two mattresses spread on the floor, side by side. These were needed for cousins, relatives or village acquaintances who descended on Delhi.

Beside the bed lay my travelling bag. It had only ever travelled to my village and back. It had a few clothes stuffed in it. The clean and relatively clean ones were hanging from hooks, but the dirty ones and winter clothes had found their way into the bag. There was some bhuja too, which Ammi had sent for me – puffed rice, gram and groundnut roasted on sand in a traditional chulha.

Next to it lay my suitcase; no longer what it used to be: compact and a beautiful black, with a pair of keys.

11

Bakchodi Days

IN COLLEGE, I FOUND myself in an illustrious gathering of about fifty failures, vying to outclass each other. Failures, because India recognises and respects only doctors engineers civil servants – and other such illustrious professions, all out of the reach of us lesser mortals. Like most medical aspirants in this country, we had failed to achieve what we set out to do. We only knew people who had got through to MBBS – a friend, a friend's friend, somebody's cousin – but none of us had. From parents and seniors, we heard stories of other people's brilliance and hard work; we ourselves had nothing to offer.

We were content with the fact that we had at least got into college, somewhere, somehow. Studying for a BSc in Bioscience, the poor cousin of Biotechnology, and still poorer cousin of Medicine. Surely, far below the poverty line.

But even among these chosen poor, while most showed signs of resilience, there were a few of us whose actions seemed to suggest we were irreparable failures. These few inevitably gelled together, hung out in the canteen, sat together during lectures and ganged up to ruin everyone else's happiness. Bullies, more or less.

I was one of the seven. A little less consequential than the others. Besides failing MBBS, we also shared a disturbing tendency finding ways to disrupt the lives of others. Others being everyone other than the seven of us: Ahmad Perwez, Alim Junaid, Asbah Faroqui, Kafil Ahmad, Rameez Raja, Shyam Prakash and me. Furquan, and at times, Inzamam, from Biotech were guest-sadists.

In short it was a mixture of: funny, middle class, Gopalganj, intelligent, seemingly intelligent, Gorakhpur, Mathura, bald, Patna, thin, aggressive, hairy, Aligarh Muslim University, Sunni, cricket, Lucknow and village.

A good, diverse mix. Like the plants in Botany classes. As poisonous as the snakes in Zoology classes. As volatile as acids in the Chemistry classes.

We all began civilly enough: reaching class in time; answering the teacher's questions; being courteous to the girls in the class. True colours still hidden. Salam, hi, bye were still to be replaced with gandu, motherfucker, chutiya.

But it unravelled quite fast.

There had been no elections to the student's union of the university for many years. Finally, in 2005, a year before we were enrolled, the newly appointed vice chancellor, Mushirul Hasan, brought democracy back to campus. But some students seemed not to grasp the fact that debates could be held in a peaceful manner, that people could listen to each other, and disagree without jumping at each other's throats. The university identified such leaders and expelled them. When we joined, there was fresh hope that elections would be held again.

Speculation about the elections kept the hopefuls hopeful. There were people in the university who had spent their entire youth in hostels and dhabas, waiting for the elections to launch their political careers. It was as if the students' union president would become prime minister of India one day.

In 2006, Mushirul Hasan expelled some forty students for indiscipline and banned their entry into campus, almost single-handedly ruining the bhai–neta–khala ka ghar culture. He also fenced in the university campus and hostels to give the amoeboid campus a physical shape, and to prevent land sharks from encroaching on university land. The fencing regulated entry and exit to the hostels, and also largely insulated the university from politics and politicians in nearby localities.

Professor Hasan was not the first VC to attempt to give Jamia a university-face and a university-feel. Syed Shahid Mahdi, the VC before him, had demolished all the illegal dhabas that lined the road running across the campus. This was where aspiring netas sat day and night, ruining their lives and setting an example for others to follow. He tried to clear the campus of unscrupulous elements, and once even allowed police into the hostels. They beat up students inside, injuring more than fifty.

Before Mahdi, VC General Zaki had struggled to bring some sanity and army-style discipline to the campus, but it needed more than mere commandeering to tackle restless, misguided young minds, charged with the vigour and brashness of youth.

In 1983, VC A.J. Kidwai established a communications institute that would go on to train well-known filmmakers and journalists in the country. He had a hard time convincing the Canadian agency that helped establish the institute that Jamia was a modern campus, devoted to secular education, with no organic link to any theological school in India or abroad. The setting up of such an institute – devoted to the study of cinema, which involves capturing and representing images of living beings – angered the godly men of Jamia and many of them reached Kidwai's door. He came out of his office and stood at the gate, defiantly puffing a pipe. The angry young men retreated.

The struggle between ideas continued, often taking ugly forms.

In 1992, some students motivated by a misguided mix of Power and God had beaten up Professor Hasan, then a history professor and pro-vice chancellor of the university, for 'defending Salman Rushdie'.

It was a time of turmoil, when competitive communalism was at its height in the country: the Hindu rightwing was calling for the demolition of Babri Masjid in Ayodhya and the building of a Ram temple in its place; the Muslim rightwing was incensed by Salman Rushdie's *The Satanic Verses* and baying for his blood.

Mushirul Hasan had told an interviewer that, as a Muslim, he abhorred what Rushdie wrote but the author had a right to say what he wished. This was read by many as an endorsement of Rushdie and his book. The then vice chancellor advised him to stay away from the campus for a while. He stayed away from university for a few months but eventually returned to his office, and this gave many an opportunity to revive their political careers. A group of students was waiting to teach Professor Hasan a lesson. They did. He had to be hospitalised. This was just two days before Babri Masjid was demolished.

He deserved it, didn't he? You can never trust a khatmal. It's not without reason that people call these Shias khatmals, bed bugs. (Those idiots call us Sunnis machhars, mosquitoes.)

A good thrashing and it ensured that he stayed out of campus for months. But the shameless man continued working, and eventually returned to the campus four and a half years later. To no particular welcome, no particular disdain.

Professor Hasan, as vice chancellor, brought funds to the campus, opened several new centres and labs, and sought to establish a culture of (civilised) debate and (meaningful) dissent on campus. And that's what he was trying to restore through student democracy.

But then the university announced that office-bearers would be chosen by an indirect election: each class would choose two representatives – one girl, one boy. If the class was not able to find a consensus candidate, an election would be held in the class. These representatives would elect a few among them to the union, one of whom would be chosen president.

As an internal student – one whose qualifying course was from Jamia – I had a certain cache in class. I knew the campus intimately and the people around. But I was not interested in the class representative business, which would mean running around with the attendance sheet or keeping tabs on whether the teacher was coming to class or not. So, this little leader gave another student in class his blessings.

But the senior named Zeeshan, who knew me, said I must fight the elections. Suddenly, the other group, led by Mama, became confrontational. I didn't like that. As an internal student, I was the one who should have been ruling, not these idiot externals who suddenly thought they could run the show.

I knew whom to approach. Let's say a Higher Authority. Like Mama and Zeeshan, he was from Azamgarh, and had been my junior in school, but his exceptional talent for inventing fights had taken him to the higher echelons of the proctorial department's list of most-hated students. His little adventures – beating up bus conductors plying on the Jamia route if they didn't allow him a free ride, picking fights in college if someone merely happened to stare at him, and harassing women students – had led the university to ban his entry into campus (though his emissaries continued to roam about freely). Of course, nobody could ban him outside.

I met His Highness at Bismillah Tea Shop near Batla House Chowk, where he and his durbar assembled every evening. Bismillah was one of the shops that former vice chancellor Mahdi had removed from campus. Outside, its watery tea and even more watery chholey still attracted nostalgic veterans as well as new students looking for cost-effective food or a few minutes of cricket on its TV. The stink coming from a garbage dump nearby only added to the flavour of the tea, and cattle roaming around the dump to your company.

Since I was his senior in school, His Highness still showed me some respect. He expressed dismay that someone had challenged Neyaz Bhai. Neyaz Bhai! And that the bugger was from his place, Azamgarh! He would teach the fool a lesson he would never forget.

The next morning, he sent his emissaries to cut Mama and Co. down to size. That day settled forever my standing in my class. Though Mama continued with his politics, he never confronted me.

People in class realised that this bright little talent had a future, and soon I had a gang.

We spent most of our waking hours together, at my place, around the canteen or outside the library. In case you wanted to study, for a change, the library had a good collection of books and it remained open till 2 a.m. during exam time (though we were strong proponents of the open-book exam policy). For those who lived nearby, the library was also a respite from the seething summer heat or the bitter cold of winter, and also from mosquitoes.

Exaggeration ruled our silly roost. Once, when Kafil had gone back home to Mathura for a minor surgery, we announced that he had died. When I was absent in class, they announced that I had gone back to the village to get engaged to be married. 'Look at his watch,' they said, pointing to it – a gift from Abbu who had brought it for me from Saudi Arabia. They celebrated my birthday in all four quarters of the year, and also with everyone else's in the group. We called Perwez a Bangladeshi infiltrator because his place in West Bengal has a namesake in Bangladesh. (Gopalganj too has a namesake there.)

We maintained our routine throughout those three years, including exam time. Two gentlemen in our group failed in one of the practical exams, something that had never happened before in the department. Another gentleman attempted all nine questions in an exam when five was all that we were supposed to write. In the religious studies exam, Alim wrote a paean to Imam Bukhari (the Shahi Imam of Jama Masjid) when the question meant the great scholar, Imam Bukhari, whose compilation of the hadees, *Sahih al-Bukhari*, Sunnis consider to be the most definitive one.

Asbah and I failed in Maths in our second year. In the finals, Kafil and I failed in Ecology – I, by one mark, one full mark. Luckily for me, the university had a leniency clause that allowed students to graduate if they failed in only one subject by one mark. So, I was able to graduate in the prescribed three years, but there is a beautiful – and permanent – red oval circle on my marksheet.

Kafil fared worse; he risked losing his admission to the Masters course in Bioinformatics. The only thing that could save him was a recheck (assuming there was a mistake on the university's part). So, he went around the campus, meeting everyone possible, putting on a face we had never seen before.

In three years at Jamia, he had figured out how to get things done. But this was an extraordinary situation, one that ran the risk of reaching his parents or local guardian. It demanded an extraordinary response: he started offering namaz. This was something he hadn't done even before the exams, as the rest of us usually did, to compensate for not studying the whole year.

While hanging around the examination department, he had learnt who ruled the roost. The big man there was a god-fearing person who offered namaz regularly during the noon break. And that's what turned our Kafil into a namazi, a complete akhlaq wala ladka. A boy of virtue. With proper tameez-o-tamaddun. A civilised and well-mannered noon-time namazi.

Finally, Kafil managed to meet the exam official while they were both leaving the masjid. Kafil offered him salam with the proper tone and tenor of a pious man: he raised his right hand a bit, bowed slightly and said, '*Assalam-o-Alaikum wa rahmatullahi wa barakatuh*.' Peace be upon you, and God's mercy and blessings. It was just the right touch. The official and his acolytes noticed Kafil and were impressed with his piousness.

And why not? How many young men offer namaz nowadays? This pious innocent boy's career was in jeopardy. He needed help. At least a chance to be heard.

As if God had unfairly picked on him.

The official heard him out that day. Hearing that Kafil had failed by a mere three marks moved him a little, and that the young man was in danger of losing a year won him over completely. Soon we heard that he had ordered prompt rechecking of the copies so that no student would lose a year. Perhaps for the first time, it had dawned on the official that their slow processes threatened so many already jeopardised careers.

Or perhaps the alacrity was due to Apoorva's efforts. She was one of four who had failed the paper, and her scientist father had apparently reached out to someone somewhere at the top in the university, requesting that the process of rechecking the papers be expedited.

To everyone's utter surprise, three of the failed innocents were cleared, Kafil and Apoorva among them. Now Kafil was back to his old self, reminding me sadistically that the red mark would stay on my mark-sheet, but not on his.

Idiot.

'So, janab, you think what Osama is doing is right?' Perwez asked, sarcastically.

It was a summer evening in 2007, about a year before the encounter, and the Delhi weather was uniformly harsh on everyone outside – with (moderate) rains, (militant) heat and (radical) humidity. The sun had gone nuts, basically.

Indoors, it created new hierarchies in society, between those with ACs, coolers or lower floors in buildings, and those without. Kafil and Perwez lived in Jullena, occupying the room closest to the sun. Their days were spent loitering in college or the library. The baking it got during the day and the sun's lingering affection in the evening made their room unbearable at night. They often stayed over at mine. At least it had a cooler, and was surrounded by taller buildings that saved it from a direct roasting for most of the day.

The day's paper lay on the floor, still rolled up. I usually read it when I returned in the evening. My morning routine did not allow for such luxuries. Kafil picked it up and joked, 'Oye, Muslim, why do you buy *The Hindu* when you don't read it?'

Perwez smiled. He used to joke that the reason I subscribed to *The Hindu* was because the city supplement of *The Times of India* turned me on. 'Achha,' he said, 'give me the supplement, Kafil. Let me see if they have any Delhi Times material in it.'

'Seriously, man,' said Kafil. 'Why do you subscribe to *The Hindu*? It's so dull.'

'Because it gives fair coverage,' I said. 'I remember they published, on their front page, the picture of that tailor from the Gujarat riots who was begging for his life. And—' Kafil interrupted, 'Achha, you were saying something about Osama. What was that?' And that brought the conversation about Osama bin Laden back.

We had had arguments about the Al-Qaeda leader earlier too. Who was Osama really, and what did he stand for? The event that had last triggered our disagreement was the screening of a movie named *Osama*. Jamia's Centre for Jawaharlal Nehru Studies had organised the screening in the university's Ansari Auditorium. It was a full house. While the fugitive Al-Qaeda leader played hide-and-seek, supposedly in the mountains of Tora Bora, and in his free time released videos on killing kafirs, his name still evoked fear and interest among the masses. The screening of the film was widely publicised and elicited keen interest amongst the students. They wanted to see the making of the man who was always in the news. The man who personified evil.

The evilest of evil.

Eviler than America.

I too went with my friends to find out about the making of Osama, the man who had plunged the world's greatest (and most evil) power into a war. Afghanistan and Iraq were already in turmoil by then, and a lot of people were angry about it. Osama was more relevant now than ever. But my first memories of the terrorist leader go back a little further. I was still in school when Osama's men flew the planes into WTC. There was a TV repair shop on the ground floor of the building we lived in. We borrowed a repaired black-and-white TV from the shop owner and tapped cable from the wires passing through the street to watch the melting towers.

The images seemed to belong in an action movie rather than real life.

The bombing of the twin towers brought Osama into every drawing room, every classroom, every space. In the days following the attacks, the US announced that it was the handiwork of Osama's Al-Qaeda. It was confusing. I had heard stories about mujahids fighting in Afghanistan against Russia, and those same men (more or less) ruled the country as Taliban. It was Afghanistan where Osama had taken shelter, that was no secret to anyone.

An acquaintance was convinced that the attack was a ruse by America to launch an offensive on Afghanistan. He gloated that, if the Americans dared to attack that country, Osama would teach them a lesson. He often visited us because we were too polite to turn him away. When we sensed he was coming, we would rush to find a book to pretend that we were studying. If our friends were around, they would vanish, saying, '*Phenku aa gya, ab lapeto beta tum log.*' Here comes the teller of tall tales, deal with him. There was just no stopping him. We would yawn, but he would never get the hint. Being younger, we couldn't call him mad to his face and just leave.

But we could not deny that he seemed to know a lot. He brought to his monologues a perspective that we didn't even know existed. He would say, for example, that Saddam was a brave man who knew how to deal with rebels. The Iraqi dictator had gassed to death hundreds of Kurds in the late 1980s. He would say the US fooled Saddam into attacking Kuwait to acquire its oil wealth. That's why they had put back-breaking sanctions on the country – but Saddam was not one to bow to them. He would talk over-enthusiastically about Saudi Arabia's laws, saying that those who criticised them didn't know that the strict punishments meted out, like cutting of hands and beheading, kept crime in check.

His theses and justifications made sense; an evil-free world was a compelling idea.

This acquaintance's vast knowledge of distant worlds impressed me. Consistency was not one of his virtues, but he confirmed what we heard here and there in incoherent voices: the West's conspiracy against the Muslim world. It was not so much religion as it was about a feeling of humiliation. Of being powerless. Betrayed. Of not being able to do anything against the might of an unjust America. The US often played – plays – a dubious role in international politics, and this is not limited to the Muslim world. But he compiled images of horror in which the US and the West were supposedly complicit – or at least, that it did not care for the Muslim world. His stories, to some degree, helped form the backbone of many of my opinions, prejudices and the sense of hurt that I acquired.

He was not talking about a revolution, neither were we interested – we did not even know what that meant in a real sense – but it was good to know the true colours of the world that surrounded us. While my flatmate heard him out and moved on, I took it seriously. It was the remnants of such stories that I carried with me. Away from the supervision of parents. Living in a hurt ghetto. I interpreted his stories through the lens of my own observations and experiences, and reacted in my own way.

In 2006, for example, when Saddam Hussain was hanged by the peace-loving Amrikkans, I protested the killing of that brave man in a letter to the editor of *The Hindu*. 'A great service to the world by US,' I wrote that very evening. 'Being a young college going student I don't know much about US or Saddam. But whatever little I know, now I can loudly say that Iran, S Korea' – I meant North Korea – 'and in some cases even Al Qaida is not at fault against US. My voice may not be important as I'm not a so called expert but this act of US I fear will poison many young minds that are future of this world.'

There were others who protested too, and did it using the easiest, cheapest, most risk-free medium: posters. Events like Saddam's hanging – or the WTC attacks, or the Afghanistan and Iraq invasions – caused posters, usually spouting gibberish, to appear in Jamia Nagar. After the WTC attacks, for example, the posters (in vague terms) supported Osama. They certainly complained that the US was leading a civilisational war against Islam. (Over the years, the wars in Afghanistan and Iraq only closed the gap between conspiracy and reality in these posters.)

Though this was certainly not the view of the majority in the locality, who in any case had more than enough to cope with in their daily struggles, it was definitely the shrillest and most attention-seeking. While the militants were fighting psychological battles with the world after the attack on WTC, desperate politicians thousands of kilometres away were fighting their own battles using Jamia Nagar's walls. They denounced the Christian Bush, in black, white, blue, using their own hypocrisy to highlight that of the US. They usually chose Urdu to communicate with the shaitan Bush. Urdu, a language few understood even in that locality.

The posters competed for the attention of passers-by. They made readers aware of the discrimination faced by Muslims in jobs and admission to institutes of learning in the country, and reminded people about incidents like the Babri demolition. They denounced political leaders, including Muslims, for their 'impotency' in not taking up the cases of riots and rights.

Few took notice of them. And the political messaging sat next to posters by coaching institutes that claimed their students had been selected to Jamia and AMU. Or those of local leaders congratulating their seniors for getting selected as party secretary or to some such office. Then there were pleading posters about lost children, promising reward for information (prorated as per the pleader's monetary capacity). And of tours and travels for Haj and Umrah.

If the walls had been flooded with posters demanding uninterrupted power supply, proper water and sewage systems, or schools and parks, the world would have perhaps been a better place. Perhaps. Instead, they railed on about distant America. America, the country that destroyed Iraq after luring it to attack Kuwait, America that supports the Jews in Israel, America that has taken over Saudi Arabia and has made all these Arab rulers its puppets.

One that stood out among the other, mostly harmless ones was allegedly sponsored by the local councillor. He had made his name by climbing on towers and water tanks, and lying in front of bulldozers to stop the demolition of homes in yet-to-be-regularised parts of Jamia Nagar. He had cases against him but probably didn't expect (or did he?) that a simple blue-and-white poster in Urdu would bring the police to his door.

He termed the WTC attack Osama's answer to America's terrorism. In his new poster, he also mocked Prime Minister Atal Bihari Vajpayee for the eagnerness of a few of his cabinet members to be part of Bush Jr's War on Terror. It read:

> *Pandit Ji (Atal Bihari Vajpayee), tum kaun?*
> *Mein Khah Ma Khah.*
>
> Pandit Ji, who are you?
> I am uninvited.

No one gave a damn about these posters usually, certainly not the police. But so soon after 9/11, the name Osama raised hackles. Internationally, Bush Jr waved his magic wand to flush out terrorists, and locally, many ended up in jail for pasting these posters – including the councillor. The police also slapped the Prevention of Terrorism Act, or POTA (now replaced by the almost-identical Unlawful Activities Prevention Act, UAPA), on him. The charge against him was spreading enmity between communities.

On the day he was arrested, as the US was contemplating the beginning of what would become its never-ending war of peace, the police also raided the SIMI headquarters in Zakir Nagar and arrested its leaders. The government then banned the organisation by an executive order. SIMI had denounced bin Laden's attack, but its statement, reportedly, came with ifs and buts.

Anyway, after the WTC attack, the conscience-keeper of the world had invaded Afghanistan and dismantled the Taliban and Al-Qaeda. Now, six years later, the bearded man was back on our campus. His name still evoked sharp reactions here.

At one level, it was hard for many to believe that someone named Osama even existed and that he was a Muslim. He must be a US creation, the argument went. They trained him, used him against the Soviets after glorifying him as a Mujahid, and now are using him to further their military–industrial complex, and to bring conflicts into Asia, where energy and future powers are. Why else does this guy always release a video when the US government most needs it? Like just before the elections. What purpose do bin Laden's videos serve for the Muslim world that he claims to represent?

On that day of the screening, I had hoped the movie might give us some clarity. What an anti-climax! The movie was about a girl in Afghanistan whose male relatives had died in the various wars, so she had to masquerade as a male to find a job and feed her family. When the Taliban forcibly recruited all the local boys, she had no choice but to attend their camp to keep up her disguise. A boy from her locality recognised her and, understanding her predicament, named her Osama. It was only towards the end that her identity was revealed.

I sat there in the auditorium, sullen, thinking: this khatmal vice chancellor can only find ways to show Muslims in a bad light. *Chutiya bana diya khatmal ne*. He's made a fool of us.

Months had passed since then. Months in which the objects of our crushes found other boys, we failed many tests, thought up and discarded several business ideas, the regimes in many countries changed, but this man Osama was not willing to leave us to ourselves. Even when he himself was on the run.

'So, janab, you think Osama did the right thing?' Perwez asked. He got an approving nod from Kafil.

They were familiar with my rhetoric. What option did he have? Haven't you seen what they are doing in Palestine? What these Western powers have done in Serbia? Chechnya? You have no idea how many children they have killed in Iraq by putting sanctions on them. Who supplied Saddam with the arms and bombs that he used to attack Kuwait? There was silence for a moment after my rant, which channelled sentiments I had unquestioningly internalised – even though the world I imbibed them from had moved on since then. At least for me, the hurt ghetto, in retrospect, was succeeding in what a hurt ghetto can do. I broke the silence. 'It's about the cause.'

'But how is killing someone justified?' asked Kafil, a staunch Gandhian in a generation that no longer believed in the old man. He found some of Gandhi's actions strange, but the honesty with which Gandhi had written about himself impressed Kafil more than anything. Besides, he had never lived in a ghetto before. Having lived most his life in an oil refinery in Mathura, his memories of an unjust world, unlike the residents of ghettos, were less bitter. (Except for when the Hindu rightwing shouted slogans like '*Ayodhya to ek jhanki hai, Kashi Mathura abhi baaki hai.*' The demolition of Babri Masjid is just a glimpse, wait until you see what we do in Mathura and Varanasi.)

'Isn't there something in the Quran that says something like killing a man is like killing humanity itself?' asked Perwez. He was not someone we expected would cite the Quran, but he still remembered a few things from his childhood or his time at AMU.

'Of course, killing innocent civilians is wrong. It is no answer to the problems. But his cause is just,' I responded.

'No one says that what's happening in Palestine is right. But the way Osama is responding is not right,' said Kafil. 'It's just wrong.'

'But what's the way then? Have they listened to anything said peacefully? And do you think Osama's response is without provocation?' I asked.

They searched for a response.

The ghetto was not homogeneous, but it was slowly homogenising the vast experiences and diversities of its residents. Its continued existence was in response to hurt and humiliation; beyond what was going in the larger world, there were the memories of violent riots in our backyard, the experiences of discrimination in housing and jobs in modern India, and there was fear of the Other – the Other that feared the ghetto equally. There was a degree of truth in what the ghetto believed, what the ghetto feared, what the ghetto said (publicly or privately). But what had the potential to make it dangerous was the juxtaposition of these beliefs and experiences and fears with violent messages and violent memories.

Intentionally or unintentionally.

'Have you ever heard of any Indian fighting global jihad in Afghanistan? Or any Muslim from mainland India fighting even in Kashmir? You hear about these terrorist networks. What about Babri? Gujarat? Have you seen those videos?' I was shouting and I didn't even know it.

They wanted to say something. But they saw my wet, red eyes.

We lay on the mattress in silence. I stared at the ceiling fan, and tried to figure out if it was turning clockwise or anti-clockwise. At some point, I fell asleep.

August 2008. As usual, we had planned to assemble at my place after attending an on-campus screening of a documentary on Salwa Judum. Salwa Judum, translated as either Peace March or Purification Hunt in the language of the Gond tribals, was a group of militia mobilised by the government to counter Naxalite violence in Chhattisgarh. Ordinary people were trapped in between. The documentary was gloomy and our heads were filled with its tragic images. The silence was broken by a squeak. '*Kya haal kar rakha hai yaar wahan pe.*' What have they done over there. It was appalling how little we knew about what was happening in our own country.

Our overflowing gutter was a privilege gone wrong, but a privilege nevertheless – our abode was intact, a home we could return to every evening, no matter the erratic electricity, overcrowded streets, lack of civic facilities like parks, banks or schools. So much better than being displaced from one's habitat to live within soulless concrete walls in lands far away – physically and emotionally. Living in a ghetto was better than being on the run, for life, for dignity. We reached home and realised the power was off, no surprise. We settled down in my dimly lit home, sweat pouring from every part of our bodies. There was lots of noise outside, and kids playing in the street because their homes were dark. As we lay still, lost somewhere in Chhattisgarh, the sounds outside were broken by the sudden hum of fans and coolers: power had been restored. The kids vanished inside to watch TV and the street returned to normal. We passed around the bottle of cold drink and cursed the shopkeeper because it wasn't cold enough.

The power revealed to us a dirty fan going berserk, from still to slow to noisy-humming at its top speed, but hardly enough to create a flutter in the spider web that decorated my ceiling.

Furquan, our friend from Biotech, switched on the music application on my desktop. Junoon's 'Sayonee' blared out. We all used to love this song, but Perwez loved it so much that he put it on loop every day and now we were tired of it. So Furquan shifted to a playlist he had got recently. The notes of 'Sunday Bloody Sunday' emerged from the injured, unwilling speaker. The cooler added its considerable voice to the air. A noisy silence prevailed. Suddenly, a rat emerged from the stack of newspapers and scurried up to Rameez. His eyes following the rat's confused sprint, Rameez got on my case. 'Neyaz babu, do something about it,' he said. 'They are dangerous; they have sharp teeth and run very fast. Someday it will bite your already cut thing.' This brought the others to life as well. Asbah added, 'And then you will keep singing Sunday Bloody Sunday.'

Everyone laughed.

'Arrey, at least Neyaz babu will finally get his thing cut,' said Alim. 'Anyway, he isn't a Musalman. Never goes to namaz. *Kam se kam isi bahane Musalman to ban jayega*.'

None of us offered daily namaz, but somehow I was the one who had gained notoriety for it.

'He reads *The Hindu*,' Asbah added. 'Batao, what kind of Musalman reads *The Hindu*?'

While we all laughed, Kafil made his contribution: 'Yaar, let's go to Azmat. I am damn hungry. I didn't even have breakfast. Due to this idiot Eco teacher.'

'Oh, Mr Rotulus wakes up. Somebody go and get paratha for him,' said Asbah.

Kafil was called Rotulus because of his roti and paratha fixation, which we believed was why he vanished to his home in Mathura most weekends. In Delhi, he usually had puri in the morning, roti at noon and paratha in the evening. It was a name we bequeathed on him in the first year.

During a Maths lecture, he whispered to Rameez that he was hungry and wanted to have roti (his generic word for food was roti). We were in our Calculus session – a subject we did not understand very much. But we had gathered that integration is an infinite sum of something something. And differentiation is more or less its opposite.

Rameez put this newly learnt Maths skills to practice. 'Aey Kafilwa, go buy roti from the canteen and apply integration on it. It will turn into paratha.'

Shyam added, 'And use differentiation on the roti to make it into a puri. Your breakfast issue solved.'

After that scholarly banter, the learned men called Kafil 'Rotulus'. From Biology, he was bestowed with the scientific name, *Rotulus rotifera*. A unique species.

As we roused ourselves to go to Azmat, someone knocked on the door.

I opened it, and saw four or five men standing at the gate in skull caps. I regretted not peeking through the window to check. They said salam and reached out to shake my hand. I responded.

Inside, my friends went quiet. These people were jamatis, the men who stroll the streets to talk to people about Islam.

Though none of us was averse to their teachings and piety, we were hungry and in no mood to go to the masjid with them. But I was stuck. One of them introduced me to the head of the group, Ameer.

Ameer Sahib took over. 'What is your name, beta?'

Neyaz Farooquee.

'Alhamdulillah Alhmadulillah. Nice name. Do you know the meaning of Neyaz?' Before I could say yes, he offered, 'Caring. Offering.'

I nodded, summoning a courteous smile.

'And you pronounce it well too.' As a child, I had been taught by maulana sahab the phonetic difference between J and Z or Ph and F or K and Q.

'We have come in Allah ki raah. To neyaz him our services,' he continued. 'Nothing happens without the Almighty willing it. He has made all the creatures in this world, the sky, the earth, animals, humans. Khudaband-wa-ta'ala made us humans and we should be thankful to Him. We all are sinners. We all commit sins which we don't even realise.'

I knew where this was going. He held my hand affectionately and spoke for a while, on Islam, God and Prophet Muhammad. He then said, 'Why don't you come with us.' I knew the drill: they would walk through the locality until the muezzin called for Maghrib prayers. I didn't want to go with them, knocking on door after door and narrating hadees to unsuspecting people. My friends were giggling now, knowing I was struggling to find a way out. Then the perfect excuse came to me. 'Actually, I have my exams,' I lied. This caused a younger member of the group to smile. He knew the trick I was employing.

Ameer Sahib then said, 'Achha achha. No problem. What do you study?'

Bioscience.

'Masha Allah. May Allah give you success. But you can come for Maghrib prayers at least.'

I knew the language. 'Sure. Sure, Insha Allah.' God willing.

He shook my hand firmly and went next door. 'Insha Allah.' God willing.

I knew I was not going. The guilt of lying lingered only a little; I had become shameless even in my own eyes, so there was no point pretending.

We waited quietly inside for the jamatis to move on so that it would be safe to sneak out. Perwez suggested that we leave from the other side. '*Bahut der ho gayi, bhook lag gayi hai, chalo iman taza karte hain*,' he joked. (It's quite late, and I'm hungry. Let's freshen our faith, our conscience.)

The tasty buff kebabs at Azmat certainly freshened up our iman. They would anyone's – they used to be that tasty. On TV was a discussion about India's nuclear deal with the

US. I mumbled, 'This government will surrender the country to America.'

'Like you keep surrendering your heart to girls?' asked Rameez. '*Yeh lo, yeh lo, tum bhi lo.*'

Asbah chuckled, then asked, 'What do you mean, selling the country to the US?'

'I am leaving if you guys start it again,' said three voices – Rameez, Kafil and Perwez – in unison. They were not in the mood for our usual debate, having sat through a serious documentary and talk today.

But I carried on. 'They are ready to accept every condition put by the Americans without bothering about what it means for the population here.'

'They need to do it to bypass the sanctions and all. And by the way, they have not accepted every condition of the US,' said Asbah. 'That's simply not true.'

Alim jumped in, 'What sanctions? It's not like Iraq where millions of children died. They are fooling us. What about if there is an accident?'

'The deal is in India's interest only. It will bypass the CTBT we are supposed to sign. Pakistan is not signing, why should we?' asked Asbah.

'So who says sign it? I am just saying that they are selling their phased-out equipment to India when it's hardly being used anywhere else in the world. This makes it all the more dangerous. I read just today about the accident in Russia which killed I don't remember how many. We are not able to cope with Bhopal Gas, do you really think we can cope with a nuclear disaster?' retorted Alim.

'You are getting too pessimistic. The speed at which we are growing, we are in serious need of alternate energy supplies,' said Asbah. 'See, these sanctions are bullying tactics. They will put sanctions on Iran but not on Israel. It's all a power game and India wants to break into that power huddle, that coterie. That's why we need the deal.'

'Fair point,' I weighed in. 'But are we prepared if, god forbid, a disaster like Chernobyl were to happen in a crowded place like India? We are talking about radioactive material.'

Alim turned to Perwez. 'You know the Left is vehemently against the deal, so what's your position? You're from Bengal. Or will you take the side of Bangladesh?' Of course, the nuclear deal had nothing to do with Bangladesh.

Perwez smiled and said he supported the deal.

'But why? When you are from the Left bastion?' asked Alim.

Perwez's family, once influential and wealthy, was torn into two by Partition. A tributary of Teesta divided his world – his branch of the family on one side, the rest on the other, first East Pakistan, then Bangladesh. His family had been fed by the job his grandfather had on the other side, in Dhaka. But Perwez's grandfather chose to stay in India after Partition. Others in the family, too, stayed where they were.

In an instant, people were turned into either a minority or a majority in the place of their birth.

Minority or majority religion.

Minority or majority language.

Minority or majority loyalty.

His family on the Indian side supported the Congress, the default party for most Indians after independence, and Perwez's father used his family's influence to enter politics. But a few decades after Partition, the CPI(M) came to power in West Bengal and harangued those who did not support them. Faced with continuous hostility, the family decided to change their loyalty. Perwez's father quit politics and the family became card-holding communists.

With a red flag flying from the top of their house. Staunchly opposed to imperial powers and bourgeoisie and corporates.

Perwez supported the left parties in their handling of communal issues – compared to other parts of India, West Bengal remained largely free from religious violence under communist rule. However, their economic policies didn't have his support. He had seen the desperate poverty of his state spill over into Aligarh, where he was sent to study for the MBBS entrance exams. He saw that most of the rickshawpullers in Aligarh were from his Bengal. They were mocked by their passengers for their language and accent, and scolded for demanding a rupee extra. Their mocking humiliated him, their scolding angered him. And he carried this feeling with him wherever he went.

'And that's why I don't support the left parties blindly,' he said.

'See, he changed sides,' Rameez said mischievously to pierce the tension. 'He says he is an Indian. You just have to grill him a little bit and he will admit he is a Bangladeshi.' We laughed.

Back home, we had nothing to do, so we decided to watch a movie.

I suggested the newly released *Khuda Ke Liye*.

Hey, get something good to watch, someone said, not this Pakistani movie no one knows. Better we watch a south Indian action movie. Dubbed dhishum dhishum. 'Or still better *Sasura Bada Paisa Wala*,' Rameez laughed. It was a superhit Bhojpuri flick. Suggestions and counter-suggestions followed. Kafil wanted some sci-fi movie but I don't enjoy those much. Perwez suggested *Lion of the Desert*, a favourite of ours.

'Again? No, we are not going to watch another Salwa Judum,' said Kafil. *Lion of the Desert* was a historical flick made in 1981 by a Libyan director but with a Hollywood cast. It was based on the Bedouin leader Omar Mukhtar's struggle against the Italian army in Libya in the years before World War II. The movie was banned in Italy till 2009. 'Let's watch some A-rated movie,' Asbah said with a wink; our joke was that the A in A-rated stood for Ahmad (Perwez).

There was not a single film that came to mind that we hadn't watched, or that someone or the other in the group had no objection to. Finally, we settled on *Omkara*. Everyone loved its dialogues – besides, of course, the acting of Ajay Devgn, Saif Ali Khan and Naseeruddin Shah.

> *Bewkooph aur chutiye mein dhage bhar ka pharak hega bhaiya.*
> *Ghaghrey me ghus ke ho rahi thi phund-raijing?*
> *Saddi ke karad batega, Kesu phirangi.*
> *Sarat ghodon pe lagate hain, kathor.*

But that ran for a few minutes and got stuck. Bad copy. With no option left, we decided to try *Khuda Ke Liye*.

There was lots of good press about the movie in India.

The story was of musician brothers whose paths diverge – partly of their choosing, partly due to fate. The elder brother goes to study music in Berklee and falls in love with an American girl. Around the same time, 9/11 happens and he ends up in jail as a suspect. His interrogator finds a tabeez on him, with Arabic numerals. A tabeez is a small amulet that contains a bit of paper with duas written on it in Arabic.

People tie a tabeez around their neck or arm, to protect them or to fulfil a mannat. Out of the jumble of numbers written on it, the American sleuth picks up two and decodes the numerical values as the date 9/11, when in fact the dua was written using the Arabic system of numerology. It's the same system that gives us the numbers 786.

The tabeez, usually worn by followers of the Sufi tradition, mostly in South Asia, is, in fact, considered by many Muslims to be an un-Islamic addition to the faith.

Meanwhile, the younger brother has turned into an extremist and tries to enforce the selective interpretation of religion to ban music, films, and paintings of humans and animals. He leaves home for what he calls jihad in the tribal belt of Pakistan.

Away from the two brothers, their uncle is in a live-in relationship with an Englishwoman in the UK, having left his Pakistani wife. But he wants his daughter to marry within his own culture. She, however, wants to marry the man she loves, a British non-Muslim. Her father deceives her, bringing her back to Pakistan and marrying her off to his nephew, the musician who is now a militant. The husband forces himself on her when she tries to run away. And the story goes on in this vein ... I loved the elder brother's part because it showed the true facets of Americanism, but I felt that the younger brother's part was an exaggeration.

Some of my friends challenged me, saying that such things did happen in our society. They felt the movie was somewhat weak on the story front, but that it tried to question stereotypes by taking them head-on.

I thought they had no idea what they were talking about. But you can't just throw your friends out of your home. While we debated, the power went out again. Rameez left for his uncle's place close by. Kafil and Perwez stayed on at my place, as did Asbah.

It was hot enough that we decided to go for a walk. There is no place in Jamia Nagar where you can sit and talk, except the tea shops, so we decided to walk to the stinking Yamuna bank, just a few hundred metres away – the only place around that has some open space to walk in. There was a battalion of the UP police posted near the canal. On the other side, the lights of the UP government officers' residential quarters glowed bright. The mowed lawns along the side of the canal hosted men – and a few women – from those quarters (on an after-dinner walk), Batla House residents (on a power-cut walk) and mosquitoes (on a malaria and dengue flight).

We sat on the bridge constructed over the canal (Opened by Sir William Muir K.C.S.I., March 1874) and watched the monsoon-river sound, heard the far-off darkness. The jungle of water-hyacinth in the water below was not visible at this hour. In the daytime, teenagers jumped into the canal and emerged covered in white pollution-foam – that too was lost in the darkness. A mandir on the riverbank blared out hymns set to Bollywood tunes. Policewallahs camping there played volleyball while people took their walks. Men and women sold roasted corn on handcarts or ice cream from ice boxes. These vendors were not allowed to come too close to the canal or park along it. And we sat on the bridge, arguing with each other – and the mosquitoes. It would be our last walk together to the canal. A few days later, among those trails of light behind us, the police encounter would take place. And suddenly the few minutes' walk in the darkness to the Yamuna would become menacing. We would stop venturing outside in the dark, let alone to the quietness of the riverbank, near a camp of policemen.

After the encounter, I decided I wanted to be a journalist. I started preparing for the entrance exam to Jamia's AJK Mass Communication Research Centre (MCRC), in the hope that the 25 per cent quota for Jamia undergrads would help me – not knowing how tough the competition in that quota was going to be. A good number of undergrads in Jamia, it turned out, aspired to the MCRC.

As a precaution, I also appeared for the MSc Bioscience and MBA entrance tests. It was a continuous dilemma for students like us – Bioscience and Biotech undergraduates – whether to go in for an MSc or to take up a job or enrol in a professional course. Rameez and Shyam were clear they wanted to do an MSc and then a PhD. Alim, also affected by the encounter, wanted to study journalism at first but then changed his mind and continued his studies in Biology.

No one knew what Kafil wanted, perhaps he didn't either. MSc or MBA or opening a garage (to satisfy his love for automobiles) or taking up a job. He eventually landed in MSc Bioinformatics, with his garage-love still alive.

Of our group, Asbah had always been the most focused. He had wanted be a doctor like his father, and his second choice was to join the National Defence Academy. He couldn't clear the last stage of the NDA, and so enrolled in BSc Bioscience. By the final year, he made up his mind to pursue an MBA, and joined a coaching centre.

Confused, Perwez and Furquan were considering MBA as well. But after the encounter, Perwez returned to Bioscience for a Masters, while Furquan turned to journalism.

I sensed that my parents were beginning to feel a bit let down by the lack of any substantial achievement on my part, so I decided that I wouldn't ask for coaching fees and the like.

Jamia's journalism course required candidates to have a portfolio of work experience or internship and participation in co-curricular activities. I had nothing. I heard they considered photography as part of one's portfolio, and so bought a small digital camera and started clicking pictures around the campus and neighbourhood.

Besides Jamia, I wrote the entrance tests for two other journalism institutes and cleared both. One of these institutes required, as part of the admission process, the candidates to present interviews with media practitioners. I knew not one journalist personally.

I asked my professor, Seemi Farhat Basir, who was the head of the Biosciences department, to help me. Her husband taught at the MCRC, and she promptly called him. I'm not sure what he said, but she responded with: 'I don't know. He is my boy. You help him out. You figure out how to do it.'

I had not done a single assignment or a single test properly, and didn't deserve this kindness.

Her husband put me in touch with many media practitioners and teachers. Two senior journalists gave me well-intentioned advice: journalism is not worth it, especially if you can do an advanced degree in Biotechnology. 'If you were my son, I would never advise you to go for it,' said one who had worked in All India Radio for about two decades.

Another said, 'Go to the US and get a good degree in your subject of study. Come back in a few years and work with the youth to do something constructive in the country. I know you are frustrated with things. But let me tell you, journalism will not let you do what you want to do and you will only get more frustrated. It doesn't pay either.' He had been writing on international affairs for many respected newspapers in India for some thirty years. When he figured out that I lived alone, away from my parents, he said, 'Beta, if you feel you need a guardian for your interview, tell me, I will accompany you. If you need money, you tell me. But think well before changing your field of study.'

In the end, I didn't join the college because of their exorbitant fees. By now I knew it would take me years as a journalist to pay back a loan.

That made it more important for me to concentrate on Jamia. Also, Jamia had a two-year degree, which would make me eligible to teach at university level – another layer of security if I failed as a journalist.

To boost my meagre portfolio of photography, I thought about doing an internship. But I couldn't really go back to the professionals I had met earlier, having disregarded their advice. I started calling newspapers. Before calling, I practised what I would say in my broken English. It kept improving as I made calls; I had to make many calls, from one department to the other, from one edition to the other. I started with newspapers where I thought I would stand a chance – *The Telegraph*, *The Statesman*, *The Indian Express*, *Hindustan Times*, *Times of India* – not necessarily in this order, but they all told me they were not hiring interns. One of them told me they were taking interns, and asked for my name and college. The person on the phone paused, and said: 'Sorry. Come next year.'

Finally I called one of the newspapers that I often read, and never hoped to land an internship with. I dialled the number that was listed in the newspaper. They kept transferring my call from one person to the other. Just when I found someone who was willing to talk to me, the balance in my cell got exhausted and the call got disconnected. I recharged and apprehensively called the number again. I reached the same person again after a few call transfers. He had a scary voice, but told me to write down an email address: 'Write to this gentleman. He will tell you more about internships.'

I knew this could be my only chance to live my modified-by-encounter dream. I wrote to the gentleman in ambiguous words that might suggest I was being recommended by Mr Scary Voice. I didn't lie but I didn't tell the whole story. However, in another way I was extra forthcoming with information: I made sure to put my place of residence in the infamous Batla House prominently in the body of the mail and in my resume.

I waited for the application to be rejected.

The newspaper responded by asking for a bonafide certificate from my college. Again, I went to Seemi ma'am, and once again she promptly gave me the certificate, no questions asked.

By the following week, I was interning at the newspaper.

12

The Cache of Memories

AFTER UN-JOINING THE PAGES on Orkut, I looked around my house to see if there was anything that could be taken as evidence of a jihadi presence. News reports had said the Terrorists had jihadi literature (though this turned out to be a copy of the *Panchatantra*, according to the information provided when my senior at Jamia, Afroz Alam Sahil, filed an RTI request).[19] We didn't know what the police meant by jihadi material. Our guess was that anything in Urdu or Arabic would fit the bill.

I had piles of Urdu magazines, on poetry, Islam, science. There were books of Islamic studies from my school days that I had not thrown away or sold as scrap because they talked about sacred subjects like Allah, Muhammad and Islam. When I looked at them with media-coloured and police-coloured eyes, they seemed suspicious.

Many reports drew attention to the number of buckets in the Terrorists' flat. Buckets? I had some too. In the bathroom and outside. Regular water supply was unreliable, so I stored a few extra litres for emergencies. No way I'd wake up early in the morning to switch on a pump when the municipality supplied water. Besides, I used to wash my clothes by hand, so I needed buckets for this too.

In one corner of the rack lay Ayaz's tools, exactly where he had left them three years ago. To me, these appeared very similar to the materials with which the Terrorists allegedly assembled bombs. Ayaz was interested in assembling and disassembling engines, motors and just anything mechanical or electronic. He had ruined my radio and rendered useless an emergency light that Abbu had bought for us to study by night, given the erratic power supply. He had short-circuited a water pump. He had built his own mini-fan using mini-motors he had bought from a nearby electrical repair shop. I had no explanation for why these odds and ends should be lying around. And I didn't know how to dispose of them.

The reports also said the Terrorists had many travel bags in their flat, suggesting that they sheltered Terrorist-friends from out of town and were themselves given to travelling to different cities in India to plant bombs. It was as if none of these reporters had ever lived the life of a middle-class Indian student. My own bag served as a cupboard. Often, there were other bags lying around, from when friends, relatives and acquaintances stayed over – a free dormitory. Few students I knew bothered with a cupboard because their landlords could ask them to leave any time; late payment of rent, too much noise, flat sold. Items that were difficult to move were considered a liability.

I had a permanent address, but I hadn't bought a cupboard either. I would like to believe it was because I preferred a minimalist lifestyle – laziness was the more likely explanation, though.

Then there was my suitcase in a corner of the room.

My small black suitcase.

The one treasure that had lasted from the time I moved to Delhi. My (little) past preserved in it (and, if I was questioned, I had no justifable reason for why I had preserved it). I had not visited this section of my past since Dada died in December 2005.

It reminded me of the hopes he had had for his grandson. It reminded me of my failure. It reminded me of the excuses, the lies that I told him and the others in the family.

It reminded me of the twinkle in Dada's eyes when he bought general knowledge books for me. He knew it would take more than general knowledge to clear the IAS entrance exam, but these were all he could find in the bookshops he searched. He had bought the suitcase for me when he came to visit a few months after I arrived in Delhi.

Black and small, appropriate for me; I could carry it around easily. It was safe and classy. There were no wheels on it, to my disappointment.

But it was my Swiss bank.

No one knows its code.

Nope, it's not 786.

No! Not even 092.

I won't tell you.

Some nights after the encounter, I felt the walls of the house closing in on me. At some point that night, I decided to finally open the suitcase. I sat on the floor, under the dim bulb, to inspect the potential jihadi evidence from my past. It was well past midnight, so I had switched off all the lights except the dimmest one; I didn't want to alarm anyone. A newspaper had reported that the lights in the Terrorists' flat used to be on until late at night. The bulb's glow was just enough for the mirror above the washbasin to reflect a scared ghost who was trying to summon a brave face to deceive his panicked heart.

The suitcase had three locks, but I couldn't find the keys. I had kept them somewhere safe, I knew – but where? They were not between the encyclopaedias. Not in the drawer of the rack. Not on the ventilator window.

I tried a kitchen knife on the middle lock. It wouldn't open. I tried a nail-cutter that Abbu had brought from Saudi Arabia. It did the trick. Then, the two side locks – clack clack – and the upper half of the suitcase jumped up a little, as if trying to escape.

The left lock had a peeling sticker with N, the right one had an A. N for Neyaz, A for Ahmad. These had satisfied the kid who had stuck them on about a decade ago that his suitcase was identifiable and safe, and that it was his. His.

The hinges of the suitcase let out a shrieking protest as I opened it further. A layer of dust that had been covering my memories escaped (as normal dust particles do) and embraced me. I coughed a little – a momentary lapse in my resolve not to disturb the silence outside.

That very moment the streetlight outside went off. Eerie.

As if I wasn't scared enough already.

No sound followed the sudden darkness. No knocking on the door or storming of it as I half-expected. I looked at the latch of the tin door and assured myself that it was bolted, and then fearfully peeked through the window. There were no dark shadows.

The street lights came back on while I was still at the window. For the first time, I realised that the bulbs used in those lights were heat-sensitive; they went off automatically when they heated up and came back on when they had cooled down.

Cursing and feeling fairly foolish, I sat down on the floor again to continue my trip down memory lane.

Inside the suitcase were letters, postcards, silliness, newspaper-clippings, innocence, pens, photos, coins – and the remains of a few other small treasures that I had once possessed.

In a flap, I found a visiting card holder and in it a photo and a visiting card of Baaji's husband, a pious man who sported a beard. Dada and Abbu wore beards too, and both were (unsaid, unasked) role models for me. But in the last few years, the beard had come to carry a negative connotation in India, just as madrasas were all painted with a single brush as schools for training terrorists. When Osama flaunted his beard on TV screens across the world, spouting violent messages, the beard was no longer seen as a sign of a Muslim man's honesty and piety.

Also in that flap was a paint brush I had bought – I felt I should have a hobby because my classmates would have some too. Like gardening, which didn't initially strike me as a hobby, being a villager. It would have been easy enough in my village, but in Delhi, where was I to plant anything?

A few classmates were fond of singing. That wasn't for me. You have the voice of a beggar, Chhoti Ammi would joke. Even beggars sing better naat sharif than he does, my cousins would say.

Baaji was a good singer, and on Independence and Republic days, she would compose naat and patriotic songs to the tune of Bollywood songs. Dada, unaware of the trespassing, loved her compositions. For many in our village, she was the gold standard for goodness: Nabib Miyan's granddaughter, she is good at everything. She is a topper, cooks well, knows how to stitch clothes in all these new styles the filmi heroines wear these days.

Painting seemed like a good idea, as long as I avoided what should be avoided – drawing the living. And so I had bought paints and brushes. But, of course, Baaji was better at that too, and the stuff lay unused inside in my suitcase and dried up.

The suitcase had a letter that was meant for Farooquee Sahab Dehlavi – Delhi'ite. It was Baaji's revenge for jokingly calling her a Bihari.

There was a pocket-sized diary in the suitcase. Its last page said:

Neyaz Ahmad Farooquee
Jamia Middle School
Jamia Millia Islamia
Jamia Nagar
New Delhi – 25
1998–99

There were illegible scribbles inside and some jokes that I had jotted down from magazines.

Inspector: If your dog has forgotten, then why are you not advertising in newspaper?
Master: My dog is uneducated.

Customer: What's this, you have sugar in a sack marked salt?
Shopkeeper: Sshh, I did it to fool the ants.

Ma: Son, why are you still sleeping? Look, the sun is up.
Beta: But, mom, the sun goes to sleep before I do.

There was one page titled 'Some facts about the human body', and a two-page description of the cleaning ritual required before reading the Quran or offering namaz: 'Notes on Ablution (wudu)'. One of the pages had 786/92 written on top.

Tucked into a diary was an unsent letter to the Children's Trust of India, Chandigarh, asking for its prospectus. I had seen an ad in which they had offered a scholarship to a deserving candidate.

There were a few train reservation slips, the negative of a passport photo – my first photo in Delhi – a few phone bills from STD booths, a few booklets that came free with Britannia biscuits and featured the schedule of the 1999 cricket world cup. Inside one of these booklets, I had noted down, 'Elizabeth Blackwell was the first lady doctor of the world.'

There was a page with incomplete Dua-e-qanoot that's read during the evening prayers or in times of difficulty or calamity. Another page listed some web addresses.

- Saregama.com
- www.hinduonline.com & www.the-hindu.com
- http://www.dailypioneer.com
- www.hindustantimes.com
- www.indiatimes.com

On the other side, I had noted a few quiz questions gathered from newspapers and magazines, among them these:

Who among the following played the role of Hanuman in the TV serial Ramayana? (A) Guru Hanuman (B) Praveen Kumar (C) Dara Singh (D) Bharadwaj

Who among the following received a Nobel prize and wrote, 'We learn from history that we learn nothing from history?' (A) G.B. Shaw (B) Winston Churchill (C) ------- (D) Ernest Hemingway.

There were two small chits. One with Abbu's address in Saudi Arabia, and the other with Chhote Abbu's. And a community library card for Mr Neyaz Ahmad. Age twelve. Not transferable.

At the bottom of the suitcase was a sheet of paper with a few couplets that I had written and compositions written by others that I had liked. Most of these expressed innocuous thoughts – on not being pious enough or being betrayed by a friend (who didn't share his notes with me when I could not attend classes due to illness or because I was away in my village).

Kabhi bhool kar kisi se na karo salook aisa,
Ki jo koi tum se karta tumhe na-gawaar hota.

Never treat someone in such a manner,
That if he did the same, it would pain you.

Ek zindagi amal ke liye bhi naseeb ho,
Yeh zindagi to nek iraadon mein hi kat gayi.

May the Almighty grant me a life for deeds,
I spent this life only in intentions.

Koshish kare insaan to kya ho nahi sakta,
Woh kaun sa aqda hai jo hal ho nahi sakta.

Nothing is impossible if man tries,
There is nothing that he can't defy.

There were more. And these couplets ranged from pure jingoism to Islamism. Jingoism was, well, okay, but now, years later, I was not sure where Islamism would land me. And how it would read to someone who didn't know me.

Khuda ki qasam, na jaane denge Kashmir hum,
Allah ko napasand ho to faryad karenge hum.

Swear to God, we won't let Kashmir go,
If God doesn't like that, we'll pray to Him so.

I even had a list of addresses and telephone numbers of important leaders of the country, copied from general knowledge magazines. K.R. Narayanan, Krishna Kant, I.K. Gujral, Mulayam Singh Yadav, P. Chidambaram, Ram Vilas Paswan. I don't know why I had kept it. Maybe just the innocent thrill of knowing where big people lived.

The police often claimed that they had recovered contacts, addresses, maps and passports from terrorist hideouts. Could my list be taken as a list of targets? A diary has been found with names of prominent leaders who were to be assassinated.

There were newspaper clippings, numbers 9 and 28 of a series on Olympians. On Dhyan Chand and Leander Paes. There was a clipping from *Sahara*, an Urdu newspaper, titled 'Malumaat-e-Aamma', General Knowledge.

There was an NBT book club membership form. An unfilled CSR Quiz Game 1 entry form. A fountain pen and a few refills.

I riffled through the paper-clippings and memories. There was a pen that Abbu had gifted me. It had a dollar bill printed on it. Mr Washington with his perpetual smile occupied most of the space. I had used the pen only on special occasions like when writing a letter or making a note in my diaries – that was as frequent as the yearly Eid. It protested when I scribbled on my palm to see if there was still any life left in it.

I was expected to understand the meaning of the pen as a gift.

The ink of a pen is holier than the blood of a martyr. Not that I was taught to be a martyr or anything, but one was supposed to know the hadees and know what's more important.

There were also a few sketchpens that had given up on life, waiting in vain to be used. Some peeped out shyly from under a paper clipping that talked about some satellite reaching some planet in some damn year. Other sketchpens playfully skated over coins that lay scattered in the suitcase.

One rupee, two rupees, five paise, ten paise, twenty paise.

Many of the coins were the ones that Dadi had given me the day I was leaving for Delhi that first time.

A piece of chewing gum, forgotten, had crawled out of its wrapper and was now stuck between one of the coins and a paper-clipping that taught English.

There was also an autograph book and a few broken chalks – I had no idea why I kept the chalks. The book was blank, except for its first page, which read:

> School is my mosque,
> Teachers are my hearts,
> Study of medical is my aim,
> Neyaz Ahmed is my name.

I had bought the autograph book when I got to know that the cricketer Virender Sehwag was coming to Jamia to play a match. *He is from Jamia, you know. I will take his autograph.* But the stupid exams spoilt everything. Like they had many planned Eid visits to the village.

There was a pocket diary that had the names of encyclopaedias I wanted to buy. The school librarian didn't allow students to take books home.

The school librarian is a witch.

I had listed books that I planned to buy at the book fair. But the titles listed in the diary never reached my bookshelf; they were too costly, some hundreds, some thousands of rupees.

Damn.

The few encyclopaedias that I had were ones that the librarian had helped me buy at a concessional rate from the seller who provided books to the school library. I just had to pay and I would get the book in my next library class.

The school librarian is not a witch.

There was a Teacher's Day memento in the suitcase, a cloth badge in blue-and-white. The blue had lost its blueness, the white its whiteness. A paper pasted on it read, in Urdu: Neyaz Ahmad, Nayab Nigran, Vice Principal. On Teacher's Day, the topper of the previous year got to be the principal of the school, and the second-ranker became the vice principal.

When I started school, I had had an image problem. I was seen as a bookworm, a bright student but a backward Bihari. Many of the classmates mocked my pronunciation: you can't pronounce R and Sh properly, they said. And you Biharis eat rice. As if Biharis are the only ones who eat chawal.

So I told them clearly, 'Don't be so proud of yourselves for eating wheat. You have no idea what you are talking about. You should know that we got thrown out of heaven only because of eating wheat.' Aadam and Hawwa lived in heaven and God threw them out onto Earth because they ate wheat, which they were not allowed to. 'So, don't act very over-smart with me.'

The teachers thought well of me, though, because I looked studious, spoke little, was a loner and hardly ever took part in mischief. All of which would change with time. The year I was made vice principal, my school wasn't able to hold elections to the student union because of violence and bullying that our seniors had indulged in. The topper of class 7 was chosen as sadar of the school, and the second ranker as nayab sadar. The rest were similarly chosen on the basis of exam-based merit.

After the school representatives were announced, the sadar and teachers chose a day to induct the team. The entire school, teachers, students and their parents attended. My parents were not in Delhi, so I went alone.

All the representatives were supposed to wear sherwanis. I didn't want to buy one for just a day, so I borrowed an (oversized) sherwani from an AMU alumnus. But by the time I managed to arrange it, it was already the morning of the day of the programme and the ceremony had started. I knew my teachers would shout at me. In desperation, I tried to lighten the mood and save myself humiliation: '*Arey bhai, sabse* important *neta* late *hi ata hai*, security issues *hote hain na. Samjha kijiye.*' The most important leader is always late. Please understand that there are security issues.

Thankfully, even the strictest teacher laughed at this, and the indiscipline was excused. A vice president being reprimanded in front of the cabinet would not have been a good sight. Made to do utthak baithak as punishment or worse, murga – in a sherwani.

In the jumble of stuff in the suitcase, there was a paper that listed a few of the Prophet Muhammad's ninety-nine names, and the benefits each would have if read. Dada had given the names to me.

> Rauf: If read before meeting anyone, he will respect you.
> Haafiz: Good source to avoid all hassles.
> Khaleel: To avoid having bad dreams.
> Qasim: If a person reads it regularly, Allah will make him a scholar. Insha Allah.

And then there was a bundle – perhaps the most important treasure I possessed. Of yellowing papers, held together with a rubber band, wrapped in some old newspaper. These were the speeches I had given in my school in Bihar on Independence and Republic days. Songs, naat shareef, qaumi ekta geet. In Baaji's handwriting, in Dada's handwriting. It was a kind of inheritance. Baaji read these speeches when she was growing up in the late 1980s and early '90s. I repeated them in the latter half of the '90s, and some of them were passed on to my younger siblings.

In Baaji's day, the speeches were called bhashan, the Hindi word, but when I was repeating them, they had become taqreer, the Urdu word. Swatantrata Diwas was replaced by Yaum-e-Azadi, and Gantantra Diwas by Yaum-e-Jamhuri.

The Hindi–Urdu divide that, without doubt, represented more than just a linguistic divide had finally reached my home – about half a century after it had other parts of north India.

Baaji's schooldays coincided with tumultuous times in the history of Indian plurality. The Bhagalpur riots in Bihar were allegedly a brazen misuse of power by the police, colluding with Vishwa Hindu Parishad gangs, under a Congress government.[20] BJP leader L.K. Advani's Rath Yatra – in which he travelled the country in a chariot to garner support for demolishing Babri Masjid to build a Ram temple in Ayodhya – was around this time too.

The yatra was a Gabbar moment for us kids. Elders warned us not to play in the vicinity of the village Eidgah, which the rath was supposed to pass on its way. They told us that if we disobeyed them and went to play there, the heavy rath would crush us.

The rath didn't come anywhere near us, though, because somewhere far from our village a new chief minister, Lalu Prasad Yadav, had come to power. His success was based on the discontent of Muslims after the Bhagalpur riots combined with backward-caste mobilisation. When Advani's rath yatra reached the borders of Bihar, Lalu stopped him, interrupting the flow of violence that had followed the rath across the country. With this one action, overnight, Lalu became a hero among the leaderless Bihari Muslims. We realised only years later what that rath of our childhood had signified, and what exactly it had crushed beneath its wheels.

Thinking back, I believe this was when Dada began to reflect upon his identity like never before. He hadn't gone to Pakistan when Partition happened, choosing to stay on in the land where he was born – where he belonged and which belonged to him. As a young man in search of a livelihood, he aspired to work in the jute mills of Bengal. He was in Calcutta when the riots broke out before the eventful day when the British finally left. He had witnessed and escaped mobs on the rampage, looking for anyone from the 'other side' to kill.

About half a century later, Dada's struggle with identity showed in the speeches – taqreer, as he now called it – he wrote for us.

Earlier, I spoke about Guru Nanak, Mahatma Gandhi, Jawaharlal Nehru, Rajendra Prasad, Abul Kalam Azad, Khan Abdul Ghaffar Khan, Indira Gandhi. Now, the list increasingly featured Maulana Mohammad Ali Jauhar, Maulana Shibli Nomani, Sir Syed Ahmed Khan, Muhammad Iqbal, Maulana Mazharul Haque and Prophet Muhammad.

The Good Muslim was clearly disappointed.

Yet, in that bundle from the suitcase was a page in his own handwriting, titled 'Qaumi Ekjehti', National Unity. I had given this speech one Independence Day. It started with a couplet:

Gul haae rang rang se hai raunaqe chaman,
Ae zauq is chaman ko hai zeb ikhtilaf se.

The many colours of flowers brighten the garden,
This garden's beauty lies in its diversity.

Another page, attached to the speech, had its own couplet:

Hasrat yahi hamari hain hum desh pe mar mitt jayein,
Desh ki khatir kam ayein hum mange yahi dua'en.

I wish I may live and die for my country,
I pray that I may be useful to my country.

The bundle also had songs that Baaji had sung during her school functions (when my turn came, I reproduced some to vastly lesser effect). There was one in her handwriting, with some errors in the scribbling. Titled 'Qaumi Ekta Geet', it was a song Abbu had heard somewhere in Mumbai, while he was job-hunting, and had brought for Baaji. It went:

> *Sawaro mil ke Hindustan suno ae Hindu Musalman bas itna yaad rahe*
> *Hamen ab ekta ke wastey har zulm sehna hai.*
> *Qasam hai ishq ulfat ki hamen mil jul ke rehna hai.*
> *Mohabbat dharm hai apna mohabbat ma ka gehna hai.*
>
> Let's build India together, O Hindus and Muslims remember,
> We must bear every atrocity for the sake of our unity,
> We swear by the longing for our love to stay together,
> Love is our religion, love is our mother's jewel.

The poem ended abruptly. It was only for her to take to practice on the day when she would lead the singing of it on stage.

The other side of the page was headlined '15 August Swatantrata Diwas'. It went on to say in Hindi, with some spelling errors: '15 August is Independence Day but it is also a day of sorrow, because on this day our land, our youth, our rich, our wise were all divided in two. The divisive policies of the British succeeded. In the name of religion, rivers of blood flowed. The pledge of Hindu–Muslim unity lost its worth. The hopes of Mahatma Gandhi remained unfulfilled … Jai Hind.'

The speeches that Dada wrote for us, and the naats and ghazals we sang, often started or ended with a patriotic couplet that celebrated diversity. In one, there was this couplet by Iqbal:

Na samjhoge to mit jaoge ae Hindustan walon
Tumhari dastan tak na hogi dastanon mein.

You will be annihilated if you don't mend your ways,
O people of India
Even your existence will disappear from people's
consciousness.

For another speech, he wrote for me the composition of Chakbast Brijnarayan who was famous for his poem on the Ramayan. The couplet that he gave me had replaced 'be-kason' (helpless) with 'Hindiyon' (Indians):

Bulbul ko gul mubarak, gul ko chaman mubarak
Hum Hindiyon ko apna pyara watan mubarak
Ghunchey hamarey dil ki isi bagh mein khilenge Is
khak se uthe hain is khak mein milenege.

To the nightingale I wish flowers, and to the flowers
the garden
And to us Indians I wish our beloved homeland
The buds of our heart will blossom only in this garden
I have risen from this soil, and will mingle with it
in the end.

And then there were words that summed up his feeling of being let down; that begged for the community's services to the country to be recognised, and remembered when it mattered. One of my speeches said, '*Tareekh mushahid hai ki jab bhi mulk ko khoon ki zaroorat padi hai, hum ne Hamid ban kar Pakistani tankon ka safaya kiya hai.*' History is witness that whenever the country needed blood, we have razed Pakistani tanks by taking the form of Hamid – the soldier who died fighting the Pakistani army in the 1965 war.

By the time my younger sisters were reading out their speeches, Dada's disappointment had deepened. There was a poem one of them had read:

> *Koi bataye bhi hamein aakhir rehzen ke hai rahbar kyun*
> *Charo janib rah-e-guzar mein aaj bapa hai mehshar kyun*
> *Kisne rachai hai ye shazish ae ahl-e-chaman*
> *Ghoom rahe hain azadi se qatil le ke khanjar kyun*
> *Kam se kam qanoon ke bandey iski wajahat to karey,*
> *Shehr mein jo mash'hoor the mujrim aj baney hain afsar kyun.*

> Someone please tell me why that ruffian is the leader,
> In every direction I look today, I see a spectacle,
> Who set this up, O my countrymen,
> That murderers roam freely with swords in their hands,
> At least the men of justice should explain this,
> Why have those infamous accused become officers.

The suitcase had a few letters from Abbu. They mentioned the bank drafts that he sent for my expenses, reminded me to work hard and live an exemplary life; he wrote of how difficult it was getting to find jobs in Saudi Arabia and he might soon be sent back. There was an undated letter that I had written to Abbu in English. This was my practice draft before I wrote out the final version. It was to show him that his son could now write in Angrezi – the ultimate sign of education, modernity, power – at least that is what villagers like us thought, and still think.

> Dear Father,
>
> Assalam-o-Alaikum,
>
> I am well and hope that you will also well. I am hard working because that is last year in my middle school and also the board exam will in this class. The rule of my school is if any student will not success in board exam he will also out from school.

And a postcard that was meant to be sent as a Letter to the Editor. The copy I had was a scribble for practice; the final version I had sent to the editor – a letter about Lalu Prasad Yadav's political career. Here in Delhi, it saddened me to read that Lalu was involved in corruption and had lost the election in Bihar's Madhepura. So, I wrote a letter to the editor of *Hindustan Times* (coincidentally the same section where I would land my first job) warning Lalua – in villages, he was called Lalua, as Neyaz would become Neyazwa: 'If your performance will continue like this, your party will fall certainly in coming MLA's election of Bihar. And if you will fall in this election, certainly you can't find the majority again in Bihar or anywhere and that will be your decay/downfall and your lantern will be extinguished.' Lantern, his party's symbol. 'So be attentive.'

To my disappointment, the newspaper never published this letter.

Even though the politics in Bihar had changed a lot in the intervening years, many Muslims and Yadavs would still rather vote for Corrupt Lalua, not Secular Congress, not Nationalist BJP.

There was more in the suitcase, and all of it only reminded me of my failure. What I had been and where I was now. I had never been open with Dada or Abbu about the extent of my failure. And now, what if all my coincidental connections to suspects or potential suspects or, indeed, Normal Human Beings, brought the police to my door?

Being reticent with one's elders is not uncommon in our culture. It's part of the reverence that you are supposed to show your elders, especially your father. And I had lived away from Abbu for years now. Before I could reach my teens, I was already in Delhi and then I was denied even the short vacations that Abbu had with us every year and a half or two – mostly during Eids. The vacations meant new clothes from abroad, chocolates, gifts and visits to relatives. Not anymore. Being away from Abbu, from the family, for so many years, I had become disconnected from the world that had sent me here hoping that I would return to enrich it.

When I did manage to meet Abbu, there was never an exchange of 'love you, Dad: love you, my dear son'. It was always there but it remained unsaid, even in the letters that we exchanged. From him, there was only advice: on being a good human, being a good Muslim, or reminding me of the expectations that people had of me. Abbu Ammi Dada Dadi Nani Chacha Chachi Phoopha Phoophi Khala Khaloo and whoever else.

That Eid, after the encounter, Abbu was home for his yearly vacation. I wanted to talk to him but didn't know how to explain all these feelings and fears. But who else could I call, whom could I trust?

How to talk to Abbu, though? On the phone? No, that would not do. And I had already abandoned the idea of leaving Delhi.

The insecurity, the fear, the paranoia if you will – I was not the only one to feel it.

There was something invisible and indescribable in the air. Almost a decade later, it's hard to recall everything, or to understand the effect of the rhetoric and stories that were flying around at the time. There was something, some lurking fear that prevented us from talking to each other freely. Who knew which of us would suddenly land in the police's net? For being an accomplice, an acquaintance … for being who knows what.

That night, I sat looking through my possessions for any clue(s) that might establish me as a Suspect. A Radical. A Terrorist. A Normal Human Being.

The masjids in the neighbourhood began to blare their sirens; sehri time was approaching. Surprisingly, the man who knocked on our doors daily to wake us up – in the hope of getting a few brownie points from God – had not yet come. Not that I relied on him to wake me up, but it was strange not to hear him. He was a middle-aged man who never missed a single roza. His duas and unintelligible wake-up calls caused us to curse him all through the month of Ramazan; he was so loud that he disturbed even those who were fully awake.

God heard our curses (when we least wanted them heard). The sehri-man vanished after the encounter, and we've never heard from him since.

His wake-up calls used to remind me of the qafila in my village. A group of men would walk through the village to wake people up for sehri. They had a loudspeaker mounted on a bicycle, through which they blared naat and Bollywoodised qawalis. I remember hearing them sing:

Ae Chand jab madeene jana
To Nabi se mera salam kehna.
Khuda teri roshni badhaye,
Nabi se mera salam kehna.

When you go to Medina, O Moon
Convey my salam to the Prophet.
May God increase your brightness
Convey my salam to the Prophet.

As children, we pleaded with our elders to wake us up when the qafila passed so that we could get a glimpse of it before it disappeared into the darkness. The naats and songs they sang were also a source of entertainment for the women who were awake and cooking sehri for the family while most men still slept.

On Eid, the qafila troop would come to collect eidi for the work they had done. And if Abbu was home on Eid, they would playfully ask him for a big eidi. 'Chacha, you are earning in Riyal. *Itne se kya hoga. Aur dijiye.*' Chacha would smile and playfully add a meagre sum to elicit a reaction from the young men. Then they would joke that the more chacha earned, the more miserly he was getting. That jibe always worked for them.

The sehri-man in Jamia Nagar too came knocking for eidi but, when he realised I was a student, he smiled and greeted us with an Eid Mubarak and rushed away to the next house.

In the dead silence of that night, I missed his annoying presence. While I sat wondering where he had gone, I heard the sound of an Enfield Bullet. The bike was getting closer. In the middle of the night, in a neighbourhood tainted by a police encounter, the sound of an Enfield, a bike used by the police, was chilling.

I threw all the speeches, letters, coins, newspaper clippings, memories into the suitcase and snapped it shut. A few papers peeked out. I slid the suitcase under the chauki and, reaching for the electric switchboard, slapped it to switch off the lone bulb.

The sound grew and grew. In a flash, I jumped onto the chauki and curled up on it. Then it slowly petered out and stopped. There was now the noise of someone pounding on a door.

Whose days are over, I wondered. Is it the Kashmiris who live a few houses away? Or my cousin who rents a place nearby?

I tried to recall Aytal Kursi. It's recommended reading for every night, more so when one is in distress. It is supposed to safeguard you from everything except death and the wrath of God.

Allah! There is no God but He,
the Living, the Self-subsisting, the Eternal.
No slumber can seize Him, nor sleep.
All things in heaven and on earth are His.
Who can intercede in His presence without His permission?
He knows what appears in front of and behind His creatures.
Nor can they encompass any knowledge of Him except what he wills.

His throne extends over the heavens and the earth,
and He feels no fatigue in guarding and preserving them,
for He is the Highest and Most Exalted.

The noise of the opening of a tin door disturbed my thoughts. I heard the sounds of a brief conversation in the distance. Then of the door shutting ... and silence.

Thank God!

It dawned on me that this was the dude of our lane. He owned an Enfield and stood at gully corners with his friends, making a mental database of all the girls who passed by.

I tried to sleep. There was more in my suitcase that I could not bear to re-see, re-read, re-remember. I tried to think of other things.

Jamia had finally acknowledged that a few of the Terrorists had indeed been enrolled in the university. Most faculty members lived in the locality; they could read the pulse of the community and sense the fear among students. A senior professor was my neighbour. Another neighbour taught at a prestigious college in Delhi University. Attendance at Jamia had dropped, landlords had asked many students to vacate their properties with immediate effect. Lying on the chauki, I thought about the meeting that khatmal vice chancellor had announced. I had no idea why he was calling a meeting and what it would mean for me and other young men like me. Still, it was reassuring that someone was willing to speak to us (publicly) – and to speak on our behalf (publicly).

His press release after the encounter had made clear how difficult his position was. He had been thrashed by Islamists, but that was not enough to assure the world of his patriotism. In the press release, I saw his national award mentioned before his name for the first time:

'Padma Shri Mushirul Hasan,
Vice Chancellor, Jamia Millia Islamia'.

13

This Side, That Side and My Side

THE AJK MASS COMMUNICATION Research Centre is a beautiful island in the tumultuous sea that is Jamia. Its dwellers can stroll down and enjoy the surrounding waters, sail, swim, or laugh at the sea, and come back and say, the sea is salty.

MCRC is one of the best in its field, and it clearly considers itself above the rest. And the Rest starts right outside its gates. Like other elite institutions, it suffers from a certain elite-institution arrogance.

This strikes you the moment you enter. On the very first day.

'The course is in English medium. Can you handle that?'

'We are the best in this country and we won't allow the sort of slackness you might enjoy elsewhere.'

'You will not find this level of instruction, equipment, these facilities anywhere else in this country.'

'We won't allow you to sit the exams if you fall below the required 75 per cent attendance by even half a per cent. Here is the affidavit form. Fill it out, please.'

And so on.

But beyond that, it is accommodating. Of divergent views and ideologies, geography and demography. From the Hindu right to the Muslim right, the Kashmiri separatist to the Kashmiri migrant Pandit. Christian, Hindu, Muslim, Sikh. From Ladakh, Kerala, Manipur. Believers, agnostics, atheists.

It prepares you for the worst that is to come: twelve-hour shifts, miserable working conditions and horrible bosses. It puts your ego in its place and demands the highest standards from you (BBC, *Al Jazeera*, *The New York Times*, *The New Yorker*, Kurosawa, Satyajit Ray, Walter Cronkite, Henri Cartier-Bresson). You are as overworked here as you are likely to be when you join the industry. It teaches you to aspire, not to a utopian world but to a utopian attitude to the journalistic profession.

But first, you have to face MCRC's signature mocktail of concern.

'Yes, Mister,' snaps the course coordinator. As Mr Mister stands at the entrance of the conference room, waiting for permission to enter. 'Why are you late?'

Twenty minutes late. Gunah-e-kabira, no less. On the very first day of the course, when the coordinator was due to spell out his (international) expectations to the twenty hopefuls present in the airconditioned room.

BBC standards. No less. That is the only measure of excellence for His Highness. All India Radio Srinagar briefly had the privilege of his services, but then he left to join the BBC just before militancy started in the valley (pure coincidence, to be clear). After years of service at the network's London office, he is back in India to share his knowledge with us future journalists, and angry at the way things are done here. Being late is one of the biggest no-nos.

So, why am I late?

'Hmm ...' I riffle through my mind for the perfect excuse. 'Sir, bus got delayed in a jam.'

'Where do you come from?'

'Munirka.' That's the far end of south Delhi, more than 10 kilometres from my place. I dare not tell him I live in Batla House.

I have lied to avoid being shouted at, but the sermon continues. 'Well, there are many who come from faraway places. I too come from ...' some place on Delhi's border, 'and I reach on time. Daily.' Silence in the class. 'DAILY.'

Standing at the doorway, I count my toes to assure myself to reassure myself they haven't fleed.

'As a journalist, you are supposed to be punctual. No bulletin will wait for you.' True, but I am already late. What now? 'It's different here. Not like that side of Jamia.'

That side.

That side where my department is. Was. The Department of Bioscience. And many other departments of the university. Like Furquan's biotech. Saiam's social work. Khalid's psychology. And most of the older centres and faculties that make the university a university: natural sciences, social sciences, Nelson Mandela Centre, Sarojini Naidu Centre, etc.

On this side: English and other languages, engineering, architecture, international studies, law, education, etc. And, of course, MCRC. Offering courses in journalism, filmmaking, television, radio, animation, acting, etc. The Brahmin among departments. You may call it the Ashraf too, but then there is no caste or hierarchy among Muslims, you know.

This side demands from you a certain level of excellence.

No mediocrity, no unprofessionalism.

Like being late. (Never mind that just the previous day, our introductory session had started two hours late.) So, I submit. As do the other twenty.

I am allowed to sit in class after a stern warning that is meant for the rest of the class too.

Thus starts my two-year journey.

The introductory sessions were hard for me. I could not help feeling a certain sense of inferiority as I struggled to express my thoughts to different teachers in front of twenty witnesses. The sessions went on for several days. Everyone spoke with a degree of conviction and, most importantly, in fluent English. I was not used to speaking the language of the influential – and sadly, by now, I had lost my fluency even in the languages of my childhood, Urdu and Hindi. Most people here took their knowledge of English for granted, but this was probably the first time I had to speak in English for so long before an audience of strangers.

I knew that what I said was more important than merely speaking correct English, but first impressions depend on presentation. Therefore, I only spoke about things that I thought were unlikely to provoke questions. I would try to keep my statements as short as possible – and my answers were mostly Yeses and Nos.

We were asked to justify in each session why we had chosen to study journalism. As if a two-part entrance test was not enough. As if a twelve-person interview panel was not enough. As if your experience, internships, writings, co-curriculars, etc. – they called it your portfolio – were not enough.

To add to my discomfort, I had committed the greatest offence of all: studying Biosciences as an undergrad. No relation at all between that and journalism, I was reminded. Have you considered your decision properly?

I feared that explaining the true reasons and circumstances for my decision would only lead to further questions, meaning that I would have to speak more. And I would run the risk of being exposed or misunderstood in the language that I was least comfortable in.

So, I took the easy way out. Science journalism. Very few people would enquire further.

The guy who actually wanted to do science journalism was Furquan, my friend from *that side*. But since I had suddenly become an aspiring science journalist, Furquan felt it would be repetitive if he said the same, so he changed his ambition. And kept changing it every session – photography, wildlife photography, *Nat Geo*, *Nat Geo Traveller*, Discovery and so on.

During the admission interview, Furquan had said he wanted to be a science journalist.

The interviewers had asked if he was sure of his choice. 'You won't change your preference later?'

'Not at all,' he had assured them. 'That's why I studied Biotech before applying for Journalism.'

But here in the introductory session, he too was dealing with issues similar to mine – language, fluency, presentation. At least he was good-looking and had some degree of confidence.

So I was the one who would be doing science journalism for now.

'Sounds interesting. We have very few science journalists in India,' said one teacher.

The next question, predictably: 'So tell us something about yourself and your background.'

'I come from Bihar's Gopalganj district.' Few knew where exactly that was. 'Better known for Lalu and Rabri.' Lalu generates smiles and curiosity among people.

'Is it? How far is your place from his?'

'My village is some 20 kilometres from theirs.' This was as good as 200 kilometres, given the state of the roads. Lalu would helicopter it to his village in his heyday.

'That's pretty close to his place. So your area must be quite developed. Why did you then choose to come to Delhi?'

'I came here because there were no good schools around my village.'

'Oh, you have done your schooling here?'

'Yes. Since middle school. From Jamia.'

Before the next question came, I tried to continue on a subject I was confident about. 'I came here in class 6 and lived with a cousin in the beginning. Then I shifted in with the extended family of my elder sister briefly, and with some other people from my place. And after that I lived on my own. Starting in 2000.'

'Alone? You must have been only this big at the time,' gesturing with hands, amid spontaneous laughter. The just-this-big insult – up to the top of the table.

My introduction was not too impressive, either in content or presentation. Nor was my appearance likely to impress anyone at all. I would run to college in whatever clothes I could lay my hands on – crumpled trousers and shirt, slippers, hair flying in all directions, moustache and beard growing whichever way they wished on my extremely handsome face, un-bathed more often than not. I mean, how are you supposed to bathe in the mornings if you wake up at 9.15 for a 9.30 class, even if you live walking distance from college?

The others in my class looked more sophisticated, better groomed. They were articulate and sounded sincere. I imagined that they must have completed their undergrad studies earnestly, that their lives had a motive.

I didn't belong here, I was sure. Even though I was one of those who had preferred Jamia over the Indian Institute of Mass Communication – as had roughly half of our class – I felt I was not brilliant like my peers were. I didn't drink, do drugs or smoke. And I was light years away from anything that even remotely resembled a fashion sense. Not to speak of my social awkwardness or conversation skills.

Those early feelings from the English-medium school so many years ago returned – now in a bigger arena.

Here I was, with nothing to show but an obscure blog that no one read, except my friends, and only when I coerced them with bribes or threats. My only qualification was my degree: BSc in Biosciences, with a glorious 2nd division. I would do no better at MCRC, achieving the second-last place in the first year, and last in the final year. All my classmates had something to show. There was Akanksha, fluently bilingual, who had been the editor of her college magazine. She seemed to know things that mattered. Zehra had been a topper throughout, and had stood second in English Literature at Delhi University. (She kept up her cruel disregard of mediocrity at MCRC, topping the course with distinction.) Aaftab had left IIT Mumbai to follow his passion. Another classmate, Chandrika, had studied at a school and a college that were both among the best in India.

Even Saiam, who like me was from 'that side', had a theatre group. People would call him Sam or Sayyam. He could mimic people, especially teachers, and sing and crack silly jokes with confidence. 'I am so dark that my face doesn't even register in photos. The studio guy told me, hey man, take back your negative, you have forgotten to click your picture.' 'What would you call Mr Kaul's girlfriend? Miss Call.' Kaul, Abhinav Kaul, our classmate, would bang his head in mock-frustration, but how can you be mad at a man who makes fun of everyone, most of all himself.

Saiam collected obscure songs, and sang them in class, peppering them with classmates' names. The Bollywood hit 'Zara Zara Kiss Me' became 'Zehra Zehra Kiss Me'. A weird Pakistani song from YouTube rhymed with Ariba's name, so it became 'Ariba Ariba Love Me'.

He would sing a funny, literary Hindi version of Enrique's 'Hero', mimicking the singer's sad, deep voice:

> *Kya tum mere sath nritya karogi agar main tumse kahun?*
> *Bachchi, kya tum mere sath chumban karogi?*

Then, on a different scale, there was Khalid. Also from that side. A sophisticated Saiam. He was a tall, walking stick, with a strong voice and a confident demeanour. Having worked already for a few radio channels as part- time jockey, he had a small fan-following among the college girls in his city, Calcutta. ('No, I still call it Calcutta, not Kolkata,' he would say.)

He also had this frank manner that won people over. 'I am Bihari but I have lived and done my schooling from Calcutta. I have graduated from Jamia. Psychology. I wanted to do Mass Communication, that's why I came to Jamia. But I couldn't crack the Mass Com. test so I took admission in MA in Convergent Journalism. It's not my first choice.'

He often joked when he was among us boys that he couldn't crack the Mass Communication exam because his girlfriend had dumped him. But he had a way with girls and flirted effortlessly. He would ask a girl for a puff of her cigarette and say, 'This is the closest I could get to your lips.' Or, 'If my Bapu would allow me, I swear to God, I would marry you. Achha, forget Bapu. Will you marry me? You are so cute.'

He would tell us that he called his father and asked him to buy him an Enfield so he could take his girlfriend on rides.

When we sat together in the canteen, or went out for assignments, he asked us for our opinion of the girls in class. 'If you could fuck a girl in the class, who would she be? And who would you want to marry, given a choice?' He would try and guess people's choices and was overjoyed if he guessed right.

We had nothing in common, except perhaps our size-zero skeleton and that we had graduated from that side.

The class was diverse. There was a girl who wanted to be an actor. Another who always sat in the front row and wanted to be a news anchor. One had prepared for the civil services. A guy from Kashmir, Gowhar. Thinly built, hair sprouting on fair face, he had a distinct accent. Within a few minutes of meeting him you would know that he wanted to free his Kashmir from India's occupation.

Azadi. Self-rule. Self-determination. The conviction with which he spoke made it seem as if his dream would come true any moment now. If not now, in the next generation. But it will happen, Insha Allah.

His views were not welcome to many in our class. Khalid was the most bitter. Saiam wanted to know why the hell he had come to ... to India. Many kept quiet. Aaftab argued that geopolitics didn't work like this. He would talk of strategic affairs, the threats around us, with keywords like Taliban, Pakistan and nukes thrown in.

Then there was Abhinav Kaul, of medium height and heavy build, totally sober and with a sincere smile. He would never let his ideology spill out. His surname suggested he was a Kashmiri Pandit, but he avoided talking about the victimhood of his community or militancy in the valley.

He had a knack for entering class late. Akanksha and he had a healthy competition going on who would make it in last. They would sneak in silently – Akanksha was mostly successful, but Abhinav was too large to escape notice. When caught, he would shamelessly start laughing. He was a beta version of Nusrat Fateh Ali Khan, in looks and in deeds. And Nusrat Sahib was his favourite singer.

Aaftab was from Mumbai and had studied Economics. He was heavier than Abhinav, was about the same height, and had a composed and mature look. In fact, he looked deceptively innocent. But it soon became obvious that he was way, way above the rest of us. That he had left IIT to pursue his choice of study was the least of it. He seemed to have an understanding of things that eluded most of us. When he talked, only he and the teacher understood what he was on about. It seemed, at least to me, like coded messages were being exchanged between two aliens.

But outside class, his talk was as trivial and jargonless as the rest of us. Many in the class called him Arnab Goswami for his capacity for relentless talk and his superior political understanding (by our standards).

One guy surprised me. 'I studied in Saraswati Bal Mandir.' What? That's an RSS-affiliated school, right? What is he doing here?

What I knew about RSS and its affiliates was the Rath Yatra, and the riots and misery it had brought in its wake, ruining the fabric of the country.

The young man elaborated, 'I cleared both the Indian Institute of Mass Communication and Jamia. I chose to come to Jamia.' Sumit who had graduated from the Delhi College of Arts and Commerce. 'My final project in graduation was on the negative portrayal of RSS in print media.' Wow! Another surprise.

'I worked for *The Pioneer* for a year as an intern.' Further consolidation. The newspaper was owned by Chandan Mitra, a BJP member of the Rajya Sabha. After the encounter, they had published opinion pieces mocking Mushirul Hasan under whose VC-ship Sumit got admission into Jamia a few months later. 'I did the entire sports section over there.' Hmm ... Had the gentleman covered the daily sport indulged in by RSS members every morning? Those morning parades?

I did not ask him that, of course. He was twice my size. But this don't-ask-don't-tell policy didn't last long. There was something that connected us, that often brought us together. Perhaps it was the similarity of our backgrounds: the aspiring middle class.

14

You Are As Patriotic As Anyone Else

IT WAS THE FIFTH day after the encounter. Jamia had called students for a meeting with the VC, Mushirul Hasan. At first, I was not sure whether I should even turn up at a meeting where terror and terrorists might be discussed. What purpose would such a meeting serve?

But then I thought, who else has even tried to talk to us? Here is someone willing to have a conversation, however belated.

It was entirely possible that those killed or arrested had been involved in the bomb blasts. But it was a serious allegation and not proven beyond doubt. There were many unanswered questions; all the rumours floating around did not help either. We all felt like potential suspects, but not a single person who could be called a Leader had had the courage to come to our locality and say, 'I will stand by you.' No one. No chief minister, no prime minister, no home minister, not even a thekedar of Muslims and Islam. The only people who showed up were rabble-rousers and opportunists. Like the sectarian Mullah Bukhari, the Shahi Imam of Old Delhi's Jama Masjid. He wanted to visit Jamia Nagar after the encounter but the police didn't allow him to enter. He shouted his usual threats, threw his hands around in the air and went back to where he had come from – the rifle-guarded imamat bestowed on his ancestors by long-lost royalty.

And the likes of freelance leader Asif Mohammad Khan. (He was the younger brother of former BJP leader Arif Mohammad Khan, who had studied in Jamia school and gone on to become president of the AMU students' union and, later, deputy information and broadcasting minister in Rajiv Gandhi's government, and then went on to join the BJP. He had resigned over the Shah Bano case and, as a result of his stand against triple talaq, had once been thrashed by Jamia students.) Asif Mohammad had a reputation for hopping from one controversial issue to the other, and for fighting it out through rabble-rousing posters in Jamia Nagar. Khan used symbolism masterfully. He had all the makings of a great leader, except that his support group was small compared to other great leaders of our time.

When no one credible spoke up, the community listened to those who made themselves available. But now, the rabble-rousers' rabble-rousing and religious leaders' religious-leading were shown to have fallen short. They had become too predictable to be taken seriously by any sensible person. Jamia Nagar's residents and university students waited in vain for someone from outside – whose patriotism was not in doubt – to come and testify to their innocence. Anyone, from anywhere: left, right or centre.

The Left often claimed to represent minorities, Muslims included, but there was no voice of political leaders worth recalling, at least not in the beginning, when we were scared even to speak aloud about it (though a few did pursue the case later). The Right claims to extend a well-meaning hand of friendship towards Muslims, but now there was none in sight. And the Centre – whether the ideological Centre or the central government – whose representatives had led the charge on Batla House, had nothing much to offer, of course. Those who spoke, did so in feeble voices. Nothing more than token whimpers here and there. No one visited the site to hear our side and console us.

Even to lie to us that justice would be served. A just justice, you know.

That no innocent would be wronged. That people's doubts about the encounter would be addressed.

No one visited the locality even to pretend that they supported us. Or to say, you are as loyal as anyone else.

That you are as chauvinistic as we are.

That you are as jingoistic as we are.

That it's all a matter of opportunity.

That we trust you and our – Our – fight is common.

So now, that job of reassuring the young people of the community had fallen to university professors.

Young men who get involved with extremism claim to have unaddressed grievances. Either there are genuine grievances, or they are misled into believing that such grievances exist. But someone needed to talk to them, offer to deconstruct it, especially in sensitive times such as after an encounter that was widely looked at with suspicion. The teachers realised they needed to talk to their students and tell them that they did indeed belong.

They called the students to the university's auditorium. I approached reluctantly – a bit late as usual. To my surprise, a huge crowd had gathered. This quelled my apprehensions a bit. At least I was not alone. There were many who were as scared as I was. Many of my friends were in that crowd.

I was able to slide my skinny body into the packed auditorium, negotiating the sea of arms and shoulders. Even the aisles were full. I could not see the stage at all, and so jumped onto the arm of a chair, like many others around me. Now, I could see the stage between several heads and necks. And the logo of the university pasted behind the podium: the crescent with a book in it and two trees emerging from it. The book had the university's motto. There was a star above the crescent and Allah-o-Akbar.

Within a few minutes, a small, plump man made his entry on the stage. There was a huge roar of applause welcoming him. The man surveyed the crowd and went to the podium. He checked the mike – takk takk – and then spoke in Hindustani.

When he spoke, he destroyed in one stroke his future prospects. Of being reappointed as VC. Or being considered for some gubernatorial or prestigious constitutional posts that ex-VCs of universities often get.

That evening he announced: 'I, as your teacher and on behalf of the other teachers of Jamia, will support you in every hour of crisis.'

The roar of spontaneous clapping from the students disturbed his flow.

'You are like my children.'

Clap clap clap clap. This I had not expected.

'And a father can't abandon his children in the hour of crisis.'

Clap clap clap.

He declared that he would defend his students unless they were proven guilty; that everyone is entitled to a defence and it's the democratic right of every citizen. In the same breath, he also warned his students to not do anything that would tie his hands and make it impossible for him to help them. 'Then I will abandon you,' he said. He asked us to abjure any form of violence and uphold the secular values of India.

He reminded us that in the eighty-eight years of its history, Jamia had gone through many turbulent periods but had always overcome these. Very few institutions had as many freedom fighters associated with them as Jamia had; the advocates of the One India theory had been among the founders of Jamia. In fact, Jamia's foundation was largely based on this ideology. Yes, the supporters of Jamia were 'conspirators', he said, but that was at the time of the freedom struggle, and we are proud of our university for having played such a role then.

He spoke. And we clapped. Clapped and clapped. After every sentence.

He taunted the media. Why are they here? When we have cultural programmes and discussions and talks, they never appear. Now, everyone is here because of one unfortunate incident.

All of us loved that jibe and we cheered our hearts out. It was our small revenge. It was unbelievable that someone was finally speaking on our behalf. Someone needed to assure us of our innocence. He did. At that moment, the entire university – whether they were machhars or khatmals, 24 number or TTS – loved that Rushdie-supporter.

Dislike of Professor Hasan had been the norm for me and many like me. Our prejudices wouldn't allow real dialogue. We casually termed him a godless communist, even an outright kafir. Infidel. A drunkard. A khatmal who can't be trusted – they always vote for the BJP. A fool who opposes Jamia's minority status. And, of course, the bastard who defended Salman Rushdie.

Here I was, clapping for him (unforced, unasked) after every sentence that he spoke.

That was a fateful day for me; that simple speech in the auditorium, his gesture of standing up for us. It forced me to think about the kind of person I had become. What I had come to represent. And where I had lost my way.

Once Dada had taught me Kabir's words:

Jati na poochho sadhu ki, poochh lijiye gyan,
Mol karo talwar ka, para rahen do myan.

Don't ask a learned man his caste, ask for his knowledge,
When you value the sword, don't go by the scabbard.

Or,

Bura jo dekhan main chala, bura na milya koi,
Jo mann khoja apna, to mujhse bura na koi.

I searched for the crooked men but couldn't find one,
When I looked inside, the most crooked was I.

And Iqbal's words:

Khudi ko kar buland itna ke har taqdeer se pehle,
Khuda bandey se khud poochhey bata teri raza kya hai.

Elevate the self to such a degree that before every decree,
God asks the man, tell me, what do you desire.

I was left only its parody, which we recited when Dada wasn't around:

Khudi ko kar buland itna ke har taqdeer se pehle,
Khuda bandey se khud poochhey, abe itna upar chadhh to gaya hai, ab utrega kaise?

The second line of which means, God asks you, hey man, now that you have climbed up so high, how do you plan to climb back down?

The meeting that day forced me to think, really think. And rationalise my thoughts and actions. It made me think about all the opinions that my friends had challenged, and my stubbornness that didn't allow me to accept I could be wrong.

Would I be able to unlearn the learnt?

Professor Hasan asked us to go back to our homes and enjoy Eid – it was only a few days away. Classes would resume after the festival, he announced. He also announced that, the next day, he would hold a rally, a peace rally.

Back home in Batla House, I wrote a report on his address (and refuted any reports if I thought they had factual inaccuracy) and posted it on my newly started blog. I had created it when I learnt through the newspapers that people earned money from blogs. If my blogs got me some income, it would lessen my parents' burden a bit, I thought – but that never happened. Two posts are not enough to earn money, it turned out.

The next day we assembled on campus for the peace rally. There was also a large media presence. During the rally, I took my first photos and added these to my blog. I didn't have a camera but a friend had a Nokia N-73, which was then a trendy phone. I asked him to lend it to me for a second and then vanished to click pictures. He did not want to take any chances, and told me to take the photos off his cellphone as soon as possible.

The coverage of the encounter in the media had affected us all. I decided I would be a journalist.

There was a couplet I had not heard since Dada died:

Ye khamosh mizaji tumhe jeene nahi degi,
Is daur me jeena hai to kohram macha do.

This reticence of yours will not let you live,
Create a tumult if you are to endure in this age.

I wanted to do my own version of kohram – a peaceful kohram. (Calm down, please!)

The write-up on Hasan's address and the next day's peace rally was my first journalistic foray. I had no illusions about changing the world, but I was sure that, at the very least, I would not be a journalist who would produce reports of the kind that had scared me – scared us.

Following the rally, while many of us hid ourselves in our homes (rented or owned), or escaped to our villages and towns (near or far), a few of our teachers came together and formed a group that would scrutinise the encounter and would give words to, and substantiate, the allegations that the residents had so incoherently made. The voluntary group had teachers from different departments, and soon they came up with a detailed report on the encounter that pointed out glaring loopholes in, and the contradictory statements of, the police and the media alike.[21]

15

What Happens in South Delhi

LUCAS'S BIRTHDAY FELL ON a cold December day. He was an exchange student from Paris's Sciences Po.

He and a friend – half Indian, half French – who shared his birthday (according to the Gregorian calendar) organised the celebrations. Four of us from Jamia were invited to the party: Aaftab, Nishath, Salman and me. The rest were Lucas's French friends, mostly exchange students at other universities, and friends of the other birthday boy, from Delhi University and JNU.

Lucas knew that I didn't drink alcohol, so he had made arrangements for me – soft drinks, lime soda, fruit juice, along with (halal) snacks like chips and peanuts.

Everyone else at the party drank. I had encountered drinking only twice before in my life. First, at Aaftab's place, and then a Diwali party at another classmate's place, which was a small family affair. Lucas's party was relatively bigger and there were many strangers from culturally as well as geographically different worlds.

I tried to fit in, but I realised I could not succeed to a degree that was agreeable to my ego. I seriously lacked party manners. Sitting with my group of friends on a couch, I watched guests smoking and drinking and wondered how to fit in here. In that crowded south Delhi flat, I was the only one who was – let's say, for the sake of vanity – pious. A cigarette and alcohol virgin, if you will.

I had poured myself a glass of cola, and suddenly it seemed to me, in that multinational, multi-ethnic group, that I was drinking something contemptible, perhaps even sinful. Every once in a while, I had to fend off the question, 'Oh, you don't drink? Why?'

There were a few girls who did not drink, but even they had the smoke of cigarettes to hide behind.

Aaftab drinks, so he started from the word go. He knew the brands, he knew the smell. He knew what to pick and what not to pick. He also knew who to pick. Within minutes he was busy with a group of girls who were smoking in a corner, having walked over pretending to look for a lighter.

Nishath and Salman had betrayed their promise to me. They were supposed to have been my wingmen, drinking soft drinks so that I would not feel embarrassed or left out. But those scoundrels couldn't resist the smell of (free) liquor.

When the girls dispersed, Aaftab joined me again. It struck him that I was drinking cola. 'You should drink Sprite,' he suggested.

'Why?'

'You can then pretend that you are drinking vodka.' I was all ears. 'But make sure they are serving vodka, or you will get exposed.' He laughed a drunken laugh.

'But what if somebody offers me one? You know, when they are drunk ...'

'If they offer you a drink, just say: I am done. If they insist, say okay.'

'And then?'

'Vanish.' He laughed and did just that.

At the midnight hour, Lucas and his friend jointly cut a cake. Lucas's jewellery almost took the cherry off the cake when he bent over it to blow out the candles. His friend wore a kurta, a Nehru jacket and a topi. He had to make sure his topi didn't jump into the cake. People called him cool.

Two different numbers of candles were blown out. And then 'Happy Birthday to You' was sung. For one less year in our friend's life.

Then, the guests and hosts were all smeared with cake. I got some on my face too. The cake found its way on to the faces, hair and clothes of people, wall, chairs, cola bottles, glasses. For a while people kept complaining, with wicked smiles, 'It's sticky.'

Music continued in the background, a mix of English and Hindi. Mostly weird Hindi songs. The lights were dimmed and a few tapped their feet.

I stuck close to my friends from Jamia, and took solace in the fact that Aaftab's dress sense was as awful as mine. But Aaftab was Aaftab – he compensated with his conversation skills. Fluent, confident, funny, he was at his best that day. He just needed a thread, and got one when someone mentioned Obama. The new president of the US had generated a lot of optimism the world over. He had just won a Nobel Prize too.

'Oh, you too like Obama?' he exclaimed. 'I love the concept that a Black man could be the president of US but I like the maverick McCain. He is a war hero and makes a lot of sense even though he is a Republican. I mean, it was a difficult battle. A woman, a Black and a Republican who makes sense.'

He kept attracting people who were willing to listen to him. I stood there in the hall and gallery with him, holding my glass of cola throughout, as if I was the one who drank the most. Aaftab was my wingman for now – a drinking wingman for a non-drinking sinner. Who hovered over his drinking wingman like Kiraman Katibeen, honourable scribes, God's Angels, who take note of everything you do. Everything.

Aaftab had told me once that he was an atheist. Then as an afterthought added, 'Maybe I am agnostic.' That conversation with him was along the lines of ones that I often had with a group of friends who taught kids living in neighbouring slums.

Similar conversations, but with different conclusions.

God and Godliness.

And His World and Worldliness.

Who is He? Is He a He or a She? Is there a life after death? Why? Will a Gandhi, a Mother Teresa, a Mandela be awarded a place in heaven? Will the Jew Noam Chomsky, the Christian Edward Said go to heaven for championing the cause of Muslims in Palestine and elsewhere? Is Osama bin Laden a Muslim? If he is, will he go to heaven or burn in hell indefinitely? Why does He allow cruelty in His name? Why does He not stop it? If my faith – or for that matter, anyone's – is the truest one, the God-sent one, why has the rest of humanity not embraced it? How differently would I have seen my own faith had I been born into another? It's the Almighty who has given us brains, and with those brains, the freedom to think, so then is it okay for me to ask these questions, and most importantly, question the answers I receive?

But in Aaftab's life, God brought a different kind of challenge. His father was a practising Muslim, his mother a practising Hindu. He went to both masjid and mandir.

Prayed to an invisible god and to visible gods. Greeting relatives was confusing – whether to say namaste or salam. Like at the wedding of his sister, who married a Hindu man. He needed to look cultured (from both points of view). Must not embarrass his sister. He chose hi-hello-bye.

The night progressed and the crowd swelled – white, black, brown. Jamia, JNU, DU, Sciences Po. We ventured into the kitchen, the only space left. Me, Aaftab, Lucas and his girlfriend, Amelie.

From Washington, the conversation had turned to Paris. We were informed by the French that their Dear Leader Sarkozy was an alumnus of Sciences Po. And that many leaders in France were alumni of Sciences Po.

Aaftab turned to me. I knew he was about to say that his Bombay University – where he had studied economics – produced billionaires instead. I whispered to him to shut up. He laughed wickedly.

He had reason to laugh. Most of us worried about expenses and came up with innovative ways to cover up our lack of funds. Aaftab, on the other hand, made no attempt to look like he had any. But he always carried the best gadgets. Not necessarily the latest ones – he would wait for months to buy a gadget, never swayed by ads or trends. The best processor, best graphics card, the highest RAM etc. Always value for money.

His banker father had taught him, even as a kid, to spend wisely. Later he taught him to invest in stocks. He gave Aaftab some money to invest on his own and learn the market. Aaftab learnt a few tricks and soon started investing profitably. Now he helped others, like his classmates in college, make investments. For his expert counselling, he charged a nominal commission. This way, he earned enough to finance his studies in Jamia. Even after that he had enough savings to go to the UK for another degree, with a little help from the bank (Jamia didn't allow him to sit his final exam as he had fallen short of attendance).

A mini-billionaire he was for us. We joked that if he went to Zimbabwe – which had a painfully high inflation rate at the time – he would be a multi-billionaire.

The conversation continued. 'Your leader is an ass. I can't believe he took this position on the burqa. You can't enforce secularism. It has to be a liberal position,' Aaftab said. 'Don't get me wrong. I find the concept of burqa regressive. But the ban diverts the debate altogether.' He added, 'The only French thing that I love now, besides wine, is the French kiss.'

A burst of laughter filled the air. Then a silence – with music in the background. Aaftab determinedly returned to his topic.

'How does a French kiss work?' he asked. 'I am not a novice but I have never experienced one.' Lucas and his girlfriend laughed. But Aaftab persisted; he wanted to know the mechanics of the kiss. The complications it involves. Its finer details.

I was a mute participant with neither practical nor intellectual understanding of such matters. Lucas and Amelie attempted to answer Aaftab's question, while I stood there sipping my cold drink, laughing at their jokes, pretending to understand all of them and fiddling with a kitchen lighter.

And then Aaftab spoke the unspeakable – at least by my standards. 'Can you help me learn it, Amelie?'

If someone like me had said this, it would have been offensive. But Aaftab's urbane manners made it seem like a genuine thought experiment.

So Aaftab hadn't been lying at that all-boys party we had. Now, weeks later, I saw that he was great at this game. Or maybe it was just the drinks that made him so persuasive.

Him persuasive and her compliant. And Lucas a bystander.

The poor boy didn't even have a lighter to fiddle with while Amelie taught her inquisitive student how to French kiss. Lucas was not sure how to react, and threw an awkward glance at me – the person who had seen it all. A person who was stone cold sober.

I missed the spectacle of the end because there was a sudden hungama in the outer room.

Woohoo ... woo ... woohoooo – Nishath was jumping from one side to the other with a camera in his hand.

In the middle was Salman. Our friend. From Jamia.

He was being – not molested – but bulldozed to drink by two French girls, tall, trendy, heavy by Indian standards. Others stood around watching the circus and cheering while Nishath tried to take pictures. Salman had already drunk some half-a-dozen bottles of beer, but the two girls were forcing him – with love, of course – to drink more. 'One more! One more!' shouted the cheerleaders.

I joined in. You can't have more sadistic pleasure than this, he deserved it for betraying his (non-drinking) wingman. One two three four five bottles, and it kept on going. Had the girls not been drunk themselves, they might have had mercy. But one of them was particularly high and it soon turned from harmless fun into something more. Confused, helpless Salman somehow extricated himself and ran into the bathroom to throw up. But then one of the two French girls followed him in and shut the door behind her.

Woohoo turned to oooooomyyyygawwwd.

What happened inside the bathroom, nobody knows, except those two. The speculation never ceases, depending upon the strength of one's imagination.

While Salman was stuck inside the bathroom, Nishath, Aaftab and I joined the girls who were taking turns dragging on a hukkah. We sat in a circle and the hukkah went around one by one. I declined, saying I didn't smoke. I knew the loophole that God can't send you to hell for smoking, which is discourged but not haram, but somehow it didn't appeal to me.

'What? You don't smoke? What kind of journalist are you?' shouted someone from the hukkah party.

A German girl next to me explained that it was just flavoured hukkah with no tobacco. 'So, you need not worry.'

'It's not about tobacco or anything like that,' I said.

'*To fir?*' she asked, in accented Hindi, flaunting her fluency in the language she was studying at Jamia's Hindi Department.

'Simply, that I have never smoked, so—'

'I see. But try it once. It's fun.'

I took a drag on the hukkah and the others cheered. 'One more drag, one more.' I had to continue as long as they cheered for me. My masculinity was at stake; even the girls were smoking it.

The hukkah didn't bother me. If it tasted of anything, it was the smoke that comes from burning hay – to which I was no stranger.

In my childhood, we would sit around a bonfire of hay cut from the fields in winter. When Dada wasn't around, we experimented with the burning bundle of hay, blowing on the fire with all our might. Or jumping across the fire. Once in a while, we would put the pipe-like rice-stalk on the bonfire and inhale the smoke through the other end. The hukkah at the party tasted much the same to me. But it had been more fun back then. With all my biases considered.

'So, you don't drink either?' enquired the German lady after I finished smoking. She insisted on knowing why.

Against a background of songs, jokes, hootings and blabberings, I explained.

I don't drink primarily because of cultural reasons. Religion is a factor, of course, but more than that, it's the culture of the place where I come from that strictly discourages, even prohibits, alcohol. Someone who drinks, irrespective of religion or caste, is considered something of a social outcaste.

He who drinks can't be trusted.

He who drinks betrays his family, his village, his society.

He who drinks comes back home every night and abuses his parents, wife and children.

He who drinks borrows money for drinking.

He who drinks can go to any extent just for a pint of the toxic stuff.

He who drinks is seen lying on the road outside the local market in the morning.

And, of course, besides all this, he who drinks doesn't go to heaven. He commits a gunah-e-kabira, the biggest of sins.

It was well past midnight, and the night only got younger. The frequency of throwing up increased. Incoherent chattering lit up the celebrations. Coordinates changed. Biology smiled an age-old smile. As old as humanity.

Nishath was still sober but Salman was missing, and Aaftab was drunk beyond recognition. He was talking about love now. Love. His secret plans with his girlfriend. We suspected that he had a girlfriend, but he preferred not to talk about her. In his drunken state, he let out that he had a girlfriend back home in his beloved Mumbai.

As Aaftab was heavily drunk, we decided to leave, a face-saver for me. We had left not because of my killjoy sobriety but his joyous inebriation. His drunken ramblings continued as we navigated the still-busy Ring Road to find an autorickshaw.

Presumably, embarrassing things had been done and witnessed at this party. So, on the way back, pledges were extracted. Whatever happened in south Delhi would stay in south Delhi.

It seemed funny enough to all of us later. But those secrets did remain in south Delhi – until now.

16

Rally, Peace Rally

THE PEACE RALLY SET out from Jamia's engineering faculty and proceeded towards Jamia school, where Jamia Nagar starts. Mushirul Hasan led the Radicals, Terrorists, Suspected Terrorists and Normal Human Beings. And our Trainers. From the engineering faculty, the rally crossed the road to continue along the Qurratulain Hyder gate, named after a writer who went to Pakistan at Partition but returned to India in a few years.

Students waved tricolours, and held posters and banners declaring their innocence, reiterating their patriotism, and even mocking what they thought were wrong portrayals of them in the media. One placard declared, 'We are masterminds, not terrorists.'

Another said, 'We oppose resignation of VC, demanded by BJP.'

While all the major leaders had attended the last rites of Inspector Sharma – as they should have – no major leader had visited our locality. The fact remains that there had not a single case against the men arrested or killed *before* their alleged role in the blasts.[22] Students asked on their banners why Sonia Gandhi did not visit Jamia (she had recently visited Delhi University).

Addressing all the political parties that were scrambling to get mileage out of the incident, students said, 'Don't make Jamia a political field.'

Many reports had claimed that the main accused, Atif, had crores transferred into his account a few days before the bomb blast. This was denied in a statement by his bank manager in Azamgarh, who said that the balance in his account was Rs 1,437.[23]

One placard read, 'Rs 1437 = Rs 3 Crore. Media and Delhi Police should be in stock market.'

Other banners and posters said:

'Do we need to prove our patriotism?'

'Until proven guilty by court of law, they are innocent.'

'We have books, not AK-47.'

'Why is govt afraid of judicial probe?'

'Spot the terrorists.'

'Down with State Terror.' 'Stop targeting minorities.'

'You can bury the dead, not the truth.'

'Special cell is a licence to Kill.'

'*Sarfaroshi ki tamanna ab hamare dil me hai, dekhna hai zor kitna bazu-e-qatil me hai.*' The desire to make a sacrifice is in our hearts, let's see how strong the executioner is. (Bismil Azimabadi)

'*Ye kiska lahoo hai, ye kaun mara, Ae rahbar-e-mulk-wa-qaum bata, Ye kiska lahoo hai, ye kaun mara.*' Whose blood is it, who died, O leader of the nation and community, whose blood is it, who died? (Sahir Ludhianvi)

Kuch hoga
Kuch hoga, agar main bolunga
Na tootey

Na tootey tilism satta ka
Mere andar ek kayar tootega.

Something will happen
Something will happen if I speak
Let it not shatter
Let the illusion of power not shatter
The coward inside me will shatter.
(Raghuvir Sahay)

The peace rally went past Ghalib Park, where a statue of the poet stands. It went past SRK (Shafiqur Rahman Kidwai!) Hostel, Guru Nanak Park, Bab-e-Azad and past the Faculty of Languages.

Then it went past Dr Zakir Hussain Library, a long-time faculty of the university who became president of India. Mushirul Hasan had got a quote from Hussain installed on its iron-grilled boundary:

> For heaven's sake, please ... build the foundation of trustworthy society, in which the weak are not afraid of the strong, the poor are not kicked by the rich, in which our own culture can blossom, and we draw out the best from all human beings, where each person's latent capacities are nurtured and where everyone is ready to be of service to the society.

The rally, the peace rally, crossed the M.A. Ansari Auditorium that had its own inscription by the man it was named after:

> I consider the brotherhood of man the only real tie, and partitions based on race and religion are, to my mind, artificial and arbitrary, leading to divisions and factious fights.

Past Zakir Hussain's tomb and mausoleum, the rally, peace rally, reached MCRC, which takes pride in throwing out its students (for inadequate attendance), among them Shah Rukh Khan and Rakesh Sharma. And in Barkha Dutt, Kabir Khan, Loveleen Tandan, Roshan Abbas, Kiran Rao and others for completing the course (without being thrown out).

The rally, peace rally, wound its way around the Premchand Archive that displayed the university's motto on its curved wall:

'He taught Man what he knew not.'

Finally, it came to a halt at Jamia's school, where Rabindranath Tagore, on a tall rock installed in front of the school gate, told the students:

> *I have felt your muffled steps in my blood, everything past,*
> *I have seen your hushed countenance in the heart of the garrulous day,*
> *You have come to write the unfinished stories of our father in unseen scripts in the pages of our destiny.*
> *You lead back to life the unremembered days for the shaping of new images.*

The rally, peace rally, didn't proceed to the other centres on campus: the Noam Chomsky Complex, the Nelson Mandela Peace and Conflict Centre, the K.R. Narayanan Centre for Dalit and Minorities Studies, or the Sarojini Naidu Centre for Women's Studies. It wasn't necessary; the point had been made.

All my friends – and most of my classmates – attended the rally.

17

Us and Them Stories

WHEN I WAS A child, my village didn't have a full-fledged mandir. During Hindu festivals, we would hear the distant chanting of hymns from neighbouring villages in the evenings. Sometime in the late 1990s, the villagers donated a piece of land near the Hindu settlements to build a proper mandir. Thus, the village had a mandir, but I had never been inside.

Even in Delhi, I had not visited a mandir. Not that visiting a mandir or a masjid makes one tolerant of the Other, but still ...

The winter after I enrolled in MCRC, I decided to visit the mandir in Okhla village, the oldest one in our locality. I had heard stories about Okhla village as a child; that men from there had gone to Ayodhya when Babri Masjid was torn down, that some of them had even brought back bricks from the demolished mosque.

The space outside the mandir was also the Ramlila ground, and I saw my first Ravana burning there while I was in school. It was so crowded that I was almost squeezed dry.

There are not many Hindus residents in Jamia Nagar, so I worried that they might be suspicious of a newcomer, especially as there had been cases of blasts across the country in the previous months. Many of them in religious places. But now that I was studying journalism, I had a good explanation; that I was doing a project on how Hindus in Jamia Nagar, a Muslim locality, celebrate festivals like Diwali.

It was noon and the puja was about to begin when I reached the mandir. The pujari asked me to wait till the prayers were over. I sat there, listening to the hymns in Sanskrit, the high and low notes of chanting in a language I didn't understand, very much like Arabic, beautiful to the ear but nothing that you could comprehend.

There was more in common than what set them – Them – apart from me. There was the ringing of bells, the reciting of prayers, the everyday mandir rituals. It was like the azaan, the recitation of the Quran, the bowing to the almighty that happens in masjids not far from this mandir.

It all seemed familiar. Like a city known by different names and reached through different routes.

I watched. Like a curious tourist trying to experience the local culture. A circumambulation of the inner shrine, bowing in front of it with folded hands. I duly contributed to the mandir fund when the bowl was passed around. Initially, I didn't know how to react. Then I recalled how, on Fridays and Eids, they ask for donations to run the masjid. I put the same amount in the bowl here as I did in the masjid.

My little blasphemy.

Or ashuddhi.

After the prayers were over, I sat with the priest and a few devotees in the mandir courtyard. We talked about much more than my project. A bhajan that I didn't understand played in the background. The pujari told me he had spent a good decade in this mandir. The devotees recalled their Khan and Ahmad friends, and the sevaiyan they had enjoyed during Eid. They summoned up memories of Ravana burnings and asked: how could there be such a rush during Ramlila if the Muslims from the locality did not attend?

Most of their neighbours were Muslim – over the years, many Hindus had moved out as more and more Muslims moved in, turning the Hindu village of Gujjars, Jats, potters and farmers into a mini-Muslim world. First, when Jamia was established. Later, when Babri happened (that I could not bring myself to discuss in the mandir). More, after Gujarat 2002 (we didn't discuss that either).

That migration didn't stop. It is still going on. Outside, I talked to the Hindu youth of the locality.

One of them I had known for some time; he was the son of a relative's landlord. He too spoke of the shared past, but added, 'There is a difference between one person clapping for you and a hundred clapping for you.' He meant that there were very few Hindus remaining in the locality and he felt that void. He proudly claimed that the Joga Bai colony in Jamia Nagar, where he lived, was named after one of his great-great-great-grandmothers. She had worked in the kitchens of the Mughals, he said, and they had gifted this patch of land to her, where a few Hindus still lived, surrounded by Muslims.

I talked to another young man who lived close to the mandir. I had always taken him to be a Muslim, as his name did not suggest otherwise, and he salam-ed like a Muslim pro. I often met him at a tea stall outside Jamia library with Saiam. The two of them had been classmates in BA Social Work. That Diwali, I called him to ask how he celebrated the festival in a Muslim ghetto. He told me that he celebrated

Eid with as much enthusiasm as he celebrated Diwali. All his best friends and neighbours were Muslim, and Jamia Nagar was where he was born. Even though many of his old Hindu neighbours had left the locality, he couldn't imagine leaving the place.

But the subtle changes in dynamics worried him. He was bursting crackers on Diwali one night when a curious kid approached him and asked if he was a Muslim. When he said that he was a Hindu, promptly the question came: 'But if you are a Hindu, why are you wearing a kurta?' Kurta-pajama, the dress of the Muslim. He had no answer to give to such (poisoned) innocence.

There is something that's taking a toll on our community life. Possibly, it's our past. Probably, it's our present. A sense of insecurity. And segregation (forced or chosen).

Our perceptions of the Other increasingly come from a distance, rather than from interaction. From hearsay. From our hysterical mass media. From our newspapers, magazines, televisions, films, internet and social media that invariably portray a stereotypical version of the Other. And rarely smooths the edges of (silent) conflicts. Even when they set out to do that, they often end up only confirming the stereotypes. There is something wrong when a human being can be turned into a minority–majority in the land where they are born. Us and Them. Anywhere. Everywhere. Jamia Nagar. Or not-Jamia Nagar.

As a journalist working for the *Hindustan Times* in New Delhi after graduating from Jamia, I visited a newly established refugee camp in Jodhpur to hear the stories of Hindus who had fled from Pakistan after telling their neighbours they were going to India on a pilgrimage.

Their situation was very different from that of the refugees who came at the time of Partition or when Bangladesh was created. As a student, I had done a story on refugees from Pakistan's North-West Frontier Province who were now settled in India but fondly remembered their place of birth. When they finally managed to get a space allotted for their settlement on the Delhi border, the migrants named their colony Pakistani Colony. Later migrants who settled nearby named theirs Frontier Colony. In the Jodhpur camp, a young girl from Sindh narrated how she felt vulnerable going out to defecate. She said the women always went in a group for fear of being kidnapped and converted to Islam. The men recalled instances of discrimination. And how they had to read Islamic religious texts in school because there was no choice.

It must have started with compulsory this, compulsory that, as it's beginning to happen in India. Some of the refugees who worked as taxi drivers told me that they avoided putting idols of deities in their taxis to avoid being identified – just as many Muslim taxi drivers in Gujarat, for example, avoid putting stickers with the crescent and moon or 786 or blessings in Urdu.

They told me that not everyone was against them: some journalists kept writing about their plight even though they were threatened by Islamists, many activists fought on their behalf, many students celebrated festivals with them. But they felt the walls closing in on them.

One family narrated how half their children were Pakistani and half were Indians as they didn't have the money to pay the citizenship fees for all of them when the Indian government granted amnesty for refugees. Their daughter could not appear for her board exam because her only identity document was her Pakistani passport, jointly with her mother's.

I learnt from the Pakistani Hindu refugees that they were often regarded with suspicion by the Indian government when they applied for citizenship. A young man told me that he was interrogated by multiple intelligence agencies in a joint session to confirm he was not an Inter Services Intelligence (ISI) spy.

Before that, while he was crossing the Attari border with his octogenarian grandfather, the customs officials termed their passport and visa fake and demanded a bribe to allow them entry into India. Rs 5,000 to begin with. The young man tried to bargain with them, but each time he spoke, the official increased the amount. When his grandfather tried to plead, he was kicked by the arrogant man. The old man fell down, started bleeding and lost consciousness. Scared now, the customs official told them to hand over whatever money they had and go – he finally paid Rs 21,000, managing to keep some money hidden.

His grandfather was declared dead when they reached Delhi. It was India's Republic Day, he said, he remembered it well. He wanted to take his grandfather's body to Jodhpur, the Indian city closest to their home in Pakistan, where a few of his relatives lived, to perform his last rites. The ambulance owner asked him to pay Rs 7,000 upfront. The young man only had Rs 6,500 left, and promised that he would pay the full amount once he reached his relatives in Jodhpur. The ambulance driver pleaded with the owner on his behalf, saying the amount could be cut from his wages if the young man didn't pay.

All the way to Jodhpur, the driver paid for his food and wouldn't accept any money from him. The driver was Muslim, the young man recalled.

Then there was Ram Bhayya's Us and Them story.

I met Ramawtar Singh, Ram Bhayya to us, in Baran, a small tribal district in Rajasthan. I had gone there with my friends from Halchal, a voluntary group that taught kids in the neighbourhood slums. We stayed at Ram Bhayya's home, and went around meeting the villagers – displaying our curiosity and ignorance about their age-old customs.

We visited the nearby jungle and stream. To our surprise, in a state known for its deserts, it rained relentlessly. The walk to the stream, now swollen with rain, was long and treacherous. But Ram Bhayya was used to it and kept going faster than we could. He told the most interesting stories, and we ran after him to keep up with all he said. That the pond we saw in front of us was so deep that, even if the ropes of all the cots in the village were joined together, they still wouldn't reach the bottom. He scared us by saying that bears and leopards and other dangerous animals roamed the jungle, so we should walk faster.

During the day-long walk, he told us that he had been a member of a rightwing Hindu youth group and was often part of their violent, disruptive acts. But he soon realised that he was being used by vested interests for their political gains. He read books, met new people, learnt new ideas, and finally left the group. Now, he lived in the tribal district and worked among the locals, teaching them and training them in skills.

He had turned into a Gandhian and ate only organic food, most of which he grew in the nearby fields. He designed books for his students. In his new avatar, he became part of a group that organised tours between India and Pakistan to advocate more people-to-people interaction, and had visited the country himself.

In 2008, when a Pakistani delegation was visiting Jaipur, there were serial blasts in the city. Ram Bhayya was one of their hosts and knew the visitors would be scared because of the anti-Pakistan frenzy such events created in the media. Indeed, a police team visited the hotel, which scared the guests even more. Ram Bhayya assured the police that he had been with the Pakistani delegation all along. That night, he stayed at the hotel to give the delegation a sense of safety and solidarity. 'I told them made-up stories the whole night to keep them engaged,' he said. 'Of spotting lions, leopards, close enough to touch them.'

(Many young men from Kota were arrested for those blasts, and most of them acquitted by a court after more than three years in jail.[24])

Us and Them stories.

Habib Muqbel was also part of Halchal. A senior from Azamgarh – that same Azamgarh – had started the group. We used to teach kids whose families had migrated to Delhi and lived in and around the university.

Habib was from Kabul and had spent most of his youth as a refugee in Peshawar. His father had been a doctor in a government hospital in Kabul; working for the government was an unpardonable sin in the eyes of the Taliban regime. His family had to flee to neighbouring Pakistan, where they kept moving around for fear of being traced and killed by the Taliban. Finally, they settled in a camp – a camp where the so-called mujahids who were now running (and ruining) his country had stayed and trained.

Habib had studied in various schools in the refugee camps and spoke Urdu fluently, if with an Afghan accent. Like an exaggerated version of the Pathan in Amitabh's *Zanjeer*.

For us, he was, in his accent, Abib Bai (he ate up the H). And we'd ask him, '*Kaana ka liya?*' (in English, you would probably say, Ave you eaten?). He would let out a light-hearted threatening laugh. Then, whatever was in his hand would go Bang on your head.

Abib Bai, the Pataan.

Once there was a Patan. A thief broke into his house. Masha Allah. Masha Allah.

The Patan caught the thief and tied him with a rope. Then he went to report the thief to the police. The policeman knew he was a Patan, so he asked him if he had tied the thief well.

'Yes, I have tied both his feet,' said the Patan, confidently.

Hearing this, the policeman got angry and shouted. 'Idiot, you have tied his feet. He can untie himself with his hands!'

The Patan thought for a moment and replied. 'Don't worry sir, the thief is also a Patan.'

Abib Bai would lunge at the mischief-maker, who ran for his life with the Patan in hot pursuit, with the rest of us laughing at the spectacle.

The Pathan would jokingly shout that just by adding Kaan to one's name one doesn't become a real Kaan – a Patan. 'We have seen your Patan. That girlie Sha Ruk Kaan!' He was our all-weather Taliban guide. Our first-hand source of stories about the group. There is a story in Afghanistan, Habib would tell us, about a fight between an Arab and an Afghan. The Afghan hurled the choicest of abuses while the Arab kept mumbling in Arabic. The Afghan thought: 'What a man! Here I am shouting abuses and he is reciting Quranic verses.'

That's the problem with the Taliban, Habib would say. They don't fully realise what they are doing. They think that anything in Arabic is pious. For them, *har marz ki dawa hai Sall-e-Allah* – the panacea for all ills is 'God's blessing is on you'.

He was ideologically opposed to them, a danger he knew all too well. Blasts and attacks had become a way of life for his countrymen even after the return of democracy. His father had miraculously survived a suicide-bomber's attack on the hospital where he worked because he happened to be out for lunch. Doctors, trainee doctors, nurses, patients and their caregivers all died in that attack.

Our friend worried about the unpredictable future of Afghanistan. What would happen after the US withdrew? Back to the Taliban age?

The Pathan didn't want to go back to that life. Where the only dress would be Pathani kurta, and the national look would be beard-face or burqa. And the overwhelming debate would be, what's the appropriate length for a beard? Is wearing a moustache Islamic or not?

Habib was studying Peace and Conflict at Jamia in the hope that one day he would return to Afghanistan and be of some use to his madar-e-watan.

His life in the refugee camps of Peshawar had taught him many lessons. Of despair. Of hope. He saw refugee-despair and refugee-hope among the slum kids he taught at Halchal, the kids of construction workers, or of the youths working in the canteen. Hundreds of kilometres away from their homes.

His past, as a political refugee. Their present, as economic refugees.

Habib was studying in India on scholarship, first from the Indian Council for Cultural Relations and then the Gandhi

Smriti Foundation. His work with Halchal was Habib's way of giving back to his host country – the country where once Kabuliwallahs came to sell dry fruits in school-stories. Where Kabuliwallahs still come, but they come seeking refuge. Where medical tourists (for lack of a more dignified word) from Kabul and Kandahar come in the hope of fixing their broken limbs, hearts and heads.

Us and Them stories.

Like the stories of Christian converts from Afghanistan who fled to India to find peace. They had been Muslim once but now found solace in Christianity. I met them to hear their stories. They had fled home fearing persecution – especially after a video of their secret churches found its way to the internet and a senior leader in the Afghan parliament had demanded that the converts be publicly executed. But the irony was that, in India, as asylum-seekers, they had to turn for a living to the people from whom they had run away. In a new land, where their existence wasn't properly recognised – India is not a signatory to the Refugee Convention, and so the refugees are UNHCR's guests – they had trouble landing jobs. As they were fluent in Dari, Pashto and Persian, the languages spoken by Afghans, the Afghan Christians acted as interpreters for Afghans who came to India for treatment. But they hid their religion, their identities, from the visitors.

I met them in a church in Delhi, led by a young man named Obaid Jan. Now he was Obaid Christ, and every Sunday he read to a gathering of some hundred-odd men, women and children from a screen that projected verses of the Bible in Dari. To the uninitiated, they looked like verses from the Quran in Arabic.

Initially reluctant, Pastor Obaid finally agreed to a meeting, but I had a hard time convincing his fellow converts to meet me. They had, after all, been attacked by fellow Afghans even in India. The pastor's companions thought it suspicious that a Muslim, and a student of a Muslim university where a number of Afghans studied, wanted to meet them.

I often bumped into the pastor at a restaurant not far from my home. His tastebuds betrayed him, I guess.

Hello, Pastor!

Salam, Neyaz!

Us and Them.

I had read and heard and heard over and over again about the treatment of Palestinians by Israel – that meant, for me, the Jews. I thought I should talk to a Jew, but I didn't know anyone in the small Indian Jewish community. I called the capital's lone synagogue. Rabbi Ezekiel Malekar didn't agree to meet me, but after I annoyed him with repeated calls – with some degree of caution lest it bring the police to my door – he agreed to talk on the phone.

But he remained apprehensive, probably because this was only a few months after the Mumbai attacks of November 2008, when terrorists had attacked a Jewish religious centre in Mumbai.

What I didn't know then was that there were Jews – and Muslims – in my own land who were silently proving my kind of prejudice wrong. The Jews of the Konkan, for example, the community to which the Rabbi belongs. They are known as Bene Israel or Children of Israel, and are mentioned in the Quran. It was not a relationship devoid of tension, but even during the worst conflicts, the two communities had managed to maintain good relations. A member of the community pointed out to me that the Bene Israel in India had always felt a close affinity to their Muslim neighbours, as monotheistic people of the Book. She said that the communities had lived in harmony for centuries, and had several customs and practices in common. Then I tried to understand the Palestinian version of Us and Them. Jamia has a good number of foreign students. I reached out to a Palestinian student in the Faculty of Architecture and Ekistics. The young man was on a scholarship from the Indian government. He was in the final year of his five-year course, and had not been back to Gaza since he arrived, fearing that he might not be able to come back, as had happened four years ago. After the confirmation of his admission to Jamia and the scholarship, he had gone back home to bid his family farewell. But when he returned, he found that the Erez crossing, the only access into Israel for Gazans, had been shut by Israel, and he couldn't leave for India.

He kept trying for weeks but couldn't get through. His admission expired, his scholarship lapsed. Still, he wanted to go to India in the hope that Jamia might still allow him to attend classes, and if not, he could try elsewhere.

He kept going to the gate whenever Israel announced it would be opened.

He tried some thirty times, he told me.

Then one night, after midnight, the Israeli government announced that the gates would be opened. He almost didn't bother to go this time, but his optimistic father convinced him to take a chance: 'What if they allow you this time? You will never be able to forgive yourself. Go son, go.' Reluctantly, without hope, the young man went to the gate – and what a surprise. He was allowed to cross. Finally.

But what a sad happiness.

He had been stuck in Gaza for months because he had wanted to say goodbye to his family, and now he had left home without it. He hadn't even said bye to his siblings this time, assuming he would return. While his family slept, all he did was exchange a hug with his father, merely as a formality. Now, on the other side, he realised he didn't have enough money. He had left home in the clothes he was wearing for the night, and had hardly any belongings other than the necessary documents like his passport and school certificates. But, somehow, he reached Jordan where many of his relatives lived as refugees. They helped him with the money he needed to come to India.

In India, the authorities in Jamia did not permit him to join the course that had already begun. He waited for the next session and applied for admission and scholarship again and succeeded. In the months before he started his course, the Palestinian savoured his freedom, a freedom that eluded him in Gaza. He roamed as far as his resources allowed him to, and joked that he got undue attention in India due to his name.

Once, he went to consult a dentist who asked him his name.

Raed Kassab.

What? Raed what?

Raed Kassab – his surname was similar to that of the Mumbai-attack terrorist, Ajmal Kasab.

He got a puzzled look first and then a generous smile. A frank conversation followed and a lifetime-discount from the dentist.

Thousands of kilometres from home, Raed was a happy man though he was unable to visit his homeland. He shared with me stories of the misery of being under occupation, being watched all the time, being categorised as either a militant or a collaborator and being confined to a small patch of land, surrendering to the whims and fancies of the occupier, Israel.

His was a physical occupation. The mental occupation is the more dangerous. This is what brings the physical occupation in the first place. It begins with promise, as a saviour, as a giver of hope. It begins, or began, when man decided to minimise nature's injustices – poverty, inequality, disability – through faith, ideology and law; through imagined realities. But it's no more about serving humankind. It's now a fight among imagined realities. It's about my imagined reality being better than yours.

Us and Them stories.

Kashmir was boiling once again. It was the year 2010. The protesters and their protests grew louder, and the deaths increased every day. News trickled into Delhi through newspapers and television sets. As also through Facebook and Twitter. And through our classmate Gowhar.

The news would upset him, and more often than not, he disagreed with us and we disagreed with him. Many discussions happened in class and they often turned louder, more bitter, more rigid and, at times, nonsensical from both ends. We avoided the subject outside class. But Gowhar's tense silence – and Abhinav's response in the same language – were hard to ignore. It was a known fact that, when they broke their silence, they differed, and differed volubly. Like the sky and the earth. Like India and Pakistan. Like the With Us or Against Us dilemma.

But they had a meeting point: Nusrat Fateh Ali Khan. When our own Nusrat, the bulky Abhinav, sang the legend's infinitely long qawalis, especially '*Tum Ek Gorakh Dhanda*

Ho', Gowhar would go into a dervish-like trance and go 'wah waaah waaaa aah aah waah'. A sound funny enough to make us grin – or record for strategic purposes. You never knew when you might need ammunition against an enemy who had access to your own embarrassing secrets, like photos or chats.

There was bitterness and it was obvious, but was there no way out?

The jokes, assignments, idleness and noodles at my house that we all recall when we meet. Over noodles, we managed to do, or fudge, our project; we discussed issues from all angles as budding journalists, and almost proved beyond doubt how toothless the government was and how the opposition was not really an opposition.

Those moments and those memories. It was a small beginning. Small in the larger scheme of things.

When I think of those days, I remember Dada quoting a couplet from Iqbal's 'Naya Sivala'.

Aa ghaerat ke pardey ik baar fir utha dein
Bichhdon ko fir mila dein, naqshdoi mita dein.

Come, let's lift the curtains of ego between us
Let's unite the sundered once more, and clean the
stains of division.

How naïve!

18

Radicals in the Aftermath

THE ENCOUNTERSHADOW HAD NOT left Jamia, at least not by the time I graduated. It came back in one way or the other, sometimes as good news, mostly as bad news. And at times, with protests in the locality, on its anniversary, or when the police filed a charge-sheet in court. Or when suspects were picked up from the locality, months after the encounter, unsettling the uneasy calm. Or when the post-mortem report was obtained by my senior, Afroz Alam Sahil.[25]

He had filed RTI applications with all the agencies that were concerned with the encounter: Delhi Police, All India Institute of Medical Sciences, National Human Rights Commission (NHRC), National Commission for Minorities (NCM), the Lieutenant Governor of Delhi.

At every turn, answers to his questions were delayed or his request was turned down, citing one clause of the RTI Act or another. AIIMS denied his request saying that they couldn't provide any information that 'has been expressly forbidden by any court of law' – even though there was no prohibition ordered by any court. After many hearings, a bench of information commissioners ordered AIIMS to release the reports after withholding identifying information. But a month later, perhaps in what was the first such case in the history of the RTI Act, the Central Information Commission sent a letter to Afroz saying that it was withdrawing its own orders.

Delhi's Minority Commission had instituted a fact-finding mission to investigate the case. Afroz's RTI requests revealed that Delhi's police commissioner had written to the Minorities Commission asking them not to go ahead with the plan to visit the site of the encounter.[26] The NHRC, on its part, said, 'The Lieutenant Governor of Delhi has declined to pass an order for magisterial enquiry' in the case. When he approached the Lieutenant Governor's office, they accepted that they had passed such an order, and added, 'In the case of Batla House, according to the Honourable High Court and Honourable Supreme Court, no judicial investigation necessary.' Again, no court had passed such an order.

The NHRC later announced that it had investigated the case and found nothing wrong.[27] It's a different matter that, in the name of investigation, all it had done was to ask the police for an explanation, and the police, a party to the case, repeated its claims that had, in the first place, made the locals demand an enquiry. The commission didn't even visit[28] the site of the encounter or meet any witnesses or relatives of the accused.

Finally, after one and a half years, the NHRC released partial post-mortem reports of the men killed but not that of Inspector Sharma.[29] The details of the post-mortem report only strengthened what the locals had been saying: that the encounter was indeed questionable. There were bullet marks on the heads of the killed men, blunt injury marks, and some missing skin on their bodies.

The repugnant smell of the incident just wouldn't dissipate. It affected everyone in the locality. And brought the realisation that even after escaping into a ghetto, one was not necessarily safe. The ghetto manipulated people's dreams. It killed them, it altered them forever – and, for many, even improved them.

It was our first encounter with the question of identity. Everyone acted, and reacted, in his or her own way. Some left their jobs, or lost them, some left the city (of their dreams) to go back to the places they had come from: Azamgarh, Patna, Sambhal, to poverty, illiteracy, obscurity. Many would never return to Delhi.

I knew a friend whose brother was in the police and had instructed him not to loiter around Batla House for the time being. The policeman brother had told him that there were too many khabris – locals, tea-sellers, general store owners and police – around the area. Don't even joke about the encounter or anything remotely related to it. You don't know what they are listening to and how they may interpret your conversations. You and your friends better avoid hanging out there, he had advised. We heeded his advice without question.

After the encounter, our hideout shifted from Batla House to Jullena (towards the Delhi side) where Perwez, Kafil and Furquan shared a room. The colony was not exactly friendly, but for now, it seemed less intimidating than Jamia Nagar. It provided a safe and dignified anonymity (to those who sought it).

It was a time when autowallahs would avoid coming to Jamia Nagar. The humiliation lay in the unsaid – a judgemental gaze, an awkward silence, a confused hmmm ... Or in some cases plainspeak, '*Yeh wohi* Jamia Nagar *hai na?*' Their expression completed what they didn't say to your face. The same Jamia Nagar that harbours terrorists. Who bombed the country. Why did they do it?

Most of us hired autorickshaws up to Holy Family Hospital, the nearest landmark outside Jamia Nagar, and then took cycle-rickshaws to Batla House.

Soon after the encounter, landlords in Jamia Nagar had started throwing out students, sometimes with no notice at all. Those who suffered the most from this housing apartheid were those from Azamgarh district. Even the once-dreaded Kashmiris were okay but Azmis were a straight no-no.

Earlier, landlords had been happy to rent out their properties to students because they were less likely to resist when asked to move out. With families, that was often a problem; when the landlord wanted the property back, the family would be reluctant to vacate. Now, out of the blue, the landlords started preferring families; for many of them, the monthly rents were the sole steady income they had.

Azmis lied about their permanent addresses when they went in search of new rooms. Or they shared with students from other places, if those others were willing to risk being in the company of an Azmi.

No one invoked his Azmi pride anymore. Boy, it's not Azamgarhi, it's Azmi. Naah naah, not Aajmi, it's Aazzmi, with a Z.

After the encounter, most Azmis I knew had vanished. They were scared, understandably, and they preferred anonymity. They sought isolation, and got it – because few were willing to be seen with them. They withdrew, as if they had accepted their guilt.

There was good reason for any young man in Jamia Nagar to withdraw into a cocoon. The encounter and its aftermath had demonstrated that once you were picked up by the police, there was nothing you could do. Your life was ruined, irrespective of your guilt or innocence.

After repeated incidents of plainclothesmen appearing in the locality, the residents in Jamia Nagar became vigilant.

Now if the police raided a house or tried to apprehend anyone, the locals demanded a court warrant and ID cards. Otherwise they wouldn't let the police take anyone away. They even beat up many plainclothesmen who claimed to be police but had no relevant proof of their identity.

Chaotic justice.

Or poetic justice?

Just two days before the hearing of a case of terrorism against senior Urdu journalist Syed Mohammad Ahmed Kazmi in September 2012, a few men in plainclothes appeared in Jamia Nagar's Shaheen Bagh. They tried to take away Kazmi's nephew, a class 11 student, as he was leaving home for tuition.[30] The boy made a noise and residents surrounded the men, who were in a vehicle with a UP number plate. The locals demanded to know their identity and why they were kidnapping the boy. The men gave contradictory answers, one of them saying that they were arresting the kid for the theft of a mobile. When more locals gathered and again asked for their identity cards, they said they were from the Mumbai Police. Why had they not brought the local police with them, according to procedure, the locals asked.

Then some from the crowd manhandled the men and forced them to produce their identity cards. It turned out, as it was reported in the media, that they were from the Special Cell of the Delhi Police – the cell that had led the charge in Batla House.[31] The Special Cell has been questioned by courts for its role in staging fake encounters, concocting evidence and torturing suspects.[32] Later, a spokesperson of

Delhi Police told newspapers that they were from the AATS, something called the Anti-Auto Theft Squad.

Kazmi was alleged to have helped bomb an Israeli diplomat's car in Delhi. He was a vocal critic of Israel, and openly supported Iran, and freelanced for many publications in that country.

There are stories, so many stories in Jamia Nagar.

Another time, in February 2012, the police came at midnight in plainclothes to Batla House to arrest a family. They tried to drag the family of eight into their van, saying they were illegal Bangladeshi migrants, even though the family had produced their passports and voter ID cards, which showed they were permanent residents of Bihar.[33]

The commotion woke their neighbours up, and a crowd assembled and protested the action. The policemen fired in the air. Some residents called the local police, who came to the rescue of the raiding team. It turned out that the raiding policemen were from the 'Bangladeshi Cell' of the South Delhi Police, while Jamia Nagar falls in the South East Delhi Police district. Later in the day, Delhi Police suspended six policemen for not following procedure, which requires raiding parties to inform the local police in whose jurisdiction the area falls.

This was three days after a group of men in a van with a UP number had tried to kidnap two car mechanics from Batla House. Locals chased down the van and released the young men.

In another case, about a month after the encounter, five plainclothesmen appeared in Shaheen Bagh around 8 p.m. in a black Hyundai car. They tried to drag a youth named Amir into their car. When he asked why they wanted him, they reportedly said they would tell him later. He shouted for help. Locals surrounded the men and demanded their IDs. The men claimed to be from the UP Police but couldn't produce any ID cards. Residents called the police, and in the commotion, four of the men vanished. One could not, and he was handed over to the local police.[34]

The man claimed that Amir was a chain-snatcher and they had chased him from Noida. But it was never explained why they were chasing him in a private car that had tinted glasses and was missing a number plate. When the locals checked the car, the papers showed it belonged to someone in Gurgaon. A number plate was found in the car's boot, with a Delhi registration number. Besides, the car was found to contain many PAN cards, debit cards and fake ID cards of an IT company, all with one name but different pictures and serial numbers.[35]

What the men's real intentions were, and even who they were, was secondary. The primary thing was that it was yet another occurrence of people coming into Jamia Nagar and grabbing residents with impunity. Each such incident left us with a feeling of uncertainty and helplessness, a worry that was becoming a near-constant in our lives.

Over the years, our fears would come true. In many high-profile cases, the accused were acquitted after years in jail. In many such cases, the courts even observed that the charges against the accused were concocted and there was no evidence against them. But how had the police claimed publicly that they had solved the case without admissible evidence?

In the Akshardham attack, for example, the Supreme Court in 2014 freed six men who had by then spent more than a decade in jail. The court observed that 'there was a serious attempt on the part of the investigating agency to fabricate a case against the accused persons and frame them'.[36] The fidayeen attack, in 2002, had killed thirty-three people in the temple, and three accused were awarded the death sentence by lower courts.

The only place that seemed safe from such scary possibilities was the university campus. The police needed permission from university authorities to enter the campus, and our VC's speech had reassured us that the university was willing to stand up for the innocent.

This was a departure from what students had experienced under the previous VC in 2000. I was in school then and heard the stories from seniors who studied in the university. The police entered SRK Hostel a few nights before the annual exams and beat up students, injuring about fifty.[37] The university claimed that the police had entered without the permission of the authorities. The police said they had come to arrest two men who had illegal weapons in their possession, a claim the students disputed. Whatever the reason, there had been an altercation between some students and the police before the raid, and the police had returned to the campus within a few hours in full force. They barricaded the exits of the hostel, shoved aside the hostel provost when he resisted their entry, and beat up any student they found. They broke open the doors of rooms, and chased and thrashed students who tried to hide in bathrooms. Scared, many jumped from the upper floors and broke their legs. One student claimed he had been thrown down by the police. Those who could escape from the exit at the back ran towards what was a jungle then, and the police set their dogs on them.

Two Kashmiri students alleged they had been dragged downstairs from the second floor, while the policemen showered them with invectives, calling them terrorists. The imam of the mosque behind the hostel was beaten up and the mosque's windowpanes, clocks and other things were smashed. The police, I was told, had abused and beaten up a disabled student. Even foreign students were attacked. Their modest valuables, like watches, calculators and certificates, were taken away.

In all, the police detained sixty-six students,[38] including schoolchildren who had been studying in the university library. They reportedly called the students ISI agents, Pakistani and katua.

There were indeed some unscrupulous elements staying in the hostel in those days, but the ones who suffered were the innocent: a topper in his class, the captain of a football team, those studying in the library or their rooms because exams were only a few days away.

Eight years later, it was a different story. Hostellers in the university felt lucky for the first time in their life. The tasteless hostel food was any day better than jail food and a terrorist tag.

One night, not long after the encounter, police arrived at the gates of the university hostel asking about some students. The authorities wouldn't let them in unless they produced a warrant from the court, or at least presented some credible evidence.

They went away and didn't come back.

My senior in the university, Mohammad Reyaz, lived in the college hostel when the encounter happened. He recalled that, for the first time, Jamia had started shutting the main gate leading to the hostel. The guards at the hostel gate would advise students to avoid going near Batla House and instead to go to Jullena, on the opposite side, if they had urgent work.

I often bumped into Reyaz while having tea at the stall outside the library. He was a good debater and knew things, especially about the history of Islam and Muslims. Often, we had disagreements, but discussions with him were always pleasant, there was always something new to learn. On one such evening, when we were returning to the library after our tea break – and a verbal scuffle over the issue of triple talaq – we saw a student arguing with the library guard. It was exam time and the reading room of the library was crowded. The authorities had become strict and checked everyone's ID to make sure no outsider occupied the already strained-for-space library.

The student was Shah Alam from the Centre for Comparative Religions and Civilisations whose blunt manner made him an excellent source of fun and stories.

He was friends with a mahant in Ayodhya, and often lived with him in his mandir. One evening, while he was at the Ayodhya Press Club, a senior office bearer of the club asked him what he was doing these days.

Shah Alam told him that he was doing an MPhil from Jamia.

The man said, 'Oh Jamia! That terrorist university?'

Shah Alam was furious, and shouted back: 'Yes, I am from that terrorist university. I had even gone to Nepal for a training camp.'

It is often said that the ISI, Pakistan's intelligence agency, is active in that Himalayan country, and that terrorists use it as a transit between India and Pakistan.

Alam shouted: 'I brought 10 lakh rupees for organising bomb blasts. I gave you that money. Sharmaji, it was in front of you, remember? Where did all the money go? What did you do with the money? Sharmaji, ask him to give me the money back, the job needs to be completed.' Shah Alam's response has become folklore among friends. He is from Basti, a district not far from Ayodhya, where he had spent most of his youth. He organised film festivals, protested unfair reporting of communal tensions in the media, opposed the Hindu rightwing in Ayodhya, and often found that he was being trailed by the local intelligence units. Friends warned him to be careful. What if the security agencies pick you up? It will take years to prove your innocence and, by the time you are out, your life would be ruined and reputation destroyed. But he would respond with his blend of bluntness and confidence, '*Is desh mein itna bhi andher nahi hai ke log bolenge nahi apke sath atyachar ho to*.' This country is not yet so conscienceless that no one will speak out if you are the victim of an atrocity.

Like us, he was returning to the library after a tea break and the guard at the entrance asked him for his I-card. He looked in his wallet and realised he had left his ID in the library's reading room. He tried to explain this to the guard, who was not convinced. Then Alam said, ill-advisedly but smiling, looking around for approval, '*Arey bhai, hum koi* terrorist *thodi na hain ke sara* ID card *leke ghumte rahenge har* time.' Man, I am not a terrorist that I keep all my ID cards on me all the time.

Usually, when an alleged terrorist is arrested, it is reported that he had an identity card with him, often a passport, and a diary that has addresses and telephone numbers, or some other identifying papers.

The guard and Alam exchanged a (secret) smile and he was let in.

This reminded Reyaz of his own small ID story. Soon after the encounter, he was going home for Eid. His father called and asked him to be careful and advised him to carry an identity card with him. Not his Jamia ID card, but the most authentic ID, his passport.

Reyaz laughed. His passport was the scariest ID he possessed. Just a few months ago, he had been to Pakistan on a college trip, representing India at a cultural festival. The first visa stamped on his passport was that of Pakistan. In the current atmosphere, the last thing he wanted was for the police, or anyone else for that matter, to know of this visit. Of all places, Pakistan! Did he have any explanation for that?

College trip? Ah, with the terrorist university?

There had been many news items stating that the Terrorists had Pakistani connections. There was so much anxiety in the aftermath of the encounter that no one wanted to be seen with anything that could be construed as anti-India. Students avoided issuing books from the library on terror, extremism, Islam or riots, even for research purposes. They were extra-cautious while talking on the phone, lest any harmless gibber-jabber be interpreted as plotting anti-national activities.

In his address, Mushirul Hasan had asked us to relieve ourselves of unwanted tensions and head back to our homes for Eid. Most of us took his advice. We travelled in groups for a sense of security. I too went with a group of students whose homes were on the same route as mine – Lucknow, Gorakhpur, Deoria, Siwan and beyond.

After Eid, I returned with the group.

On the return journey, the train halted at Gorakhpur for the engine to be changed. Being a news junkie, I went for a stroll on the platform to buy something to read. I saw a cart with books, magazines, Premchand's short stories, pocket-sized Gitas, Abul Kalam's autobiographies; along the handcart's sides hung *Saras Salil*, *Hindustan*, *Navbharat Times*, etc. There was also an *India Today*, its banner partly visible, with the cover-headline 'Inside the mind of bombers'. The cover had picture-sketches of the Terrorists arrested from Jamia Nagar. I picked up the magazine and casually turned its pages. Inside were highlighted quotes supposedly elicited from the Terrorists in police custody.

One of them was quoted as saying, 'If Allah wants, I'll bomb the market where my mother buys vegetables. She will be sent to paradise.'

It was a story by the same reporter who had approached the police as a social worker and had been allowed to meet the Terrorists twice. The story inside said: 'What is more frightening is that they could be young men you meet in a local Barista café or see working on their laptops at a cybercafé.'

It was frightening for anyone, no doubt. But for us, there was another reason to fear. Because, in place of these young men, it could have been any one of us. Normal Human Beings. I had enjoyed Eid back home and it had helped me put the terror of the post-encounter days in Delhi out of my head – but the magazine brought it all back in a flash.

I bought the magazine out of curiosity but I didn't want my fellow passengers to see me reading it, what with Terrorists on the cover. I wasn't even comfortable carrying it. Eventually, I clambered onto the upper berth and read the piece.

One story was headlined 'The ancestry of hate'. It described the district in the news, Azamgarh:

> Look around before you whisper it. Be afraid if the place appears in your permanent home address.

> Escape its drabness only to be awakened by a knock on the door – or a gunshot – in your most isolated, unguarded moment, when you are trapped in that space between faith and anger.
>
> It is a place where martyrdom can be booked in advance – or victimhood is a constant anticipation. It is where those who hear the call of the Book buy their one-way ticket to paradise from the nearest travel agent.
>
> It is where the terror of Islamic radicalism is a distant echo and the terrorist is an intimate loss. And its mythology continues to be co-authored by the god, the cop and the journalist.

The cover story said:

> A seminal report, 'The Homegrown Threat', prepared last year by the New York Police Department's (NYPD) intelligence division bursts these three myths about homegrown terrorists:
>
> They began as radical or devout Muslims, came from economically destitute backgrounds and were poorly educated.
>
> In reality, the terrorists were all under the age of 35, seemingly well-integrated local residents of liberal western democracies, came from reasonably well-off middle-class backgrounds and were high-school graduates.

There was more in the magazine. I fell asleep skimming through the pages. Someone from the group woke me up for dinner. I ate sitting on the upper berth, and went straight back to sleep. I didn't want to be awake with the still-fresh memories of the EncounterDays crowding my mind. Next morning, a call from Perwez woke me up. I was supposed to have reached Delhi in time to attend my morning class, but the train was delayed, par for the course on this route.

Perwez had not gone home for Eid. Getting a train ticket to his place was not easy, and also, he didn't want to travel alone. He asked me how far I was from Delhi. I shouted into the phone, to compensate for the bad network and the noise of the train, that I was still a few hours away. He told me the Biochemistry class had started.

'Oh, Seemi's class?' I asked him, worried.

And instantly regretted it. Seemi sounded a lot like the dreaded SIMI, which was in the news after the Delhi blasts and the encounter.

The anxiety about missing class became anxiety to save ass.

I tried to unsay it. 'Oh okay, so Seemi Farhat Basir ma'am is taking her class. Biochemistry, na?' I added a few more words to sound convincing. 'Yes, yes, she is very strict about her classes.'

Soon, I realised that Biochemistry was another dangerous word. In proximity with the word SIMI, you never knew, it could well have to do with bio-warfare. The consolation was that my co-passengers were a mixed crowd of migrant labourers and young students like me, so there seemed little possibility that anyone was reading meanings into my phone conversation.

But I had the magazine too from last evening, which shouted Terrorists on its cover.

Now, after the call, I wanted to get rid of it more than ever. I waited for the train to move fast, and slid into a window seat. After making sure the others were busy – on the phone or bitching about the lateness of the train – I took out the magazine, slowly put my hand out of the window, and let it go.

I could hear the fluttering of its pages for a few milliseconds.

Jamia had changed. Leadership had once again been handed over to a bureaucrat, Najeeb Jung. He was the third non-scholar to head the institution since I had joined Jamia School in 1997.

Of the four VCs appointed to the institution since then, Mushirul Hasan was the only scholar and the only VC appointed from within the university. Lt General Zaki, who was appointed in 1996, was an army man; Syed Shahid Mahdi was a bureaucrat. Mushirul Hasan, a professor of History in the university, was VC from 2004 to 2009. Now again, a bureaucrat was heading the institution.

Jung had been a joint-secretary in the petroleum ministry, and then joined the Asian Development Bank before going to Oxford to do a PhD in Energy Studies. He returned to join Reliance, and then Jamia. After Jamia, he would go on to become the (Honourable) Lt Governor of Delhi, replacing Tejendra Khanna, the man who had declared that no judicial enquiry was needed in the Batla House case.[39] Under him, the university (indirectly) discouraged all platforms that, in the absence of a students' union, gave students space to voice their opinions. University guards turned stricter, shooing away anyone who stayed on campus after class. CCTVs were seen all over the campus.

Elections were never held again, on one pretext or another. But the authorities kept talking about student democracy; they even organised a talk on the importance of student leadership. The Left leader, Sitaram Yechury, who had been a student leader in JNU, was invited to address students on the subject.

While the talk by Yechury was going on, a student rose to ask a question: so, when is the university planning to hold elections? He was immediately summoned by the proctorial department, warned and let off. He had come from Kerala, they said, and would be sent back there. He had come to study, so he should do that, not try to be too smart.

But such actions by the authorities faced little opposition there was no student representation, and teachers' tongues were tied too.

Afroz Alam Sahil, my senior, was part of the whiff of opposition that existed. He had filed an RTI application on the students' union election but it yielded little result. The authorities knew how to delay their response indefinitely. In 2011, the university invited Tejendra Khanna as chief guest at its annual convocation. Afroz protested, saying it was Khanna who had obstructed the investigation into the encounter.

By noon, he got a call from the Special Cell of the Delhi Police to report at their Lodhi Road office. Afroz didn't know how to react. He posted on his Facebook page about the summons. A lot of people commented and shared their concerns. Soon, he got a call from the Special Cell that he need not come. It was simply a call to question why he was protesting against the Lt Governor, Afroz told me. Afroz had enrolled in the university for MPhil, but in protest against Jamia's submission to power, he left, abandoning the course midway.

A few weeks later, when the encounter was back in the news before the 2012 UP state elections, Afroz asked a few questions in a debate on national television. What happened to the voluntary donations that Jamia had received for fighting the cases of the Jamia students arrested in the encounter case, he asked. What happened to the money? How was it used? Were there any funds left?

We had all wondered about this but he had asked these questions publicly, and so the university slammed a case of defamation against him.[40]

A case seeking damages of Rs 50 lakh against someone who was still struggling to pay off his education loan.[41] Someone who had barely survived in Delhi by writing stories for different Hindi and Urdu newspapers that paid him hardly anything.

Apologise or pay was the question in front of him. He apologised and went silent.

He now worked full-time on his news website, *Beyond Headlines*, which Reyaz and he had started. They wanted to cover the news that was neglected in the rush of breaking news. Afroz used to publish an occasional newspaper and a blog named 'Leek Se Hatke'; the name of their website was derived from there.

Reyaz was already working with a news production firm run by journalist Karan Thapar, and worked on the website in his after-office hours. They kept it going for a few months until they went their separate ways. The question then and now: how long can idealism survive without funding?

Afroz continues to struggle for his Ideal world, still without monetary or moral support.

His small effort. Small in the larger scheme of things. Afroz is one of the many stories of those who adjusted their dreams to the tune of the encounter and its aftermath however uncomfortable it may make those who are not forced to dream EncounteredDreams. It was a reiteration of the fact (to those few who listened) that young people here believed in democratic means and were willing to fight it out within the democratic spaces. Militantly democratic, if you will.

Almost two and half years after the encounter, Delhi held municipality elections. While the rest of the capital city fought for water supply and cleanliness, candidates in Jamia Nagar debated the issue of young Muslim men being picked up by the police from the locality.

In the same election, a young man named Zia Rahman decided to stand for elections. He had been in jail for bombing the city, and was on the cover of the *India Today* story I had thrown out of the train window. He fought valiantly and many campaigned in his favour. Eventually, he lost by a few hundred votes.

But the questions that the encounter raised never went away. The fear and mistrust it created remained.

We stopped making Osama jokes. We had a friend named Osama, a classmate of one of the accused. When we met, we used to make fun of his height: oye chhotu. He would respond jokingly, 'Boy, don't go by my height. You know who I am? Don't you? I will blow you up.'

Haha. We bow to you, sir, we know.

We stopped calling him chhotu.

Perwez too – we stopped calling him Bangladeshi.

We were never as conscious of our identity as we were then. We had to be. One harmless joke could well turn the course of someone's life in a matter of minutes. And none of us would have the power to undo that. And un-truth that.

We returned home on time. We locked our doors as early as possible. We avoided talking about encounter-related subjects in public.

It's a process that continues. More or less.

Epilogue: So, You Are Having Tea? I See!

It was a pleasant winter's night, the sort that warranted chai. More than that, though, it was an excuse to meet my friends, and do what we had been doing since our graduation days – talking politics, dissecting our (failed) love-lives, disparaging our teachers or bosses, discussing Islam and Muslims, and making fun of each other. Like Normal Human Beings do.

Like most evenings, I called everyone to meet at Hotel Taj, a small teashop in Batla House that is open late – and so is a favourite with students and young professionals like us. It served chai, cold drinks, rusk, cookies, boiled eggs (in winter), pouches of water (in summer) and paratha-kebab (during Ramazan).

Alim was there first, having arrived early from his lab in the Indian Agricultural Research Institute where he was working on a PhD. Asbah joined us from his office; he worked as an analyst. Perwez was still in his lab in Jamia, where he was doing cancer research for his PhD, and joined us after he got my message. Rameez was training to be a teacher at Jamia's Education Department. Kafil's shift at a Noida firm, where he worked as a copy-editor, was to start early next morning, so he planned to go straight to office from here. Saiam was now a radio producer and comedian, and came along as well.

By midnight, the seven of us were gathered at the tiny one-room teashop, cursing the winter. But Asbah still ordered his usual drink, ThumsUp. Irrespective of the weather, he always had a cold drink. His addiction had all of us hooked to the unhealthy habit, sip by sip. After cold drinks, chai was also given its due. 'A bit strong. Less sugar.' The steam from the hot tea merged with the fog, our winter-breath and a dying bonfire (surrounded by the laughing mourners).

The Community Centre nearby was still alive with noise. This unobtrusive one-room space on the corner of the street looked as if it was built on stolen space. The muffled sound of young people singing and dancing to music was audible. In the distance, at the other end of the street, Bismillah Tea Stall was faintly visible through the fog. We sat outside our teashop on creaking benches, below the high-tension wires that crossed the colony. And as usual we talked trash, peppered with some sensible conversation, and made fun of each other. Like Normal Human Beings do.

That night I was the butt of their jokes.

Rameez used the fact that I had called everyone for chai to rib me. He said I drank so much chai that chai must run in my veins. 'If Neyaz meets with an accident, we will have to organise a chai-donation camp,' added Asbah. 'He will need a chai drip.'

Then Furquan arrived from work – as a journalist, he had to stay late once in a while – and joined the gang. He asked me how long I was going to take to finish the book I was writing. Before I could offer a believable excuse for my procrastination, Asbah offered: 'Neyaz follows the Infinite Monkey Theorem.' No one knew what that was, so Asbah explained. In its essence, it is this: if a monkey is given a keyboard and an infinite amount of time, he will eventually produce a best-selling novel.

Hahaha.

Amidst our silly conversations and laughter, someone's eye wandered to the first floor of the teashop, where the owner lived. Something winked unevenly in the glow of the street light. It was not clearly visible at first. But when he fixed his eye on it, he realised it was a CCTV camera.

He quietly alerted us all.

Silence.

A what-to-do, what-not-to-do moment.

We had never noticed a camera here, and we were regulars. The teashop owner had never informed us that one had been installed. We looked around and realised that there were more cameras.

One.

Two.

Oh, three!

No, four!

On his teashop roof and the floor above that.

There was nothing to hide, but it was still scary that we were being secretly recorded. The next day, we went to check if cameras had been installed at other teashops, like Lajawab and Bismillah. There were none; none that we could spot. We confronted the Taj teashop owner and asked him about the CCTV cameras.

Who installed them?

The police did.

Why had he not told us?

Hmmm, actually, um ...

It could well be a simple, routine security measure, but it could also be pointed surveillance. For us, it was a mini-encounter moment.

When we spotted the cameras that night, we tried to act normal, as if we had seen nothing. The words dried up. We finished our tea, cold drinks, gossip and left soon after.

We don't visit Taj anymore.

Radicalism [mass noun] The beliefs or actions of people who advocate thorough or complete political or social reform. (Oxford dictionary)

Bits and Bobs from the Suitcase

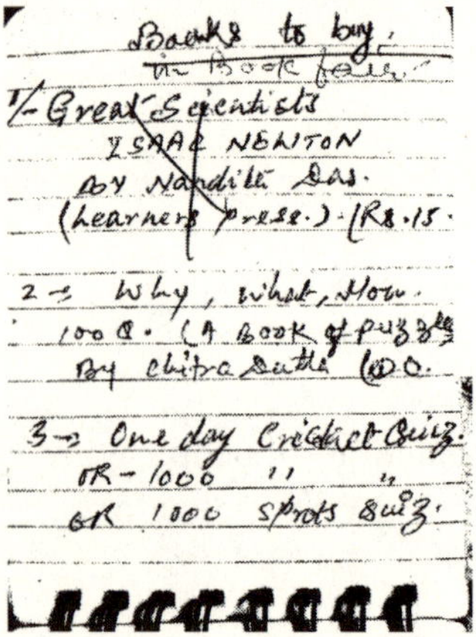

Books to buy.
~~in Book fair~~
1/- Great Scientists
ISAAC NEWTON
by Nandita Das.
(Learners Press.) (Rs. 15
2 - Why, what, How.
100 Q. (A Book of puzzles
By Chitra Sathe (DO.
3 - One day Cricket Quiz.
OR - 1000 " "
OR 1000 Sports Quiz.

A pocket notebook in which I had made a list of books to buy

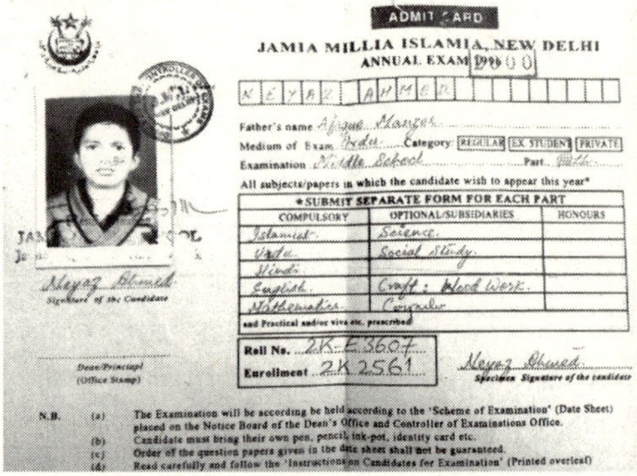

ADMIT CARD
JAMIA MILLIA ISLAMIA, NEW DELHI
ANNUAL EXAM

NEYAZ AHMED
Father's name Afaque Manzar
Medium of Exam Urdu Category: REGULAR / EX STUDENT / PRIVATE
Examination Middle School Part
All subjects/papers in which the candidate wish to appear this year*
* SUBMIT SEPARATE FORM FOR EACH PART

COMPULSORY	OPTIONAL/SUBSIDIARIES	HONOURS
Islamiat	Science	
Urdu	Social Study	
Hindi		
English	Craft: Wood Work	
Mathematics	Computer	

and Practical and/or viva etc. prescribed
Roll No. 2K-ES607
Enrollment 2K2561
Neyaz Ahmed — Signature of the Candidate
Dean/Principal (Office Stamp)
Specimen Signature of the candidate

N.B. (a) The Examination will be according be held according to the 'Scheme of Examination' (Date Sheet) placed on the Notice Board of the Dean's Office and Controller of Examinations Office.
(b) Candidate must bring their own pen, pencil, ink-pot, identity card etc.
(c) Order of the question papers given in the date sheet shall not be guaranteed.
(d) Read carefully and follow the 'Instructions on Candidates for Examination' (Printed overleaf)

My admit card for the class 8 exams (what a handsome lad!)

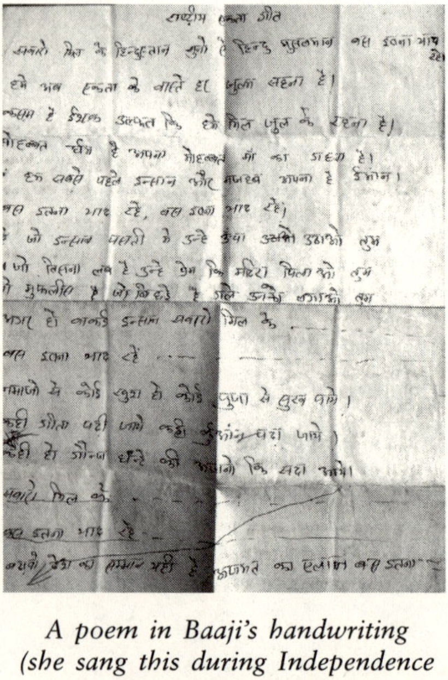

A poem in Baaji's handwriting (she sang this during Independence Day celebrations)

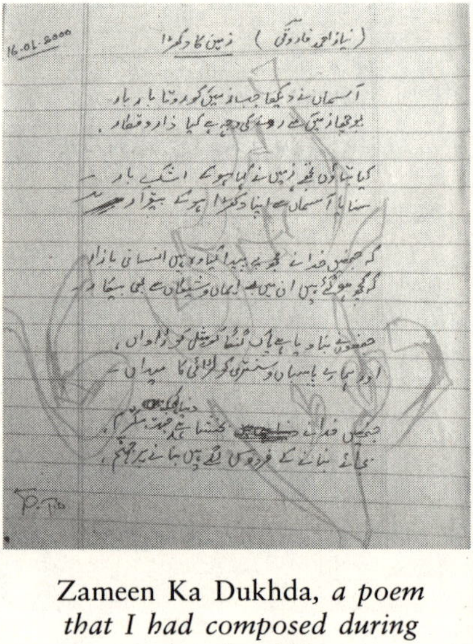

Zameen Ka Dukhda, *a poem that I had composed during my schooldays*

Notes

All urls in the footnotes were last accessed on 20 December 2017.

1. 'The Court asked the police to allow Zia-ur-Rehman and Saqib Nissar to meet their relatives and advocates in the evening': http://www.rediff.com/news/2008/oct/03delblast1.htm
2. http://indiatoday.intoday.in/story/Inside+the+mind+of+the+bombers/1/16662.html
3. On the allegations of questionable encounters: 'Close Encounters, a Report on Police Shootout in Delhi', PUCL, Delhi, October 2004, http://www.pucl.org/major_reports/ close_encounters.pdf; Prashant Bhushan, 'A Rogue Police cCell', Outlook, 21 February 2005, https://www.outlookindia. com/website/story/a-rogue-police-cell/226552; Vijaita Singh, 'Terror-busters with Chequered History of Own', *Indian Express*, 21 May 2015; Jamia Teachers' Solidarity Association, 'Delhi Police Encounters', *Outlook*, 20 May 2015; 'Framed, Damned and Acquitted: Dossiers of a Very Special Cell', A Report by the Jamia Teachers' Solidarity Association.
4. http://www.firstpost.com/india/ahead-of-independence-day-celebrations-police-raid-jamia-milia-islamia-hostels-students- see-a-dangerous-pattern-2955280.html
5. http://indiatoday.intoday.in/story/3+dead+17+injured+in+Mehrauli+ blast+in+Delhi/1/16293.html
6. http://indianexpress.com/article/india/india-others/2008-malegaon-blast-case/
7. http://indianexpress.com/article/india/india-others/nia-closes-modasa-blast-case-in-which-hindu-extremists-suspects/

8. http://indianexpress.com/article/india/india-others/2008-malegaon-blast-case/
9. http://indianexpress.com/article/india/india-others/nia-closes-modasa-blast-case-in-which-hindu-extremists-suspects/
10. http://beyondheadlines.in/2013/07/batla-house-encounter-and-beyond-shahzad-sentence-tomorrow/
11. https://www.outlookindia.com/newswire/story/judicial-remand-of-varanasi-blasts-accused-extended/405757
12. https://timesofindia.indiatimes.com/india/UP-government-calls-CBI-to-probe-Khalid-Mujahids-death-in-custody/articleshow/20143080.cms
13. http://www.thehindu.com/todays-paper/tp-national/tp-newdelhi/11-acquitted-in-jaipur-blasts-case/article2702913.ece
14. https://www.outlookindia.com/magazine/story/no-cover-under-fire/238559
15. http://archive.indianexpress.com/news/-delhi-encounter-hero-sharma-died-of-heartattack-/364473/
16. https://jp.reuters.com/article/us-india-blast/india-police-raid-slums-relatives-angry-after-bombs-idUSLD36237120080914
17. '"Encounter" at Batla House: Unanswered Questions', Jamia Teachers' Solidarity Association, p. 37, https://ia802705.us.archive.org/32/items/encounterAtBatlaHouseUnansweredQuestions/Batla_House_encounter_report.pdf
18. Link to the B.N. Srikrishna report: https://www.sabrang.com/srikrish/vol1.htm
19. https://mumbaimirror.indiatimes.com/mumbai/crime/suleman-usman-bakery-raid-court-puts-the-cops-who-opened-fire- on-trial/articleshow/48429443.cms & http://www.asianage. com/mumbai/1993-riots-inquiry-offi -gets-2nd-showcause- notice-076
20. Arrest of the caretaker: '"Encounter" at Batla House: Unanswered Questions', Jamia Teachers' Solidarity Association, p. 6, https://ia802705.us.archive.org/32/items/encounterAtBatlaHouseUnansweredQuestions/Batla_House_encounter_report.pdf. He was recently released: https://www.outlookindia.com/newswire/story/batla-house-encounter-court-discharges-caretaker-accused-of-harboring-terrorists/969390

21. http://www.openthemagazine.com/article/india/open-s- response-to-an-investigation-bias-charge & http://www. rediff.com/news/2008/sep/20delblast.htm & http://epaper. timesofindia.com/Default/Layout/Includes/TOI/ArtWin. asp?From=Archive&Source=Page&Skin= TOI http://epaper. timesofindia.com/Default/Layout/Includes/TOI/ArtWin. asp?From=Archive&Source=Page&Skin=TOI& Continuation=1&BaseHref=CAP%2F2008%2F09%2F22&ViewMode= HTML& PageLabel= 1&EntityId=Ar00100&App Name=1
22. http://www.milligazette.com/Archives/15012001/Art12.htm. Also see: http://www.tribuneindia.com/2000/20001228/main1.htm (the last story) and http://www.frontline.in/static/html/fl2620/stories/20091009262002000.htm (the report from Delhi).
23. http://www.firstpost.com/politics/batla-house-jihadi-literature- had-one-exhibit-panchatantra-88806.html & http://beyondheadlines.in/2011/09/the-irony-of-rti-in-batla-house-encounter/
24. http://www.unipune.ac.in/snc/cssh/HumanRights/04%20 C O M M U N A L % 20 R I O T S / A % 2 0 - % 2 0 % 2 0 A N T I - MUSLIM%20RIOTS/02-BIHAR/02b.pdf & http://www.caravanmagazine.in/vantage/bhagalpur-1989-bihar-police-massacre
25. https://ia802705.us.archive.org/32/items/encounterAtBatlaHouseUnansweredQuestions/Batla_House_encounter_ report.pdf & http://www.yorku.ca/drache/Canada%20 Watch/canadawatch/pdf/fall2011/Sethi.pdf & https:// timesofindia.indiatimes.com/interviews/Manisha-Sethi-Theres- no-mechanism-to-support-those-falsely-accused-of-terrorism/ articleshow/16480724.cms
26. Shahzad Ahmad was convicted not for the blasts but the killing of the inspector during the Batla House encounter: http:// www.thehindu.com/news/national/batla-house-shahzad-ahmad-convicted/article4952500.ece. However, the Jamia Teachers' Solidarity Association has questioned the evidence against him: http://www.thehindu.com/news/cities/Delhi/evidence-against-shahzad-not-beyond-reasonable-doubt/article4977049.ece
27. https://www.outlookindia.com/magazine/story/no-cover-under-fire/238559

28. http://www.thehindu.com/todays-paper/tp-national/tp-newdelhi/11-acquitted-in-jaipur-blasts-case/article2702913.ece
29. http://www.rediff.com/news/report/batla-accused-were-assaulted-during-encounter/20100318.htm & http://www.hindustantimes.com/delhi-news/batla-autopsy-report-out/story-2WNB5MDXCAMhAIYu5o5OmN.html & http://beyondheadlines.in/2011/09/post-mortem-reports-raise-serious-questions-on-the-authenticity-of-the-batla-house-encounter/
30. Afroz's report on the matter: http://beyondheadlines.in/2011/09/why-delhi-minority-commission-inquiry-into-batla-house-encounter-never-happened/
31. NHRC proceedings on the Batla House encounter: http://nhrc.nic.in/batla.htm
32. Ibid. The NHRC proceedings on the encounter do not mention a visit to the site. Also see Afroz's report: http:// beyondheadlines.in/2011/09/why-delhi-minority-commission- inquiry-into-batla-house-encounter-never-happened/. See criticism of the NHRC report here: http://www.thehindu. com/todays-paper/tp-national/NHRC-report-on-Batla-House- encounter-flayed/article16562981.ece
33. https://timesofindia.indiatimes.com/city/delhi/Batla-House-encounter-Militants-postmortem-report-raises-questions/articleshow/5703697.cms
34. http://archive.indianexpress.com/news/shaheen-bagh-erupts-as-police-team-tries-to-detain-syed-mohammed-ahmed-kazmi-s-nephew/1001345/
35. http://indianexpress.com/article/india/india-others/shaheen- bagh-erupts-as-police-team-tries-to-detain-syed-mohammed- ahmed-kazmis-nephew/
36. https://blogs.economictimes.indiatimes.com/et-commentary/punish-the-delhi-police-special-cell-for-framing-sayyed-liyaqat-shah-set-an-example/
37. http://archive.indianexpress.com/news/batla-house-raid-goes-wrong-cops-fire-shots-again-/913113/
38. http://twocircles.net/2008oct16/jamia_residents_foiled_encounter_attempt.html#.VhGgL-yqqko

39. http://twocircles.net/2008oct17/shaheen_bagh_kidnapper_cops_had_fake_ids.html
40. http://supremecourtofindia.nic.in/jonew/judis/41558.pdf & https://thewire.in/1838/escape-from-the-pota-archipelago/
41. http://pudr.org/sites/default/files/pdfs/jamia.html
42. Ibid.
43. http://indianexpress.com/article/cities/delhi/lg-might-say-no-to-judicial-probe-into-batla-encounter/
44. http://jmi.ac.in/upload/publication/pr_2012january25.pdf
45. http://www.thehindu.com/todays-paper/tp-national/rights- group-slams-jamia-for-harassing-rti-activist/article13376296. ece

Acknowledgements

BEFORE I BEGIN THE many thank yous that I owe people, I would like to note that this book is not in the English language. It's in Hindustani, the language that I speak naturally (oh, maybe we should have told you that before you bought the book).

On to the gratitude now.

I am thankful to the good people of the world who agreed to be part of this book. To recall events mentioned in the book accurately, I relied on them wherever my memory faltered or I was not present as a witness. This list includes my family, friends, future friends, and many knowns and unknowns.

I have changed the names of a few of them to protect their identity and privacy. The rest waived this privilege, as they really loved the idea that they are being written about until they read, well, the actual manuscript. One of them is Furquan (name changed in a couple of places, though); those who know him know where exactly he features in the book.

I consider writing books a collaborative project, and many people (and places and events) have played crucial roles in making this one. Allow me to name a few: Bush brothers (in Washington), Osama Bin Laden (Afghanistan), Narendra Modi (Gujarat), Delhi Police and sister concerns (Delhi and elsewhere), Gabriel (somewhere in sky), Babri Masjid (?), Leaders of the independence movement (British

India), Mohammad Iqbal (British India), Kabir (Mughal India) and farmers (everywhere).

I would also like to specifically acknowledge the roles played by a few more people, so you know where to direct the blame. If you meet Ramachandra Guha, ask him if is it true that he believed in me when I had nothing much to show. At the New India Foundation, he encouraged me, mentored me, allowed me to take my time, read the manuscript closely and suggested changes as minute commas and full stops, and directed the manuscript to the kingpins of the trade.

My agent Shruti Debi, I mean, of course. (Don't hire her as an agent, by the way.) Or V.K. Karthika – my publisher, who decided to acquire this book as soon as she read it. And of course, Rivka Israel and Ajitha G.S. – my editors, who made the book readable. During the lengthy editing process, they were more patient – all the while nitpicking, what else? – than I ever was. What errors remain are mine. Vishwajyoti Ghosh, who had us spoilt for choice with his many covers.

I am glad to have known people who selflessly gave their time and opinion whenever I sought it. Ajaz Ashraf, Manisha Sethi, Neha Dixit – and Shuddhabrata Sengupta, who gave me first words of encouragement at Sarai-CSDS. Afroz Alam Sahil, for sharing a wealth of information. And Sadia Akhtar for fact-checking the book.

My editors where I worked or contributed – Basharat Peer, Kanika Gahlaut, Rajesh Mahapatra, Sanjoy Narayan some of whom showed me undue favours.

Dharam Arora, Hulchul members, Javed Sultan, Mazhar ul Haque, Kunal Majumdar, Nakul Sawhney, Shiraz Babu they often showed me way.

Gowhar, Reyaz and Zehra, my critics-on-demand. I'm certain I would have completed this book even without your help, but – what the hell, let me admit it – you did help me shape the book. Thank you for the time you spared for me from your (haha) busy schedule.

The many curious questions from my little sisters and cousins – Tayammum, Tanazzum, Wahdat, Shafqat, Rafat, Rifa – were always a push for me to complete writing it; I believe they will grow up to write their own stories, their own books. My parents, family and extended family members, who continued to trust me, and tolerated my long absences.

Thank you – you – for your time (I hope you didn't jump to the acknowledgments directly. You will burn in hell if you did so. Reference: page numbers 37, 47 and 162).